Ivory Towers and Nationalist Minds

Ivory Towers and Nationalist Minds

Universities, Leadership, and the Development of the American State

MARK R. NEMEC

THE UNIVERSITY OF MICHIGAN PRESS   *Ann Arbor*

Published in the United States of America by
The University of Michigan Press
Manufactured in the United States of America
⊚ Printed on acid-free paper

2009   2008   2007   2006   4   3   2   1

A CIP catalog record for this book is available from the British Library.

Library of Congress Cataloging-in-Publication Data

Nemec, Mark R.
    Ivory towers and nationalist minds : universities, leadership, and
the development of the American state / Mark R. Nemec.
        p.   cm.
    Includes bibliographical references and index.
    ISBN-13: 978-0-472-09912-2 (cloth : alk. paper)
    ISBN-10: 0-472-09912-4 (cloth : alk. paper)
    ISBN-13: 978-0-472-06912-5 (pbk. : alk. paper)
    ISBN-10: 0-472-06912-8 (pbk. : alk. paper)
    1. Education, Higher—Political aspects—United States.   2. Higher
education and state—United States.   3. Education, Higher—United
States—History.   I. Title.

LC173.N46   2006
379.73—dc22   2005024421

In loving memory of Kristen Diane Nemec (1971–1997)

Contents

Acknowledgments

Any project of this nature depends on the support and patience of those around the author as much as it requires the effort and dedication of the author himself. With that in mind, I would like to take this opportunity to thank those who have helped me over the years in bringing this project to life. While I hope to be comprehensive, I realize that no catalog is complete. I apologize to any whom I might have overlooked in this one exercise of memory. Please rest assured that your support is not forgotten.

I would like to begin by thanking those most involved in this project from the outset. From my earliest days as a graduate student, Nicholas Steneck, John Kingdon, Ann Chih Lin, and Douglas Dion showed remarkable interest in my work and tolerance for my work patterns. Additionally, their respect for my ideas and opinions as well as for each other's helped enormously in the formative stages of this work. Individually, they contributed in a marked fashion.

Nick Steneck has been an exceptional champion whose enthusiasm and encouragement beyond my years as a graduate student have brought this work to fruition. I never took a course from Nick, and yet he has taught me a great deal. From allowing me to serve as a perennial graduate student instructor for their course on the history of the University of Michigan, to tolerating my occasional frustrated outburst on the golf course, to helping guide my research and application of the historical method, Nick and his wife, Peg, have been enormously useful and encouraging resources.

In taking his seminar on American politics, serving a number of semesters as his graduate student instructor, and working with him as chairman of my preliminary and dissertation committees, I have found John Kingdon to be a model as a scholar and teacher, and I am grateful for his guidance. I had the privilege of taking Ann Chih Lin's first graduate seminar in public policy and her ambitious (in the context of Michigan's research tradition) seminar in qualitative methods. Beyond her courses, Ann has always been an exceptionally attentive and challenging reader, offering insight and demanding clarification in a most sympathetic and supportive way. From conveying the fundamentals of linear algebra to surveying the details of American political development, Doug Dion broached questions in a creative and unique way. His suggestions for this project have continued in that tradition and have helped significantly.

Maturing this work into a manuscript has been a pleasure. I have had the good fortune to find assistance all along the way. Notably, Scott Allard has brought unwavering encouragement and enormous discipline and insight as a reader. The support of my editor, Jim Reische, and all at the University of Michigan Press has been invaluable. The anonymous reviewers Jim selected were exceedingly attentive and helpful.

For affording me a unique opportunity to witness the modern administrative state in action, I thank Los Angeles County Supervisor for the Fourth District Deane Dana and his successor, Don Knabe, along with their staffs—especially Anna Cervantes, Gail LeGros, Mishal Montgomery, and Tim Riley.

I wish to acknowledge the support of Tiffany Pollard throughout much of this process. While we somewhat abruptly found ourselves taking separate paths before it was completed, I am grateful for her patience and involvement in the time we shared.

Writing is a state of place as much as a state of mind. For their hospitality to me and my laptop, special mention is due to Michael and Ann Finson of Concord, Massachusetts; John Hittell of Rincon, Puerto Rico; and Bill and Susan Wheeler, sometimes of Chatham, Massachusetts.

To the members of the Michigan, Santa Monica, White Plains, Charlotte, and Potomac Athletic Club rugby sides, I offer thanks for the invaluable diversion they provided.

My parents, Richard and Constance Nemec, encouraged my academic bent (I still remember a family tour of the University of Oregon in the summer of 1976, after I had just turned seven) and supported my undergraduate and graduate studies with exceptional excitement and confidence even in the most difficult times. Their unceasing faith has been of value beyond calculation. I only hope I can offer some sense of its worth.

In addition to sharing the immeasurable gifts of our sons, Alexander and Theodore, my wife, Suzanne, was instrumental to the completion of this manuscript, thanks to her humor, her generosity, and her passion. She is the subject of my utmost gratitude.

Finally, I dedicate this work to the memory of my sister, Kristen Diane Nemec. While she never read a page of this work, her spirit is in every word. I miss you, Kristen. I am always grateful to be your brother.

1 Ideas and Institutions in American Political Development

As the Civil War ended and the antebellum state declined, various nongovernmental institutions, both newly founded and newly defined, positioned themselves for the coming era. Seeking to establish their significance, American universities and the institutional entrepreneurs who guided them nurtured an expertise that helped to further the developing state at the turn of the twentieth century. Universities served the national state as an active partner and worked on its behalf as an independent agent. In these efforts and in their relationships with one another, the nation's leading universities initially worked through informal associations, often based on the close friendships and social ties of their presidents. However, as the demands of academic leadership and the complexity of institutional tasks continued to rise, the nation's leading universities formalized their ties.

Though the relation between universities, the state, and expertise may seem obvious to the contemporary observer, there was nothing inevitable about it. Alternative sources of expertise and alternative approaches to education certainly existed. The emerging universities' support of the developing American national state at the turn of the twentieth century has broad implications, since contemporary institutions, credentials, requirements, and expectations of expertise and higher education evolved from this era and since the founding premises of the universities still define the parameters and the procedures that influence politics and policy today.

Generally speaking, scholars of politics and history have underscored the relationship between ideas and institutions but have not necessarily explored their interactive effects. Specifically, scholars of American political development have recognized the relationship between the emerging universities and the national state but have not detailed or fully explained its significance. Nevertheless, a consensus has formed around the belief that there was an effort to expand the capacities of the federal government and the related autonomy of its bureaucratic agents in the era of "building a new American state" (roughly 1870–1920) and that such efforts were highly dependent on expertise. Broadly defined, national state capacities have been seen as the ability of governments and their agents to influence the practice of politics, the formation of groups, the identity of individuals, and the demands of society.[1] Though helping us understand attempts to build a national state, this consensus still leaves us with some basic questions: how did expertise come to be the basis on which federal authority and related bureaucratic autonomy were extended, from where did this expertise emanate, and how was it defined?

Governmental authority is vested in ideas and institutions. Since the state itself is not necessarily fully equipped to substantiate and perpetuate the intellectual basis of its own authority, conceptions of national political institutions must recognize the fundamental role nongovernmental institutions play in the establishment, furtherance, and reform of governmental authority. In this book, focusing on American political development, I underscore the place of emerging universities in the evolution of the national state and detail the extent to which and manner in which universities legitimized and formalized the state's authority.

The Emerging University

While highly intertwined, the relationship of universities to the national state was not all-consuming. Universities did not exist solely to develop, provide, and enforce research-based expertise. They also pursued courses and curricula that emphasized mental discipline, utility, and liberal culture.[2] However, by the second decade of the twentieth century, research and the pursuit of expertise had become defining missions. The university became known as the research university, spurred on by coordinating organizations, such as the Association of American Universities and the National Research Council.

The contest between academic proponents of research and expertise, service and utility, liberal culture, and mental discipline continued even after research gained prominence—and to some extent, it still continues today. Proponents of research stressed systematic examination of social and scientific problems. Proponents of utility stressed the pursuit of knowledge and the provision of skills that would not only enable students to "make their way" in society but also contribute to the general welfare. Proponents of liberal culture stressed the creation of the "gentleman scholar" through instruction in the developing fields of art, literature, and history. Proponents of mental discipline stressed repetition and memorization of classical texts in keeping with earlier collegiate traditions.

Members of these various camps battled not only between institutions but within them as well. In this era, for example, Yale supported economist Arthur Twining Hadley, who would serve as an advisor to the Interstate Commerce Commission before becoming president of Yale; provided agricultural instruction with land-grant funds given to its Sheffield Scientific School; fostered the Elizabethan Club, which was dedicated to "free conversation of literature and the arts amongst its members"; and continued a tradition of commencement orations in Greek and Latin.

These were not pitched battles, however. The university was marked by a "diversity of mind" that not only allowed for clear lines of debate but also encouraged a general expansion of the reach, breadth, and depth of higher education.[3] Thus, whatever the extent of these internal struggles, the university still promoted research-based expertise and its relevance for the developing national state. The institutional entrepreneurs who guided higher education not only promoted their schools but also promoted the expertise their schools defined. Expertise was not the only intellectual resource they offered, but it was the most prominent one.

Ideas, Institutions, and Authority

Those who examine the institutional and intellectual apparatuses of the developing state at the turn of the twentieth century acknowledge the significant role of the university in this era. Stephen Skowronek recognizes the importance of universities as a home for intellectuals concerned with the formation of a national state.

> The challenge of building a new kind of state in America was taken up in the post–Civil War era by an emergent intelligentsia rooted in a revitalized professional sector and a burgeoning university sector. These intellectuals championed a fundamental reconstruction of the mode of governmental operations to be centered in an administrative realm possessing "finish, efficacy, and permanence."[4]

Eldon Eisenach reflects a similar train of thought. He suggests that universities represented "the organization of specialized knowledge as a political force outside of the party and electoral system."[5] In attempting to redefine American life, Progressive political ideas required institutional support. Primary among these institutions was the newly emerging university, which, Eisenach maintains, served "as something like a national 'church'—the main repository of common American values, common American meanings, and common American identities."[6] Universities did not simply support and transmit the ideas of this new, American, nationalist "regime in thought." Instead, Eisenach maintains, they navigated the divide between these ideas and the state: "political ideas and the identities they carry become altered when they become institutionalized. Most obviously, when institutionalized governmentally and enforced, these ideas become quite literally authoritative."[7] Eisenach observes that the university lectern became a "public pulpit" and that academics at the turn of the century "were compelled to address their competitors more directly."

> As more direct competitors for institutional political power (e.g., expert bureaucracy) and as intellectual underwriters and publicists for institutional reforms across every area of American political and economic life, they . . . had to engage in direct competition with jurists and with partisan carriers of American political life.[8]

Eisenach and Skowronek's assessments are highly complimentary and interrelated. The university was more than simply a pulpit and/or home for the new American state's intelligentsia. The prominence and authority of the university grew along with, if not in direct connection to, the prominence and authority of the national state. Determining and detailing the specific nature and significance of such correspondent evolution is the fundamental concern of this work.

Higher Education's Formative Years

Histories of higher education have recognized a significant relationship between the evolution of universities and the development of post–Civil War America, especially notions of the state and public service. George Marsden[9] focuses on the rise of secularism in the mid- to late nineteenth century. Appealing to conceptions of national service was an effective method for newly founded public universities to navigate around local sectarian concerns and squabbles that had hindered state supported institutions in previous years. Julie Reuben[10] considers the same process of secularization but suggests that the marginalization of religion was the end result of universities pursuing objective science. According to Reuben, among the consequences of this secularization was a social science that attempted to merge science and ethics in pursuit of public policy. Jon Roberts and James Turner[11] extend this idea, arguing that secularization was the driving force behind the expansion of the curriculum. Looking beyond American higher education's religious origins, Roger Geiger[12] suggests that private donations and state funds were more significant than federal sources, such as the Morrill Act of 1862, which he argues primarily spurred, rather than maintained, the movement toward research and service. Roger Williams[13] finds the Morrill Act to be highly influential but stresses that its implementation was far less tidy than commonly recalled, as its beneficiaries had to fight both national and local political battles to build their institutions. Looking beyond the Morrill Act and focusing, respectively, on California and the American South, John Aubrey Douglass[14] and Michael Dennis[15] focus on the state and local influences that defined state universities' research and service. Summarizing the era, Laurence Veysey acknowledges that the federal state took an interest in higher education, but he also refers to government reports and publications regarding higher education in this era as "a wasteland of noncommitment."[16]

In detailing the rise of national higher education associations, Hugh Hawkins to some extent answers Veysey's complaint, by noting the limited reach and authority of the United States Bureau of Education (USBE): "Problems of international academic relations would in many nations have been treated by a ministry of education. In the United States, where the USBE was restricted to gathering and dispensing information, these issues suggested the formation of a voluntary association."[17] The lack of a strong state organization regulating higher education was one of the primary factors leading to the formation of the Association of American Universities (AAU). Actively lobbying and partnering with the federal government, the AAU consisted of the nation's elite universities. Soon after its founding, the AAU became a defining force for the goals and standards of American higher education.

A more universal awareness of universities' impact on state authority exists beyond the specific context of American political development. The most adamant proponents of "bringing the state back in"—Evans, Rueschemeyer, and Skocpol—recognize universities' impact on state capacities. They do not examine the role of universities beyond consideration of social knowledge, but they do suggest that further studies should attend "to the interplay of state agencies with institutions and professions oriented to the production and dissemination of knowledge" and should detail "the inter-relations of officials with all groups that advance claims over information and social theories in connection with political struggles over state action."[18] By focusing on the American state and the institutions primarily responsible for the production of social knowledge, my study furthers some of these universal interests.

State Authority and the Rise of Institutional Entrepreneurs

Clyde Barrow's *Universities and the Capitalist State*[19] is one of a few studies to detail and specifically consider the relationship between American higher education and government authority. Barrow's work is useful for my consideration here, as he examines the university's role in furthering the "capitalist state," balancing capitalism and democracy, and transforming American economic structure at the turn of the twentieth century. I would argue, however, that there are limits to his approach. Barrow assumes that the relationship between prominent capitalists and universities was unidirectional, with the universities being co-opted by industrialists who Barrow believes were directing the state.

Building on the "garbage can model" of organizational choice[20] and on John Kingdon's[21] application of this model to public policy, I would argue that the relationship between universities and capitalists worked both ways and often in the opposite direction. Academic leaders acted as entrepreneurs, often seeking out wealthy patrons and offering their programs and institutions as solutions to the problems of complexity that events at the turn of the century posed. In my study, I am concerned with the state's relationship to institutions and ideas, whereas Barrow is concerned with its structuring of markets and capital. Barrow's arguments do not contradict and in fact can be incorporated within my consideration of university support for the intellectual and institutional apparatuses of the state.

I should stress—in regard to the expansion of the American national state—that though the intellectual apparatus of social knowledge was the primary component of universities' support; it was not the only component. The institutional apparatus provided by credentials, partnerships, and training was also essential. In other words, universities not only legitimized but also formalized expertise, creating structures—both as active partner and independent agent—that extended the state's authority further than it would have gone on its own.

University leaders often worked as institutional entrepreneurs. Attempting to establish and build their fledgling universities, these entrepreneurs needed to find relevance for their school's research-based expertise. By offering their institutions as a solution to the problems of American state expansion, they found this relevance. The university did not necessarily pursue research and expertise in response to the demands of building the national state, and the national state did not always look to the university as an immediate solution to the problems inherent in such expansion. However, university leaders gradually linked the solutions their institutions offered with the various problems and challenges the developing state faced.

American Political Development, 1870–1920

Current models of and rationales for governance have their origins in the era of building a new American state. The institutional and intellectual forces that define contemporary public policy, bureaucratic autonomy, and reform efforts were developed at the end of the nineteenth and beginning of the twentieth centuries.[22] This period of redefinition saw the beginnings of federal government expansion and a related shift in state authority.

There exists some dispute regarding the extent to which the federal government was able to establish central state authority;[23] these efforts were often met with resistance and limited success. However, a general consensus has formed around the belief that such attempts at centralization were driven by rapid economic expansion, industrialization, and urbanization.[24]

America's initial experiment with bureaucratic order was derived from the regulative, hierarchical needs of urban-industrial life. Supporting this order was a newly emerging "national class." This class helped to define the expanding national state, while it valued and promoted expertise that "carried the burden of hopes for a new era of specialized parts and systematized wholes where nothing worked without carefully mastered bodies of knowledge."[25] With the rise of this order, political life and public institutions offered prominent roles to men who were interested in ideas and scholarship.[26]

This new bureaucratic order was fundamentally national in its efforts and orientation.[27] However, the institutional and intellectual apparatuses that furthered this new national authority should not simply be equated with the federal government. Proponents of the new American state sought to standardize and rationalize not only federal procedures and activities but also those of state and local governments, through incentive-laden land grants, specialized journals, "good-government clubs," and schools of public administration. The development of the new American state thus meant not only the expansion of national administrative capacities but also the reform of existing modes of local governance.

The Fundamentals of the New American State: Ideas and Institutions

Skowronek and Eisenach provide the broadest assessments of the structures and philosophies underlying the new American state. Skowronek surveys the institutional developments of the period but also acknowledges that the state "is an intellectual enterprise."[28] Eisenach primarily examines the intellectual roots of the period but also grants that political ideas are greatly impacted through institutionalization.

Both Skowronek and Eisenach not only recognize the relation between ideas and institutions but also stress the importance of universities in developing this relationship. In an effort to bridge the gap between the two authors and assess the dynamic relationship between ideas and institutions, I concentrate on one institution—the emerging American university—that was essential in establishing the institutional and intellectual frameworks that marked the national state in this formative era.

Scholars of American political development have long acknowledged the influence of universities and expertise but have not detailed the process by which they came to be influential. In this study, I detail the processes by which universities established such influence; thus, this study sheds light not only on the formation of universities but also on the development of the American administrative state itself. Understanding the development of the administrative state is fundamental for contemporary conceptions of politics and policy. Brian Cook notes: "the administration of government is a prime target for agitating for change in the American polity. Indeed, the question of how the Republic can best administer its affairs has been at the center of nearly every political conflict that has marked a new stage in the nation's development."[29] Administration is not simply an instrument of political actors, it is itself an independent actor with constitutive force. Thus, the origins of administrative authority are relevant to anyone with interest in current governmental activity.

According to Skowronek, efforts at building the new American state and the expansion of national administrative capacities from 1877 to 1920 attempted to place power in the presidency and federal bureaucracy while wresting control from the locally oriented Congress, courts, and political machines. Relying on organizational, procedural, and intellectual redefinition, this building and expansion sought the concentration of authority at the national center of government, the centralization of authority within the government, and the specialization of institutional tasks and individual roles.[30]

As Skowronek states, "providing the national institutional capacities commensurate with the demands of an industrial society required nothing less than a different kind of state organization."[31] New, bureaucratic forms of government needed to be adopted. These new forms represented, "the great departure in American institutional development," as "new national administrative institutions first emerged free from the clutches of party domination, direct court supervision, and localistic orientations."[32]

Intellectual support was crucial for the development of the state. Skowronek aptly articulates its overall significance to state building.

> Associated with all highly institutionalized states is a special intellectual cadre that maintains an underlying continuity in governmental activity through social and political changes. The intellectuals must be recruited through an established church, an aristocracy of birth, or a university. Such institutions tend to confer legitimacy on the state as they generate the personnel to operate it. By their education and their social status, the intellectuals come to embody the special identity of the state.[33]

In the expansion of the federal state at the turn of the twentieth century, this cadre did not come primarily from the church or aristocracy. They came from the university. During this era, "new communities of intellectual competence—socially differentiated and internally ordered— were heralded in broad-ranging movements to establish formal professional recruitment and practice, and to build universities that would train specialists and define expertise."[34] I would stress that universities were built to do more than simply train specialists and define expertise. Universities also sought to build character, provide skills, and elevate "gentleman." Seeking to establish their fledgling research universities, the institutional entrepreneurs who led higher education needed to emphasize their relevance to the newly redefined frameworks of the national state; training specialists and defining expertise was the most effective way to do this.

Eisenach stresses that commensurate with creation of this new American state were new ideas of and new approaches to politics and public life. Comprised largely of academics and other public intellectuals, a Progressive "regime in thought" focused on creating a nationalist ideological framework. Seeking common American values, meanings, and identities, this "regime in thought" created institutional locations, primarily within universities, for a new form of social knowledge that articulated ideas of a national public good unmediated by party, interest, region, or sectarian religion.[35]

The emergence of this "regime in thought" was crucial in the United States, according to Eisenach.

> Our only source of a common American identity is political; our fundamental political ideas are largely constitutive of our personal ideas as Americans. If the moral and intellectual integrity of our most basic political ideas is in doubt, so, too, are its ideological products and the authority of political groupings organized around those ideologies.[36]

Extracting from Eisenach, we see that political ideas shape not only the state but also the identities of the citizenry, the values of the public, and the meanings of the civilization.

Tensions certainly did exist between the various strains of Progressive political thought.[37] However, these tensions were joined in a common belief that the previous American state of courts and parties and its spoils system were corrupt and needed to be replaced by a more efficient, expert, and fair national system of government. "Efficiency," notes Cook, "was in a very real sense a moral concept."[38] Correspondingly, it was also a national concept. For Woodrow Wilson, Henry Carter Adams, and others of this era, the challenge was to incorporate European models of rational, bureaucratic, and expert governance while maintaining American democratic values.

Because of the "moral" and nationalistic components of the push for efficiency and expertise, universities and their institutional entrepreneurs were uniquely well positioned to support this pursuit. Institutions of higher learning already produced good and patriotic young men. With the establishment of new schools and credentials, the production of good and patriotic experts was an appropriate and logical next step.

Institutionalizing the Authority of Expertise

Rapid economic expansion, industrialization, and urbanization expanded interdependence and increased complexity in most all aspects of American life. In response to such forces, Skowronek's "new American state" and Eisenach's Progressive "regime in thought" developed as capstones to a "broad movement to establish or reestablish authority," a movement that "made some people receptive to expert advice about human affairs and provided others the confidence to give it."[39] Such expertise was more than simply specialized knowledge. It was specialized knowledge codified and formalized primarily through the university and its credentials.

The new American state developed from the acceptance of expertise and the formalization of this acceptance through institutions in which "experts were heavily represented and the official language and justifications for reorganization were apolitical, couched in efficiency terms rather than policy terms."[40] As the new American state developed, expertise became almost a "habit," structuring individual and institutional preferences and alternatives.[41] March and Olsen explain that the authority of experts stems from knowledge that was defined through "a collection of rules": "Although . . . rationalized to some degree, rules [were] learned by experts as catechisms. . . . The rules [were] enforced by the standards of professions and the expectations of patrons.[42]

The emerging university and the federal government were both standard enforcers and expectant patrons of such expertise. As the state expanded and the university emerged, producing experts meant more than simply educating smart men, it meant educating men in particularized bodies of knowledge and training them in the best manner and methods to apply such knowledge.

By developing and nurturing expertise, the university did not simply produce trained personnel for government employment. It also defined national standards and expectations for a widening array of disciplines, fields, and professions. These efforts were often driven by coordination among the leading universities. Such coordination meant that national systemization of knowledge did not necessarily include the federal government. In some policy domains, such as forestry, the federal government was intimately involved in defining expertise. Universities worked as active partners of the national state in developing standards and expectations. In other domains, such as education, the federal government was only marginally involved in defining expertise.

Universities coordinated with one another to develop national standards and expectations; thus, they served as agents of the national state. In assessing the influence of university-based expertise, one must consider not only how institutions of higher learning supported the formal apparatus of the federal government but also how they supported the less structured networks that would serve to extend the reach and the authority of the national state.

The Apparatuses of the State

Before discussing my particular examination of universities' contribution to the development of the American administrative state, it is worthwhile to place such examination in a broader context. The relation between institutions and ideas is not simply defined by historical perspective. The power of political institutions and public ideas can also be discussed more generally. It has been widely recognized that the structure of institutions and the construct of ideas can possess authority and influence on their own. However, by defining what political institutions and public ideas mean, we create new questions as to how their influence is enhanced by one another. Institutions need intellectual support, and ideas need an institutional home to develop and thrive in the world of politics.

The Institutional Apparatus

Whether viewed as a single entity seeking a particularized set of agendas and goals or as one of a series of institutions that influence and structure politics and policy, the state has been recognized as a distinct element outside of the individual citizens who comprise it, the particular leaders who govern it, and the various state organizations that exist to petition it. As Weber observes and as Poggi, Skocpol, and others reiterate, the state does more than simply claim control over territories and the people.[43] It is more than "government." It is a series of administrative, legal, extractive, and coercive organizations.

The ability of these administrative, legal, bureaucratic, and coercive systems to establish policies and goals as more than simply conduits is characterized as "state autonomy." The ability to implement such policies and goals is characterized as "state capacities."[44] In defining the state, the distinction between autonomy and capacities is not as significant as the understanding of the state as a political actor somewhat independent of the citizens, leaders, and groups that constitute it.

Within these conceptions, the whole of the state is greater than the simple sum of its political parts. Its authority is defined as the ability to influence the practice of politics, the formation of groups, the identity of individuals, and the demands of society. The state is more than simply the activities of governmental officials and institutions. Theories of state building recognize that educational institutions often supplement and extend such state authority. They contribute to the sum of the state's overall authority. Thus, in examining here the institutional development of universities closely tied to the national state, I also consider the broader development of the state itself.

The Intellectual Apparatus

The ability of the state to influence the practice of politics, the formation of groups, the identity of individuals, and the demands of society does not rest solely in its institutional activities and structures. Public ideas greatly influence these abilities as well as the activities and structures themselves. Whether we consider the state to be a single entity defining other institutions or only one of many institutions shaping society, changes in the state's ability to exert authority and establish constraints do not depend entirely on its own structural characteristics and activities. Reforms also depend on the power of public ideas that exist beyond it.

Politics and policy should be seen as more than the conflict and ordering of interests. It should also be seen as the conflict and ordering of ideas. While focusing on individual and collective interests who petition the state, Kingdon finds that ideas are crucial. Major changes in public policy often occur when the power of an idea whose "time has come" bowls over existing interests and constituencies. The power of ideas is not limited to their ability to influence the outcomes of conflict between interests. They also greatly influence institutional structures and activities, as well as political outcomes. For Kingdon, "it is difficult to understand the origins, attraction, and tremendous power of such movements as abolition, civil rights, environmental protectionism, feminism, and consumerism without resorting to the power of ideas."[45] I would add that it is also difficult—well-nigh impossible—to understand the origins, attraction, and power of the state without including the role of ideas.

Mary Douglas[46] attempts to parse out the specific influence of ideas on institutions. She does not disagree with Skocpol, North, Jackman, and others who argue that institutions can structure ideas as well as outcomes and activities.[47] Rather, she emphasizes the reciprocal relationship between ideas and institutions. For Douglas, the formation and maintenance of institutions is an intellectual process as much as an economic and political one. That politics and policy are, as we can infer from Kingdon, an intellectual enterprise does not mean we should disregard institutions. Rather, as Douglas underscores, it means we must examine how ideas affect the state's ability to structure outcomes and activities, as well as consider the state's ability to influence ideas. Douglas thus offers a method for understanding social, political, and economic puzzles: "half of [the] task is to demonstrate this cognitive process at the foundation of the social order. The other half is to demonstrate that the individual's most elementary cognitive process depends on social institutions."[48]

In other words, when examining questions of politics and policy, we must acknowledge that ideas are shaped by their institutional context and that institutions are shaped by their intellectual underpinnings. Therefore, whether considered as a series of institutions or as a single entity, the state, as an independent actor, is more than just an institutional construct. It is also an intellectual construct in which ideas as well as institutions influence the practice of politics, the formation of groups, the identity of individuals, and the demands of society.

From these various approaches to the question of what defines "the state" and its relation to institutions and ideas, a useful definition emerges. The state operates as an autonomous actor whose institutions exert authority and structure conflict. Ideas have weight on their own and can shape politics and social interaction. State authority is grounded in the interplay of institutions and ideas. More important, for this discussion, the state depends on social knowledge that is supported primarily by nongovernmental institutions. The institutions that support such knowledge are not beyond the influence of the state. State action creates demands for knowledge about the social processes and structures that state interventions seek to influence. The knowledge basis of such action, as well as the processes by which the state affects the development and application of social knowledge, are of central importance to state authority.[49] Most succinctly, to understand state authority, we need to consider more than state institutions. Puzzles of state authority are also puzzles of social knowledge and of the institutions that create and disseminate such knowledge.

Research Design

In addition to rendering an overview of political institutions and ideas at the turn of the twentieth century, Skowronek and Eisenach also present a useful methodological framework. Skowronek employs case studies of selected governmental agencies to assess the structure of the new American state. He focuses on governmental reform and expansion in civil administration, the military, and business regulation. Skowronek explains why he elects to use this approach.

> By identifying patterns of development over three distinct areas of administrative innovation, we can move beyond a history of each towards a cross-sectional view of a transformation in the integrated networks of institutions, procedures, and human talents that constitute the state as a working organization. In a comparative framework, the reform efforts complement each other in illuminating a single political process of reconstructing the American state around national administrative capacities in the industrial age.[50]

Incorporating an approach similar to Skowronek's, I employ case studies of distinct schools to illuminate the coordinated process of university support for national state authority.

Eisenach uses case studies of selected individuals to examine the ideas of the era. In selecting writers and writings, Eisenach attempted to identify "potential candidates for the title 'inventor' of Progressivism." The final short list of candidates he focused on "is not intended to be 'representative' in the sense of encompassing the entire range of reform movements, causes, or ideas." Instead, it represents "a core group whose writings and institutional innovations first defined the larger terms by which Progressivism was defined in all its variety and conflict."[51]

In this project, I parallel Skowronek and Eisenach's methods and attempt to build on their analysis. I rely on historical, archival case studies of individual schools. Previous archival histories of the research university at this time—such as Laurence Veysey's *The Emergence of the American University,* Roger Geiger's *To Advance Knowledge,* and Julie Reuben's *The Making of the Modern University*—furnish background as well as guides to pertinent collections. These works emphasize the unique influence of the American university in the post–Civil War era. Veysey aptly characterizes the challenge inherent in examining the university and its relation to society when he asserts, "the university must be understood as a magnet for the emotions, not alone as a project of conscious definition."[52]

Case-Study Selection and Rationale

To understand the emotion and conscious definition of the university's relation to and support of the national state, I compare schools drawn from four distinct groupings. Three are drawn from Geiger's categorization of early members of the Association of American Universities (AAU): older eastern elite institutions; newer private institutions; and newer midwestern and western state institutions.[53] The fourth grouping—antebellum southern state institutions—is comprised of schools that at the time of their founding lagged behind the expansion and research that marked the AAU schools. The members of each category are as follows:

Older Eastern Elite Institutions	*Newer Midwestern and Western State Institutions*
Columbia University	University of California
Harvard University	University of Illinois
University of Pennsylvania	University of Michigan
Princeton University	University of Minnesota
Yale University	University of Wisconsin

Newer Private Institutions	*Antebellum Southern State Institutions*
University of Chicago	University of Georgia
Cornell University	University of North Carolina
Johns Hopkins University	University of South Carolina
Massachusetts Institute	University of Tennessee
of Technology	University of Virginia
Stanford University	

These four categories allow me to draw cases from a core group of institutions that defined the university's relation to the national state both formally, through the AAU, and informally, through their institutional leadership and training of faculty and administrators who would staff schools across the country.

Obviously, the universities from this group do not represent the whole of higher learning at the turn of the twentieth century. Women's colleges, urban Catholic colleges, and historically black colleges emerged at this time, and many existing liberal arts colleges flourished. Therefore, I also include broader considerations of these institutions, along with detailed examinations of research universities, in order to develop an understanding of how this core group of schools came to define higher education and its relation to the national state in this era and for generations to come. The influence of the leading universities and their leadership on other schools was summarized by Wellesley College president Caroline Hazard in her conclusion to a letter asking Harvard's Charles Eliot for advice about the organization of her faculty, where she stated, "everyone in college work looks to you as the ultimate authority."[54]

By focusing on more established schools, I am not suggesting that these were the only institutions that influenced American political development. I am, however, suggesting that to some extent, research universities grew out of a desire to serve the state. Since this period witnessed the rise of more coordinated efforts and an increased awareness of "peer institutions," these particular studies also incorporate more general considerations of the other institutions within the group.

Using the preceding institutional categories enables both generalization about universities' role in the institutionalization of the American state's authority and examination of particular institutional differences in their approach and commitment to this role. The categories allow for consideration of distinctions that might have influenced the relation of the university to the national state: regionalism, age, and funding source. Regionalism has long been considered a factor in American politics and state building.[55] Organizational age is often considered a significant institutional characteristic.[56] Funding sources clearly can impact a nongovernmental institution's support of state authority.[57] Categorizing the institutions as I have done allows for comparison of southern schools where the national state was being reconstructed, western schools where the state was being newly settled, and eastern schools where the state was being reestablished. It also allows for comparison of institutions built from public munificence with those built from private generosity. Finally, it allows me to undertake a particularized as well as a comprehensive consideration of the manner and method in which universities further the development of the expanding national state.

University Archives and the "Golden Age" of Presidents

In examining the role of the university in American political development, I relied heavily on university archives as well as contemporary accounts and writings of academic leaders. Owing to their long tenures in office and their prominent positions in public life, such collections as the James Burrill Angell Papers at the University of Michigan's Bentley Historical Library, the Arthur Twining Hadley Papers at Yale's Sterling Memorial Library, the Benjamin Ide Wheeler Papers at the University of California's Doe Memorial Library, and the Charles Eliot Papers at Harvard are all major sources of academic correspondence from this period. These collections contain more than personal letters; they also serve as the primary repository of institutional reports and academic addresses of the period and therefore as the best resource for capturing the diversity of academic and political debate among university leaders and faculty in this period.

The university presidents of the late nineteenth and early twentieth centuries came to embody their institutions in a way not seen before or since.[58] Ralph Waldo Emerson once referred to institutions as "the long shadow of men." In considering the university's role in state building at the turn of the twentieth century, one can see the long shadows of university leaders stretched not just over the ivory towers of academia but to the White House, the capitol, the courts, and the executive offices of the new American state. Though certainly the most high-profile example of an academic leader defining an institution and stretching into the public sphere, the election of former Princeton president Woodrow Wilson to the presidency of the United States in 1912 simply reflected the very active role university leaders took as "public men" in the politics and policy of the new American state.

In taking such active roles, university leaders were greatly assisted by lengthy tenures that allowed them to both establish and perpetuate their personal and institutional identities. Having established their identities as "public men," the leading administrators and educators of the era often became prominent figures in the new American state. Such men as Daniel Coit Gilman, who twice was "runner-up" for the Yale presidency and who served briefly as president of the University of California before guiding the newly founded Johns Hopkins University for twenty-seven years (1875–1902), served among the longest tenures that have ever been seen at their respective institutions. Gilman's initial contact with California came on an assessment visit sponsored by the United States Department of Agriculture. While head of Johns Hopkins, he served on a number of boards and commissions concerned with the promotion of rational and "good" government. After retiring from Hopkins at the age of sixty-five, Gilman served as founding president of the Carnegie Institution. Gilman's good friend and fellow Yale alumnus Andrew Dickson White had a similar record of pubic service. White served as president of Cornell for its first seventeen years (1867–85). In this time, he also was drafted to run for governor of New York but declined, and he served as the State Department's minister in Berlin. Later, he served a lengthy stint as minister to Russia.

Newly founded and privately capitalized universities, such as Johns Hopkins and Cornell, were not the only institutions to witness such long shadows. James Burrill Angell guided the University of Michigan for a remarkable thirty-eight years (1871–1909). The exceptional length and breadth of his shadow over the Ann Arbor campus can be seen in the fact that though he chaired the Deep Waterways Commission in 1895 and took significant leaves of absence to head diplomatic missions (in China in 1880–82 and in Turkey in 1897–98), he remained a hands-on administrator who was seen as so indispensable to the institution that his initial letter of retirement in 1905 was unanimously rejected by the university's elected Board of Regents.

Though the discussion in this book relies extensively on Angell's papers, it does so without overstating his influence and reputation. Angell was, by any measure, a national figure. His leadership of the University of Michigan and his governmental service helped establish his reputation as a leading man of letters and public service. Early in his career, many suggested he return to his native Vermont to run for the United States Senate.[59]

Perhaps the best reflection of Angell's stature was the nationwide outpouring of editorials that greeted his retirement in 1909. The *Port-*

land Oregonian noted Angell's departure with regret and with praise for his work and for the university it saw as his legacy.

> The University of Michigan is the immediate model which all successful state universities have followed. . . . The university was the creation of the common people of Michigan, led by a great commander. Like the career of Lincoln, it [Angell's career] shows the inner meaning of democracy. The University of Michigan is typical of the future wonders which the people shall work not only in education, but in everything else.

The *Wheeling News* in West Virginia characterized Angell as "one of the most imposing figures in the realm of education in America" and praised him for the "reforms introduced and results produced."[60]

Angell's influence and stature were heightened by his unique position in Ann Arbor and by the incredible length of his tenure. The leaders of fledgling western and southern universities often referred to him as the "father" of public higher education and sought to draw on his remarkable experience. The leaders of established eastern schools similarly trusted his experience but also valued his position detached from their own rivalries. Perhaps no one expressed this sentiment better than Harry Pratt Judson, who served as the University of Chicago president from 1906 to 1923.

> Pres. Angell we feel is not solely the property of the Univ. of Michigan. He belongs to all of us who are interested in educational work in the west and throughout the country. His ripe experience, his rare personal qualities, his sound judgment have endeared him to all. We look to him for leadership and regard him in a very large sense as one of the most trusted leaders and advisors of educational thought in the entire nation.[61]

It would not be uncommon for Angell to receive correspondence from two academic leaders each expressing frustration with or skepticism about the ideas or plans of the other. Angell, therefore, is not only a central figure but also a linchpin for understanding the process of university support in the development of the national state.

The oldest and most established schools in the country were also witnesses to lengthy presidencies. Charles Eliot ran Harvard for forty years (1869–1909), and Frederick Barnard led Columbia for twenty-five years (1864–89). Arthur Twining Hadley guided Yale for twenty-one years (1899–1920),[62] during which time he also actively served the federal government in various capacities—most notably, chairing a special commission established to direct reform of interstate railroad rates.

Even the relatively languid schools of the South reflected this significant trend of strong and continued academic leadership. Thanks largely to Chancellor David Barrow's patience and longevity in dealing with a conservative legislature and public, the University of Georgia, though "remaining behind national norms," evolved beyond a school once described by one of Barrow's predecessors as "a scheme that sets up an aristocracy of pretensions to culture."[63] Recognizing that "every other leading institution of higher education in the country was operating under this form of governance," the University of Virginia's Board of Visitors appointed Edwin Anderson Alderman as its first president.[64] Alderman oversaw the university for twenty-seven years (1904–31) and undertook efforts to establish it as a "full university of national prominence."[65]

The significance of such lengthy tenures does not lie in the fact that these academic leaders had a monochromatic vision of higher education and its relation to the federal state. These leaders and their institutions represented the various strains of academic emphasis—mental discipline, culture, utility, and research—that melded into the emerging American university. Such lengthy tenures often meant that academic leaders came not only to embody the particular institution they served but also to represent higher education as a whole.[66] Thus, no matter what emphasis his particular vision for higher education reflected, the university president was often speaking on behalf of both his particular institution and his vision for the American university in general.

Overview of This Book

My purpose in this book is to develop a systematic understanding of the university's role in American political development. Building from general considerations of this role, I argue that the university provided both intellectual and institutional apparatuses that legitimized and formalized national state authority. Defining state authority as the ability to influence the practice of politics, the formation of groups, the identity of individuals, and the demands of society, I argue that such nongovernmental institutions as universities are crucial for modifications of and reforms to state authority. I also contend that the support of these institutions was not necessarily co-opted by the state as much as it was offered by institutional entrepreneurs seeking to establish the societal relevance and significance of their institutions. To illuminate these discussions, I examine the university's role as agent and partner in legitimizing and formalizing the new American state in first the "loosely coupled" era (1862–99) and then the "formally aligned" era

(1900–1920). I conclude by discussing the evolution of this role and its consequences for American political development and policy.

In simplest terms, scholars of politics, history, and many other disciplines have recognized the importance of expertise in the expansion of the American state. However, in acknowledging this relationship, most have posited that the state recognized the need for experts and then turned to universities who dutifully obliged in their provision. Examining the period between the end of the Civil War and the end of World War I, I note that just as often, universities and the institutional entrepreneurs who guided them developed experts and then worked actively to create a market for their services. This shift to a more shared causality has significant implications not only for our historical understanding of American political development but for our current assessment of public policy and of higher education's impact on it.

2 Why the University?

A Uniquely Positioned Institution

To modern ears, Grover Cleveland's assertion "When I was in trouble and needed help, I usually turned to the University of Michigan" and such speeches as Woodrow Wilson's "Princeton in the Nation's Service" may border on platitudes.[1] After all, it has been commonplace to find universities promoting their "service," allowing faculty to take sabbaticals to work in government posts, and inviting public figures to address commencement. However, in their time, these presidents' words reflected a new role for higher education.

The conception of the emerging university as an institution directly involved in the political, economic, and industrial development of the nation was essentially new, replacing the antebellum belief that colleges should primarily produce theological leaders and upstanding local citizens. Debate certainly had existed about what was meant by a college education and about how best to develop character and morality among students. Nonetheless, the scale and reach of American higher education was appreciably smaller in the colonial, Revolutionary, Jacksonian, and antebellum eras. Some people—most notably, Henry Phillip Tappan (at the University of Michigan in the 1850s)—did attempt to bring the "university idea" to America before the Civil War. However, not until the founding of Johns Hopkins University in 1876 and the passage of the Morrill Acts in 1862 and 1890 did the national research university, focused on supporting the American state and directly serving the government, became an established alternative to the local college, focused on building morality and serving God.

To fully appreciate the role of the university in the development of the new American state, one must appreciate the massive institutional change that transformed American higher education. The university of today is fairly similar in its curriculum and mission to the university of the 1920s. The same certainly cannot be said about the relation of the university of the 1920s with the university of the 1850s: "to paraphrase Henry Adams, Harvard in 1850 was in many ways closer to the Middle Ages than to the Harvard of 1900."[2]

While the nation's leading universities came to this political role naturally, they did not do so effortlessly. The institutional entrepreneurs who guided higher education worked continually to elevate their schools internally and to define their relevance externally. Additionally, these leaders created and furthered both structural and societal roles that placed the university in a privileged position and allowed it to work as an active partner and independent agent of the burgeoning American state.

Universities and the Institutionalization of Expertise

Studies of American political development have long recognized the role that university-based expertise played in the expansion of the American state and in related reform. Skowronek neatly summarizes the rationale for such a focus.

> The obvious fact [is] that American institutional development did not stop in 1920. Indeed, the institutions that have been added to the state apparatus and the functions that have been assumed by the national government since 1920 may seem to dwarf the significance of the state building episode [between the 1870s and 1920]. The expansion of national administration accelerated dramatically in the 1930s and again in the 1960s. *Yet, the course of institutional development . . . [is] rooted in this turn-of-century departure* [emphasis mine]. The internal governmental changes negotiated between the end of Reconstruction and the end of World War I established a new institutional politics at the national level that has proven remarkably resistant to fundamental change. They have also raised questions of political authority and the capacity for direction within government that have yet to be firmly resolved.[3]

Strikingly, a very similar story can be told regarding the development of higher education. As I discuss throughout the course of this book, such similarity is more than the product of coincidence. Universities did not simply mirror the growth of the state; they both facilitated it and capitalized on it.

Contemporary observers and scholars of reform—including, to some extent, Eisenach and Skowronek—assume an inevitability in universities' rise as supporting institutions for the national state. In part, such an assumption is understandable, for one of the primary goals of their works is to underscore the intellectual and institutional apparatuses that were integral to the expansion of American state capacities. Skowronek states in his introduction:

> The routine work of government is primarily a mental rather than a manual labor, and the intellectual talent available in government for problem solving and innovation is critical to the capacities of a state to maintain itself over time.

Skowronek notes that such "intellectual talent" can come from an established aristocracy, a state-supported church, professional and trade organizations, or educational institutions.[4] However, he also stresses that in the case of American state building, this talent came primarily from the emerging university and the related professional associations. As mentioned earlier, Eisenach takes Skworonek's emphasis even further, describing the university as akin to a "national church,"[5] providing the state not only institutional and intellectual apparatuses but also moral and cultural support.

I do not quibble with Skowronek and Eisenach's characterization of universities' fundamental role in the state-building era. In fact, I use their arguments as both a springboard and a frame for my own discussion. Appreciating their general discussion, I seek to move the consideration of universities a step further. Seemingly, Skowronek, Eisenach, and others take the role of the university in state building for granted. They maintain that the state needed intellectual talent and that the university provided it. In this work, I highlight the fact that the situation was not necessarily that simple.

First, before the later half of the nineteenth century, American universities were not necessarily in the business of developing and defining "intellectual talent." Instead, American higher education devoted itself to developing character, instilling morals, and defining a gentleman class. University service on behalf of the new American state was not merely an extension of its previous work. Rather, it was a product of the university's own institutional redefinition.

Second and correspondingly, universities were not the only potential source of institutional and intellectual support. Today, it seems natural and almost inevitable that universities would define particular bodies of knowledge and provide credentials testifying to individuals' expertise. However, it would be a mistake to assume that no alternatives ever existed. In the development of the new American state, one could imagine a system whereby the knowledge and skills required by teachers, foresters, civil administrators, and others were defined and credentialed either by national government agencies or by a federally chartered university. But instead, the nation's leading universities came to define appropriate knowledge and skills. The possibility of such an alternative imparts greater richness to the study of universities' contribution to the development of the American state, because it frames universities' contribution to the development of the national state not as a simple mechanism for reform but, rather, as a piece of a complex puzzle within which universities helped to define and establish the parameters of reform itself. Crucial to this effort was the universities' intimate relationship with other organizations dedicated to reform and to the development of the national state.

Professional, disciplinary, and civic associations were also actively involved in the process of building a new American state. The membership and, more important, the leadership of these associations were drawn from what was described as the class of "university men." Institutions of higher learning served as a defining and driving force. To borrow from Brian Cook's distinction, the American university was not simply instrumental to but, rather, constitutive of the administrative state.[6] In other words, the university did not simply provide manpower and transmit knowledge at the behest of the national state. Rather, by defining new bodies of knowledge, establishing new degree programs, and granting new credentials, universities defined the agenda for state capacities. University-based expertise thus provided the state not only with particular capabilities and rationales but also with direction, establishing priorities and defining the appropriate reach of its administration.

Universities' efforts to define their contribution and forestall potential competitors placed a premium on institutional entrepreneurship and organizational coordination. Such entrepreneurship and coordination were not simply crucial for the growth of universities and their service to the state; they were also fundamental to establishing the nature of such service. First through informal means and later through structured efforts, universities were often able to determine to which public concerns specialized knowledge would and would not be applied.

This agenda-setting function may seem so readily apparent as to be almost unworthy of mention. However, it is important to illuminate its effect. For example, scholars of the late nineteenth and early twentieth centuries were highly interested in making government more efficient, applying expert techniques for land use in forestry and agriculture, and establishing standards in such professions as law, medicine, and education. They were not interested in issues of contemporary concern, such as the political participation of ethnic minorities, the effects of smoking on public health, and the best way to educate citizens for whom English is a second language. Though it might seem almost absurd to imagine either early university scholarship focusing on such issues or early academic programs dedicated to such fields, the peculiarity of this conjecture stems in no small part from the universities' extensive influence on the public agenda. The efforts of advocates and the force of social movements certainly have been essential in bringing such matters to public attention. Nonetheless, the power of such public ideas is greatly enhanced by their institutional locale. Since the end of the antebellum era, the American university has been arguably the most authoritative of public institutions.

Developing Structure: Coordination, Agency, and Partnerships

In undertaking this study, I initially expected to focus on each institution separately, comparing their individual relations with the state. However, as my research progressed, I realized that the coordination of and relationship between universities was essential to understanding their interactions with the state. Moreover, I also discovered that the relationships between universities themselves and between universities and the national state evolved significantly with the founding of the Association of American Universities in 1900. I therefore frame my discussion around this founding. I build from studies of individual schools to consider the general role of the university in the legitimization and formalization of the national state in the "loosely coupled" era (1862–99) and in the "formally aligned" era (1900–1920). While the state developed, the notion of universities' public service as active partners and independent agents evolved as well.

Nongovernmental institutions play a significant role in the establishment of state authority. Mediating interplay between political institutions and public ideas, nongovernmental institutions take on a "parastate" quality,[7] acting as partners of or agents with the state. In American political development, the role of such nongovernmental institutions is intensified. The public good is not always democratically defined, especially during eras of reform. Nongovernmental institutions are largely free from the immediate concerns and whims of electoral politics and thus can better support changes in the foundations of state authority.

In the era of building a new American state, existing democratic institutions were seen as corrupt and inefficient; thus, new institutions needed to be created.[8] New institutions would not just spring to life from the demands of the electorate. They had to be nurtured by non-governmental institutions that fostered new institutional and intellectual apparatuses for governance. Additionally, because of the various stratifications and constraints imposed by American federalism, shifts in the basis of governmental authority are not necessarily unitary and immediate. Instead, they are often scattered and gradual.

University Coordination: The "Loosely Coupled" and "Formally Aligned" Eras

Though not formalized until the formation of various higher education associations, such as the AAU, the contributions of universities to the new American state were coordinated throughout the state-building era. Initially, this coordination was based largely on the personal and social ties of university presidents. A telling example of such familiarity was the friendship of Andrew Dickson White, founding president of Cornell, and Daniel Coit Gilman, founding president of Johns Hopkins. The two were friends at Yale and traveled together to Europe after graduation, before embarking on their academic careers. In no small part due to such familiarity and in response to the uncertainty of their expanded role and mission, universities consciously modeled themselves on one another in terms of curriculum, structure, and relations to the state.

Coordination helped spur what DiMaggio and Powell characterize as institutional isomorphism.[9] The nation's leading universities were close enough to learn from one another. They were also complex enough to harness variation that (to borrow from Axelrod and Cohen)[10] would allow for institutional adaptation and evolution. University presidents would send one another their annual reports and budgets, but formal collection of such materials or meetings regarding similar administrative concerns rarely, if ever, took place. Universities and their leaders handled between themselves, rather than through internal committees, questions ranging from whether to add courses in political economy, to the appropriate role for summer sessions and extension programs, to the appointment of naval engineers to the faculty through informal communications and letters. Even when internal committees were formed to examine such matters as coeducation or fraternities, among their primary duties was to poll other schools to learn how they addressed such issues. This loosely coupled coordination not only meant there was institutional similarity; it also meant there was informal regulation, as universities standardized their curriculum, their campus life, and their relations to the new American state.

Interestingly, despite increasing complexity in the size and scope of universities, the move toward more formally aligned coordination was not prompted by difficulties between the loosely coupled elite universities. Rather, it was prompted primarily by difficulties certain universities had encountered in gaining credit for their course work and acceptance of their degrees at the leading European universities, especially German ones. In the United States, if a student sought to transfer or to pursue graduate studies at an institution different than where he or she had done undergraduate work (a practice that was much less common than it is today), the leading universities would accept that student based on a simple letter from their former institution. This letter often came personally from the university's president. Such an approach did not necessarily work for students seeking to study at European universities.

Responding to a report on the difficulties of American students abroad by his university's Graduate Council, University of California president Benjamin Ide Wheeler suggested a conference of the nation's leading universities. Writing to the presidents of Harvard, Columbia, Johns Hopkins, and the University of Chicago in October 1899, Wheeler suggested that a meeting was necessary because it would be impossible to discuss the value given American degrees by the German ministers of education unless a more formal standard for scholarship was set among the leading American universities.[11] Other university leaders agreed, and by February 1900, fourteen of the nation's leading research universities met in Chicago and formalized their coordination by establishing the Association of American Universities.

Between initial discussions and its first formal meeting, the organization's purpose had grown beyond simple concern with European respect for American degrees; matters fundamental to relations between American universities, such as standardized admissions, degree requirements, and graduate migration, were all included on the agenda for its first meeting. Recognizing the potential importance of such discussions for their relations with the national state, university leaders included the U.S. commissioner of education among their numbers at the conference.

Formally aligned coordination meant that the leading institutions of higher education could now set an agenda of issues to be addressed, rather than haphazardly waiting for issues to arise. They could formally standardize degrees and curriculum, rather than handling credentials on a case-by-case basis. They could also define their relations with the state through a collective approach, rather than through disparate efforts.

The University and the National State: Active Partners and Independent Agents

Whether coordinated through loosely coupled personal affiliations or through formally aligned associations, universities helped to establish the new American state and its authority of expertise. Universities functioned as both active partners and independent agents of the state. The role taken by the university was usually determined by the availability of resources. In addition to coordination, universities utilized access to highly generous benefactors, such as Andrew Carnegie, Paul Mellon, and John Rockefeller.

Such access did not mean that university leaders had limitless funds. New buildings, new problems, and new faculties stressed academic budgets. Therefore, institutional entrepreneurs sought patronage whenever necessary but not exclusively. Generally speaking, problems that cost a great deal to handle, such as the training of university students for military leadership and service or the expansion of scientific agriculture, were tackled through partnerships. Problems that cost little or nothing for the university to deal with through its expertise, such as the quality of secondary education and the standards of the professions, were tackled by the university as an independent agent. The application of expertise in these roles was driven by problem identification and entrepreneurial choice on behalf of university leaders and government officials.

Working in conjunction with the new American state sometimes meant that universities simply pursued a shared interest in national standards of rationality and expertise; at other times, it meant more direct partnerships with the national state. These partnerships began in earnest with the establishment of land-grant colleges through passage of the first Morrill Act in 1862 and continued after the Civil War, reinforced by the second Morrill Act of 1890. Though various experiment stations accompanying the creation of the land-grant colleges represented a prominent partnership between universities and the government, they were far from the only ones. During the late nineteenth and early twentieth centuries, federal departments and bureaus—such as the Departments of the Interior, the Treasury, Agriculture, and Commerce; the Bureaus of Education, Mines, Fisheries, Forestry, and Public Health; the Geological Survey; the Weather Bureau; and the Departments of the Army and the Navy—would all work in conjunction with universities to gather, assess, and disseminate expertise and information.[12]

In an effort to maintain relevance and patronage as well as serve the state, universities sought to develop relations that moved beyond simple research partnerships and into the establishment of whole schools, degree programs, and credentials. The efforts of University of California president Benjamin Ide Wheeler to establish a school of forestry in Berkeley present a fine example of this. Writing to the head of the Bureau of Forestry, Gifford Pinchot, Wheeler proposed that the bureau provide foresters to serve as faculty.

> I think it represents at any rate a line along which much can be done in bringing the United States departments into closer relation with the universities. The department at Washington would be benefited often by closer relation to the universities and the universities would be benefited quite as much.[13]

As Wheeler's letter to Pinchot indicates, university leaders saw such partnerships as beneficial for both their schools and the federal government. Wheeler never could convince Pinchot to fund faculty for a whole school, but various agencies made numerous contributions to Berkeley and other universities in terms of manpower, money, and resources, solidifying relations between universities and the federal government.

Building on earlier partnerships, universities offered their service to the nation in the preparation for and eventual entrance into World War I. Some faculty opposed such efforts and were relieved of their duties. Interestingly, other faculty felt universities were not doing enough and should direct all resources to the war effort, abandoning the study of literature, art, and the like. Between these two views, university leaders sought what was arguably a somewhat middle ground, by developing the Student Army Training Corps and the Reserve Officers Training Corps. The aim of the SATC was to develop "as a military asset the great body of college men throughout the country and to provide a reservoir from which officer material could be selected" and "to prevent wasteful depletion of the colleges through indiscriminate volunteering perpetuation."[14] As the war continued, the partnership between universities and the federal government continued and in fact grew. In an editorial entitled "Drafting Our Universities," an anonymous Columbia University professor, "on leave in the nation's service," stressed the need to perpetuate these partnerships.

> We spell Government with a capital "G" these days and the habit will continue until the war becomes a memory only in the mind of the oldest inhabitant. And the universities have been recognized in the general division of things essential and unessential for the public welfare.
> The universities after this war will be recognized by the Government as

the training schools for national efficiency. The mere will to live and to pay our debts is going to see to that. Trade, commerce, manufacture, science, national welfare in general are going to require such stimulation that they will have to be nationally organized; and the roots of their successful growth are going to be imbedded in the university. The universities of the country will have busy days before them after peace is declared.[15]

The partnerships that fostered such "busy days" represented not only direct institutional and intellectual linkages between the university and the national state but also direct efforts by the university to help legitimize and formalize the authority of the national state.

Working as independent agents meant that universities acted on behalf of the American state, regulating and coordinating policy areas in keeping with national reformers' desire for standardization, rationality, and efficiency, but not with direct authoritative governmental sanction. For example, the era of the new American state not only saw the expansion of national administrative capacities and the emergence of the university; it also witnessed an extraordinary boom in public and private secondary education. In 1870, there were 72,156 students in 1,026 high schools; by 1900, there were 519,251 students in 6,005 high schools. In the next twenty years, the numbers doubled for each decade.[16] Though interested in the quality and nature of secondary education, the national government did not have the resources to regulate high schools. As mentioned in chapter 1, the United States Bureau of Education was an agency of limited means and reach within the Department of the Interior. Responsibility for regulation, however, was simply given to the states.

In the East, the Middle States Examination Board, comprised of the region's major universities and colleges, created standardized entrance exams that drastically reshaped secondary school curriculum. In the Midwest and West, universities began accrediting public and private high schools through a system of admission by diploma. Many of the universities that adopted the diploma system were public, but in curricular matters, these institutions were often more concerned with pleasing their peer institutions than with pleasing their state legislatures. Started in 1869 by President E. O. Haven of Michigan, the diploma system meant that high school graduates who had taken the requisite courses from an accredited high school would be admitted to the university without having to sit for the entrance examinations.

Simply offering course work that universities prescribed, however, was not enough for high school accreditation. The high school or local alumni association would sponsor accreditation visits whereby faculty or select alumni representatives would visit local high schools to determine if their graduates could gain admission. The visits meant that universities were actively overseeing the quality of secondary education. For example, when A. F. Nightingale, superintendent of Chicago high schools, wrote to the University of Michigan president thanking him for renewing his school's accreditation as a "diploma school" and for providing him a detailed report by the faculty members who had assessed the school, he also asked for the names of two teachers the report had found unqualified, so as to be sure to not rehire them for the next year.[17]

Visitation reports did not simply comment on the quality and content of instruction; they also assessed the quality and size of the physical plant, especially libraries and laboratories, as well as student demeanor. Reports were frequently shared between universities, as high schools often would use their "diploma relations" with one university as the basis for seeking similar relations with another. Thus, universities acted as a regulatory agent, ensuring standards of quality, efficiency, and rationality.

Regulatory activities were not limited to secondary education. Such rising professions as law, medicine, and public administration found themselves regulated not by government agencies but by universities coordinating their efforts through their own schools and related professional associations. The development of a national, professional bar was fundamental for the new American state and its efforts to replace the existing state of courts and parties.[18] The formation of the American Bar Association was crucial to this effort, but just as important was the development and expansion of law schools, which stressed a standard and formal notion of legal expertise. Law schools helped the bar enforce these notions by producing credentials that allowed the bar to distinguish those who did have such training from those who did not. Similarly, the development of medical education, spurred by social critic Abraham Flexner's scathing report on the quality of medical training in the United States, created standard expectations and requirements for those who would possess the doctorate of medicine.[19]

Universities not only provided credentials; by regulating and standardizing their admissions and curriculum, they gave value to those credentials. It was not justice, health, or education departments that were setting the standards for lawyers, doctors, teachers, and others; it was universities who were doing so, as independent regulatory agents. However, because of the intimate ties between leaders of the university and leaders of the new American state (oftentimes they were one and the same), universities did so not in competition with the state but in conjunction with it.

Whether as an independent agent or as an active partner, universities expanded the scope and reach of the national administrative state further than it would have been able to go if it had relied on its own institutional and intellectual apparatuses. Universities' extension of the state was primarily directed by academic leaders seeking to establish their own institutions as well as the state itself. Pursuing the expansion of expertise and cultivating the patronage of private benefactors and public officials, institutional entrepreneurs offered the resources of their universities. In both the "loosely coupled" and the "formally aligned" eras, universities coordinated their efforts and resources and thus accentuated and systematized their support of the national state.

Universities and the American Aspiration

When considering the contemporary context for university-based expertise and support of state authority, it is crucial to build on our understanding of how and why universities were essential to the development of the national state. However, it is also important to understand the unique societal position universities held at the time of such development. As universities developed greater awareness of their identities as national institutions serving more than a local or regional elite, their entrepreneurial leaders offered university expertise not just to the federal state but to the nation as a whole. Expertise alone was not enough, and thus university leaders and other advocates also stressed the contributions that the emergence of universities as national institutions made to a national democratic identity, to national economic and industrial competitiveness, and to a national intellectual vanguard. Not only is this auxiliary support essential for our understanding of universities' role in the process of building a new American state at the turn of the century, but it is also fundamental to our examination of current questions about the relationship between the nation's academic and governmental institutions.

The Rise of Institutional Awareness and National Identity

Universities were structurally well positioned to support state authority founded on expertise. However, this alone was not the reason they were integral to the national state's development. In addition to promoting an expertise that placed authority in the hands—or more specifically, the minds—of trained specialists, the emerging university also fostered a culture of aspiration and a perception of accessibility that helped position it as a national institution. Critics, especially populists, would decry universities and their focus on expertise as elitist and undemocratic. Nonetheless, by the turn of the century, these criticisms had been largely diffused, as university leaders argued that the promotion of expertise was democratic, since training was supposedly available to any and all who were gifted enough to pursue it. Class and social status certainly still had a large effect on the institution, but the creation of fellowships, grades, and a general move among university leaders to stress academics and "merit" meant that the emerging university was more open than its antebellum predecessor had been.[20]

Universities also offered a unique nationalism grounded in intellect and collegiality. The national reach and ambitions of the emerging university offered the new American state not only expertise but also a possible institutional base for reconciliation of the Union. Soon after the Civil War, the University of California's eager search for faculty led it to the Harvard educated Joseph LeConte, who had served with the South Carolinian regiments during the Civil War. LeConte even briefly served as president of the University of California. Yale's War Memorial built in 1901 honored alumni who had died serving both the United States of America and the Confederate States of America. At his inauguration as the University of Virginia's first president, which was attended by President Theodore Roosevelt, Edwin Anderson Alderman reflected a desire to create a national institution.

> The Americans of the Southern States are the only Americans who have known in the direct form the discipline of war and the education of defeat. They alone of the unbeaten land have had intimate experience of revolution and despair.
>
> There is still the Republic to be served, venerable now, for all its brilliancy, and literally made over in outward form, in spiritual purpose and in industrial capacity since 1850. Who shall leaven this tumult of peoples with soberness and simplicity and Americanism? What is Americanism coming to signify spiritually to the world? Shall it be alone pride of power, passion for achievement, genius for self-indulgence, mad waste of energy, as in the ant hill, or shall it mean steadfast justice, respect for law, sober discipline, responsible citizenship, and moral sturdiness?
>
> The building of a National university of modern type in the South is the great opportunity to benefit the Republic now offered to the wisdom of States and imagination of far reaching men.[21]

Such nationalism was not limited to grand general conceptions of the university and its relation to the nation. It was imbued even in consideration of specific university programs. Describing the work of the

University of California's School of Agriculture and explaining the significance of agricultural research, acting president David Barrows stated in 1912:

> It is the country even more than the city which is menaced by the migration of the more active elements from the rural districts into the urban. It is the rural districts moreover which may be prejudicially affected by the settlement of foreign immigrants. . . . Foreign immigrants located in communities in the country tend to remain foreign, to perpetuate their foreign speech and prejudices, and to long resist incorporation into the American nation. All of these considerations give the highest importance to the work which lies before the Department of Agriculture of the University of California.[22]

In other words, the university was not operating experiment stations in rural areas simply to teach people how to farm; it was also operating them to teach people how to be good Americans. As Barrows's comments reflect, these programs offered more than just expertise to the various regions and people served. They also promoted a national state and identity. The university thus not only helped establish the new American state; it helped define what it was to be American.

With the Morrill Act of 1862 leading to a conflation of curricular, institutional, and political forces, the research university began to emerge in the aftermath of the Civil War. Professional and graduate schools, research laboratories, structured disciplines, and specialized faculty reflected the response to and demands of a more industrial and complex society. Additionally, the end of the Civil War and the push toward the twentieth century witnessed the beginnings of self-conscious institutional identity. Active alumni associations, the rise of extracurricular programs (especially intercollegiate athletics), and the move toward public ceremony gave institutions both organizations and identity beyond their own hallowed halls.

The University of Michigan's various alumni associations outside of the state—most notably, the Alumni Association of the Southwest (Kansas City, Missouri)—would sponsor accreditation visits whereby faculty would visit local high schools to determine if their graduates could gain admission by diploma. For a number of years, beginning in 1887, the Harvard Club of San Francisco sponsored a scholarship to send a University of California student to Harvard for a master's degree. At Harvard and Yale, only clergy served on the governing corporations until a push by alumni for representation ended with elected alumni representatives being seated—first at Harvard in 1867 and later at Yale in 1889. The relative power and influence of such graduate organizations could also be seen by the fact that in addition to inviting the U.S. commissioner of education, the founders of the Association of American Universities also invited the Federation of Graduate Clubs to send a representative.

The rise of extracurricular programs, especially of the sport of football and the activities surrounding the game, also reflected the growth of institutional self-awareness. School nicknames, fight songs, and colors all developed quickly after the first game between Princeton and Rutgers in 1869. Correspondent to the rise of alumni associations, football became a focus for loyalties and socializing. The Princeton-Yale game in New York and the Michigan-Chicago game in Chicago were highlights of the elite social calendar. Extensive coverage of college football in newspapers across the country surpassed every other sport of the early twentieth century. Such coverage not only stoked the fire of alumni but gave the mass public who might never have set foot on a college campus an image of and identity with the elite universities.[23] Football was not without problems. In fact, rampant abuses of rules, excessive alumni boosterism, and, most significantly, player deaths troubled academic leaders. For a number of years, California and Stanford abandoned football and instead played rugby, a game that Stanford's president David Starr Jordan felt was morally superior and that he characterized as demanding a much higher grade of skill and alertness and being far more interesting to watch.[24] Eastern schools did not take such a drastic action, but a significant increase in on-the-field fatalities led President Theodore Roosevelt to convene the athletic managers of the leading football schools—Harvard, Yale, and Princeton—at the White House in 1905.

The rise of alumni activity and of athletics was not necessarily essential to the emergence of the research university. However, it demonstrates the development of universities as national institutions that self-consciously created and nurtured an identity beyond their own walls. Institutional image and prestige became commodities that were linked to the value of university-based credentials. The elite institutions sought to establish national reputations for their schools; alumni associations and athletic success were one way to do this. National reputations were critical not just for attracting new students but also for maintaining the value of credentials and furthering the authority of expertise that these credentials helped create. Football success did not necessarily make degrees more valuable, but University of Chicago president William Rainey Harper courted Alonzo Stagg, for example, in an effort to build a successful football team that the president hoped would both bring great national notoriety and, in its own way, build legitimacy for the school.[25]

Correspondent with such concerns, the overall size and geographic diversity of universities' student bodies were of interest to their leaders. In an era before reputation rankings and college admissions guidebooks, these statistics were a measure of a university's prestige. For example, responding to enrollment figures showing a marked increase in overall student population and in the number of students coming from outside the Northeast, Columbia president Seth Low declared that the figures were "evidence that the great development of the university . . . has become widely known," and he maintained that "it [was] a fair inference from [the] figures that Columbia's national reputation [was] on the increase.[26]

Heightened awareness of institutional identity could also be seen in university ceremonies. In the mid-1880s, the leading American research universities adopted standards for academic costume, corresponding to the degree received and the school from which the degree was conferred. Additionally, the commencement address, rather than student-based activities, became the focus of graduation ceremonies. The influence universities held as national institutions was both summarized in and symbolized by the comments made by President Rutherford B. Hayes at Yale's commencement in 1880.

> Any administration and any country is more indebted to the man who is engaged in educating the people than to those who are its executive and administrative officers. The executive officer is but the figurehead at its best. The Government are the men who, figuratively speaking, run the machine, and the boilers of the Government. The head of such an institution as this, where moral and intellectual culture are committed, is the man who forms the men who control not only the figurehead but control the nation. . . . Any administration that is a good one or desires to be a good one, must ever be grateful to an institution such as this.[27]

Like Cleveland's comment and Wilson's address mentioned at the beginning of this chapter, Hayes's sentiments here might be dismissed by contemporary readers as empty rhetoric common to political speeches at university events. It is important to note, however, that the notion of a public commencement address from an outside notable developed in this era. Previous to this era, commencements were fairly insular activities comprised essentially of student oratory and a farewell address (often in the form of a sermon) by the university president. The rise of the university as a national institution led to an effort to bring in outside speakers and to a recognition of the university dais as a platform from which public figures could receive attention for their remarks.

Universities and the Democratic Community

The multiple contributions of the universities to the nation were often discussed in regard to the primary object of providing expertise. Nowhere was this more readily seen than in discussion of the university's ability to produce active and educated citizens. Responding to those who feared that university promotion of expertise would be undemocratic and would lead to a lazy and compliant citizenry, university advocates argued that expertise and citizenship education not only could go hand in hand but were in fact related.

Speaking of the limits to expert training, the annual 1880 commencement editorial of the *New York Times* praised the American system's pluralistic attainments: "But it is not so much the purpose of the educational system of this country to produce ripe scholars and men of great learning as to turn out citizens well equipped for the work of active life and qualified for the most exacting duties of citizenship."[28] The editorial was not dismissing the value of expertise. Rather, it was stressing the ability of universities to both examine politics through special study and contribute to the more general political awareness of all its students. University leaders and proponents of expertise have argued, even today, that specialization is useful not just for those who pursue detailed examination but for those who receive a more general grounding in a subject and take such grounding to the world around them. In the view of the *Times* editorial, such scholarship would benefit the nation not only by producing experts who handled the great public questions of the day but also by producing citizens more likely to contribute to and participate in public life and the political process.

As the university became more specialized and as its production of expertise grew, university leaders emphasized that the notions of service and community were enhanced, rather than overwhelmed, by their expansion. Building from the rise of institutional identity, university leaders saw the growth of the university as an opportunity to further community and enhance citizenship. Speaking at Boston's Old South Church in 1901 on the "development of the college spirit," Yale president Arthur Twining Hadley argued:

> It is perhaps the greatest merit of the typical American college that it exercises a powerful influence against selfishness, whether physical or intellectual, and in favor of the development of a community life. . . . The majority

of those who attend our universities are ready to enter into the spirit of the place, and they demand their fellows do the same thing. Man is a political animal: and the boys entering into a group of this kind at an impressionable age become part of a close community whose public sentiment and code of ethics take powerful hold upon them. . . . it has this result: that the boy, at a most impressionable age, forms a conception of public conscience and a code of honor which carries him outside of himself: a code which leads him, not by physical compulsion but by influence of public sentiment, to do things in which consideration of personal convenience are purely secondary.[29]

As Hadley continued with this message, he emphasized that in addition to training specialized experts in the fields of medicine, science, literature, the arts, law, and public life, universities trained all students, no matter what their specialty, to be experts in democratic citizenship.

We have seen how our colleges give their men a training in just this sort of public spirit which is so necessary to our welfare as a nation. . . . We are in the midst of difficulties that cannot be checked by law—difficulties that grow greater as the years go on. Individual efforts at reform seem helpless and hopeless. We need a sound public opinion to meet them. We must have large bodies of men who will fully accept the principle that we are members one of another, and insist upon applying it to the problems of practical life.[30]

Like the *Times* editorial twenty years earlier, Hadley stressed that in addition to expertise, notions of citizenship and democratic community were promoted at research universities, and he maintained that the relation of these two purposes was not mutually exclusive. In securing public acceptance for the authority of expertise, Hadley and others argued that while training students to be experts, the university also trained students in the proper way to employ this expertise—for the betterment of fellow Americans. Hadley's "public spirit" was thus an extension of the *Times* editorial's notions of citizenship. Both sources were concerned with the university's ability to produce students who looked to the nation's welfare, and both maintained that the legitimization and formalization of expertise based in research and specialization advanced, rather than hindered, this ability.

Universities and National Economic and Industrial Competitiveness

The university offered itself—and was looked to—for more than promotion of participation, citizenship, and democratic community. As the Industrial Revolution expanded both products and markets, American business, political, and academic leaders became concerned with their nation's economic and industrial competitiveness. Their most specific concern surrounded America's position relative to other nations in regard to industrial productivity and advances in technology. While issues of character, national will, and natural resources concerned these leaders, the nation's ability to produce men who could develop new technologies as well as harness manpower and other resources was also a major concern. The classrooms and laboratories of the emerging university offered a source of hope and comfort.

Similar to notions of democratic community, the university's contribution to the nation's industrial and economic competitiveness were a compliment to, rather than a competitor with, the university's efforts to further the federal state through research-based expertise. After the Civil War, among the major educational policy concerns was the fact that a number of Americans—including such academic leaders as Andrew Dickson White, Daniel Coit Gilman, and Arthur Twining Hadley—had received their graduate degrees in Germany. Writing in 1883 about Columbia's plans to turn Columbia into a full-fledged university with graduate and professional schools, the *New York Times* celebrated the value such a university would offer.

> It comes as no beggar, but to ask the room be made for it, and strength be given it until the day when it shall be the City's pride and glory, when it shall draw from every part of the country and from other countries and shall furnish here upon our own soil the post-collegiate education which American students must now seek abroad. This latter fact alone is reason enough for establishing such a university.[31]

The question of what would drive the professional and scientific training that helped define the emerging university led advocates to urge that universities stress industrial and economic development, which, in keeping with the dominant current of the time, fostered a concern for utility and relevance that encouraged universities to expand the objects of study and research. The *Times* was a primary advocate of universities' pursuing such diversity.

> It is plain that our higher educational institutions, if they would conform to the progress of the world and the demands of the times, must extend widely the limits of their field of study so as to include within its scope those subjects which really constitute now the body of human learning. If they do this, they must of necessity allow a wide liberty of choice.
>
> It is certain that the institution that best meets the requirements of modern life and best fits its students for the variety of tasks and provides them will meet with the greatest favor and do the most useful work.[32]

Curricular expansion alone, however, was not a solution. As the *Times* would note a few years later, studying multiple subjects was not enough. American universities needed to study multiple subjects well, and there sometimes were limits to an institution's ability to do this. In an editorial regarding the appointment of President Low as president of Columbia, the *Times* used the opportunity to speak of American higher education's limitations compared to other nations.

> It is no secret that our educational institutions all through the country cannot for a moment compare in respect of endowments and appointments with similar institutions in England, France, and Germany. . . . it is possible to organize instruction here that is on scale with the University of Berlin. It is one part . . . of the needed work to be done in America.[33]

The comparative lack of resources available at American universities were a problem for institutional entrepreneurs, such as Low, but they were also an opportunity. Appeals to both public and private benefactors would stress institutional competitiveness with other American universities and would also appeal to a patriotic obligation to ensure that American higher education—and by extension, American industry—was competitive with other nations.

The call for competitiveness was not simply articulated by the mainstream press. University presidents themselves highlighted the economic and industrial advantages of advanced research and training. Of course, part of this emphasis stemmed from an institutional desire to raise funds and build programs. However, these leaders also spoke of a collective necessity. American higher education could serve the nation in many ways, and enabling America's industries to compete with those abroad was a major goal. In an enthusiastically received speech given to an audience including the leaders of other major colleges and universities at a National Higher Education Conference at Association Hall, Brooklyn, in December 1891, Brown University president E. Benjamin Andrews addressed the importance of universities for economic competitiveness.

> Nearly all the great advances in industry which make goods cheaper and life happier involve principles which have been wrought out in the study or the laboratory. Edison could do little but for the science of physics, which less practical men elaborated and made ready for use. . . . the power of research in high realms pays. Witness the case of Germany, which manufactures 83 percent of the chemicals used on the Continent of Europe because of the chemical discoveries made and the knowledge of chemistry diffused among her people through the agency of her universities. In the effort of America to compete industrially with European nations no one thing is more important than the promotion among us of scientific training in its highest forms.
>
> No tongue can tell the debt which the practical, everyday science on which the world now lives owes to the great masters and law givers of sci-

ence and the departments of mathematics and everyone of them was the off-spring of some institution for higher learning. The same, if not a closer relation, exists between good schools and practical science in the department of sociology.[34]

When considering the emergence of the American university, one cannot overestimate the importance of comparative sensibilities. As Andrews emphasized, the university's support of economic and industrial development was justified not in response to a need to serve the marketplace or support capital expansion, though these certainly might have been implicit. Instead, the obligation to help America compete against other nations drove such concerns.

Interestingly, just as notions of democratic community were linked to the expanding federal state's authority of expertise, so was concern regarding America's industrial and economic competitiveness. Building on their belief in a greater need for efficiency, both institutional entrepreneurs in academia and leaders of industry argued for university-developed expertise that would support state expansion and industrial competitiveness. Needless to say, national state capacity and industrial capacity were seen as connected. Universities and institutional entrepreneurs helped promote that connection as essential to their societal contribution. Concerns over American scholars being trained in foreign universities and concerns about the quality of American education in comparison to foreign universities were not limited to institutions of higher education but were shared by the national state and by American industry as well. The more stakeholders universities could find for its efforts, the more support it could garner.

Universities and a National Vanguard

In expanding the federal state, "an emergent intelligentsia rooted in a revitalized professional sector and a burgeoning university sector . . . championed a fundamental reconstruction of the mode of governmental operations to be centered in 'finish, efficacy and permanence.'"[35] However, this national vanguard based in the professions and universities did not limit its attention to state building. In developing acceptance for their pursuit of efficiency and expertise, universities and their supporters stressed the diversity of intellectual leadership that these growing national institutions provided.

Partially, this intellectual leadership was to be directed toward democratic citizenship and industrial development. However, universities did not limit their national service to these areas. Additionally, they sought to perpetuate their support of all that was "useful" by producing scholars and disseminating knowledge. Speaking at an anniversary celebration at Columbia University, Francis Courdet articulated this ambition as the defining function of the university.

> If I could venture to give a definition of my own, I should proclaim that the true university is that which teaches nothing that is useless and everything that is useful and good. That its aim should be to form a class of men who, by their training, moral and intellectual, would be the model men of the country in the government of which they might be expected to take a large and useful part. I would be bold enough to say that the real university should concern itself in ripening useful talents, in eliminating useless and idle theories. Law, medicine, theology, literature—surely all these things, in all their branches and offshoots, form useful subjects to the student. To elevate the standards of all professions and ennoble the pursuits of study loving men, to arm these with weapons, offensive and defensive, which experience has proved to be available in battle, public or private life—these are the aims which may well encourage the founders of the ideal university.[36]

Courdet did not limit the universities' intellectual leadership to affairs of the state. Instead, he outlined multiple areas of service a university could provide. Driven by increasing specialization and the rise of professionalism, universities helped create a national vanguard that served as leaders in a variety of fields, from law to agriculture, medicine to religion. Many of these leaders would be involved in the expansion of the federal state, and many of the advances in their particular fields would contribute to the state's development. Notably, just like notions of democratic community and industrial development, the university efforts to develop a national vanguard were portrayed as one of many different contributions.

Reflecting on the growth of Johns Hopkins University, founding president Daniel Coit Gilman saw the growth of higher education as essential to the furtherance of intellectual leadership. It was the importance of knowledge, not character or social standing, that Gilman and other proponents of a national vanguard stressed.

> Twenty years ago students in colleges were said to be diminishing in numbers. Now careful statistics show a marked increase. . . . Think for a moment what this means. Think of the large additions to Church and State. Think of the large additions to human happiness by keener intellectual enjoyment and nobler love of life.
>
> We need more knowledge. The paths of inquiry are clear; the route has been surveyed. Now for detailed investigation.[37]

While governor of New York, Theodore Roosevelt also stressed the need for intellectual leadership in all fields of endeavor. Speaking at

Cornell's commencement exercises in 1899, Roosevelt showed characteristic enthusiasm when stating the case for such leadership.

> Our country could better afford to lose all of the men who have amassed millions than to lose one-half of its college-bred men. We can get along without men of enormous wealth, but not without men of brains.
>
> Above all, do not become of the class of so-called highly educated and cultured, who sneer at American institutions and American customs. If you recognize fault, come forward and expose it and strive to remedy it.[38]

As Roosevelt's words underscored, the need for "college-bred men" and "men of brains" was universal, not limited simply to the creation of an expanded state based in expertise.

Structuring a Unique Position

The era of building the new American state witnessed an effort to bring expertise to most all of America's institutions and customs. The university's support of democratic community, industrial development, and a national vanguard might not have been directly linked to the formal structures of the federal state, but it was linked to issues of national pride and national capabilities, which in turn greatly influenced these formal structures. University support of expertise and its promotion of administration were closely tied to all these aspects of public service.

When assessing contemporary conceptions of administration and the role of universities in advancing these conceptions, it is critical to recognize that the origins of such service lie not only in the entrepreneurship and coordination of universities and their leaders at the turn of the century but also in the development of the university as a national institution dedicated to the promotion of America's democratic community, industrial competitiveness, and an intellectual vanguard. Expertise and specialized knowledge were essential to the university's service. This service was enabled and enhanced by its unique structural and societal position.

3 The Morrill Act of 1862 and Coordination

*Shaping the American University
and the American State*

A variety of forces drove the emergence of the American university, the expansion of the American national state, and their shared development. While no single event was the catalyst, the origins of such development can be traced to the passage of the Morrill Act in 1862. Beyond being the most extensive and ambitious federal education program undertaken to that point in time, the Morrill Act helped spur the coordination and entrepreneurship that would be essential for the formation of research universities and for these universities' evolving service both to and with the national state.

The Morrill Act and the Origins of Entrepreneurship

The American university's fundamental contribution to policy and governance stemmed from institutional coordination and entrepreneurial maximization of resources. The roots of this contribution lay in a Vermont congressman's stubborn pursuit of agricultural legislation. A shopkeeper from Burlington, who received no formal education beyond the age of fifteen, Justin Morrill originally introduced his plan to establish agricultural colleges in 1857. The legislation passed both houses but was vetoed by President James Buchanan. Five years later, Morrill tried again. With the southern delegations having already seceded, Morrill's legislation this time passed as the first piece of an extensive Republican development program.[1]

The Morrill Act provided land grants within each state and required that the funds from sale of these lands

> be inviolably appropriated by each State . . . to the endowment, support, and maintenance of at least one college where the leading object shall be, without excluding other scientific and classical studies, and including military tactics, to teach such branches of learning as are related to agriculture, and the mechanic arts, in such manner as the legislatures of the States may respectively prescribe, in order to promote the liberal and practical education of the industrial classes in the several pursuits and professions in life.[2]

Morrill was not necessarily a visionary. He was not seeking to build large research universities, nor was he seeking to create a national system of schools that would develop multifaceted expertise. In fact, early proponents of academic research, such as Henry Tappan of the University of Michigan, dismissed Morrill's legislation. Interestingly, funds were not dispensed by a national agency that standardized the land-grant colleges and their curriculum. Nor were the funds spent on establishing a federally run college of agriculture. State governments were responsible for surveying the lands, selling the tracts, collecting the proceeds, and establishing the colleges.

Each stage in the development of the Morrill institutions was fraught with opportunities for political intrigue. In most every state, competing local agricultural groups, religious groups, and others sought to secure funds for their particular vision of higher education. The act was vague, leaving the actual design of colleges to individual states and institutional entrepreneurs. A primary challenge to building institutions dedicated to an expanded curriculum and research was the expense of the laboratories, libraries, faculty, and other resources.

The land grants provided by the Morrill Act were to raise funds for colleges offering instruction in agriculture and the mechanic arts. Many university presidents, led by George Atherton of Pennsylvania State University, developed schools that fulfilled Morrill's legislative vision.[3] Other institutional entrepreneurs, with the help of cooperative legislatures, attempted to use the grants as seed for an institutional expansion of service and mission much broader than Morrill had intended. Cornell in New York, Yale in Connecticut, and the University of California, Berkeley, represented various approaches available to states for those utilizing the resources the act generated.

Maximizing Implementation: Andrew Dickson White and Cornell

In New York, Andrew Dickson White parlayed a federal grant and funds from a private benefactor into what many educational historians describe as America's first research university. The founding of Cornell has been labeled "the best use of the funds made available under the act."[4] New York State maximized its public funds by combining them with the private gift of philanthropist Ezra Cornell, who hoped to "found an institution where any person can find instruction in any study." White's efforts are significant not only because they created, arguably, America's first research university but also because they reflect broader trends in universities' contribution to American political development. Specifically, the story of Cornell's founding underscores the importance of institutional entrepreneurship by and coordination between academic leaders. The federal government did not systematically pursue research and expertise with the Morrill Act. Rather, institutional entrepreneurs took a simple educational subsidy and shaped institutions of learning with a new notion of service to the national state. In other words, while the federal government was a patron of university-based research and expertise from the outset; it was not necessarily involved in defining the nature and structure of its pursuit.

The son of a wealthy Syracuse banker, White graduated from Yale in 1852 and then traveled extensively throughout Europe, accompanied by his good friend and classmate Daniel Coit Gilman, the future president of Johns Hopkins University. While oversees, White studied for a semester at the University of Berlin. Upon his return to the United States, White went back to New Haven for a year, before securing a professorship at the University of Michigan. In Ann Arbor, he taught under the highly influential Henry Tappan. White would later write in his autobiography, "to no man is any success I may have afterward had in the administration of Cornell University so greatly due as to him."[5]

White left Ann Arbor in 1862. After a brief sojourn to Britain, he returned to his family home in upstate New York. He was the Republican nominee for that state's senate soon thereafter, in November 1863. White won election easily and took his seat in January 1864. Among those joining him in the state senate was fellow Republican Ezra Cornell, who had served the previous two years in the state assembly. Though raised on a small farm and without formal education, Cornell was also exceptionally wealthy, from having helped develop the telegraph with Samuel Morse. In the senate, Cornell was made chair of the Agriculture Committee, and White was made chairman of the Literature Committee, which included education.

While the Morrill Act was a federal initiative, responsibility for implementing its provisions and establishing an educational institution dedicated to agriculture and the mechanic arts fell to state legislatures. The act provided a grant of thirty thousand acres for each senator and representative a state had in Congress. New York's share was thus by far the biggest, but it was also highly contested. Two upstate schools, New York Peoples College in Montour Falls and New York State Agricultural College in Ovid, claimed to be the most deserving schools for receipt of the grants.

Founded in 1853 by Charles Cook and counting Horace Greeley among its initial supporters, the Peoples College was founded to train students in "practical" arts and sciences. The college opened in 1860, with an impressive main building donated by Cook. However, it had four professors, no endowment, and no students of college age.

Also founded in 1853, the Agricultural College was similarly struggling. Established with a decent endowment of forty thousand dollars, generated through local fund-raising, it began offering classes in December 1860, with four faculty and twenty-seven students. The advent of the Civil War called away the institution's president as well as most of its students, and the school closed its doors in November of 1861.[6]

The leaders and many well-placed supporters of these two institutions—one struggling and one dormant—saw the Morrill monies as an opportunity to ensure what had been a questionable existence. Land grants provided a means for raising funds but were not direct revenue. In fact, for New York and most eastern states, there were not enough public lands to satisfy the grant. Instead, the grant served as scrip for acreage that was in the western territories.

Nonetheless, the promise of revenue from 989,920 acres, whatever the form, was highly coveted. Charles Cook—who had been elected to the state senate in 1862—and the supporters of Peoples College possessed a fair amount of influence within the legislature. In March 1863, the institution was given the rights to the grant. However, this victory was not absolute, as skeptics of Cook's college required that the grant be presented only when his institution had hired ten full-time professors, attracted 250 students, and built a 250-acre farm. These conditions might possibly have been met, but in January 1864, Cook had a stroke, and doubts regarding the Peoples College's ability to meet its obligations grew. These doubts meant that as White and Cornell took their seats in the state senate, the legislature began considering alternatives.

To this point, White had been an active outside observer. He wrote about the general need for a "truly great university" modeled after those in Germany in the breadth and depth of its work, and he corre-

sponded at length with his good friend Gilman about the higher education opportunity that he feared his state was missing. Cornell was
more intimately involved. Since he served on the Agriculture Committee of the state assembly, he was also on the Agricultural College's state
Board of Trustees and had signed a petition supporting the school's
efforts to obtain the Morrill funds.[7]

After Cook's stroke, Ovid's supporters mobilized. In the spring of
1864, Cornell introduced a bill proposing that the funds be split
between the two institutions. He also offered to supplement Ovid's
funds with a sizable personal donation. As chair of the Literature Committee, White buried the bill, arguing that the funds should not be split
and that neither of the "existing" institutions would be an appropriate
recipient of the money. Detailing his efforts, White wrote to Gilman: "I
am fighting like a terrier against those who would tear that noble donation into bits. I do so for a good college in this state."[8]

With White stubbornly refusing to release Cornell's bill, the trustees
of the Agricultural College met in September, ostensibly to bury their
dying institution. Before the meeting, White had heard from Cornell
that an alternative would be suggested. White appealed to Cornell to
use his proposed gift to the fullest and create a university that pursued
the finest scholarship in not only technology and science but also literature and the arts, encouraging him to use the full share of the state's
Morrill funds as support.

Following much lobbying and debate, White succeeded. He wrote
Gilman, "You will be glad to hear that Sen. Cornell offered $300,000 on
condition that the whole Agricultural fund go to the Ag. college and
that it be placed in his part of the state." White, recognizing that the
"fate of the grant" depended on strong leadership, asked Gilman for
his suggestions.

> Do you know any first rate man or do you know any one who knows such a
> man to take the presidency of the NY State Ag. Coll. Said institution will
> probably be a consolidation of Agricultural and Peoples College and will
> have besides other funds the $800,000 land grant. A first rate man who
> understands agriculture and something besides. Salary whatever is neces-
> sary to get and keep such a being.[9]

White had been trained as a historian, so he turned to Gilman, who, as
a member of the faculty at Yale's Sheffield Scientific School, was more
familiar with the practical implementation of the Morrill grants.
Reflecting the origins of coordination, White asked for his good friend
Gilman's assistance in finding a leader for New York State's land-grant
college, and he also requested that Gilman pass along "any document

useful in relation to Agricultural colleges."[10] At the meeting of the Agricultural College's Board of Trustees, Cornell solidified his commitment of three hundred thousand dollars, and the consolidation plan was formally approved.

White was elated, his efforts to use the Morrill monies for something more than an agricultural college were moving forward. He also realized that the consolidation proposal needed more detail, and he turned to Gilman for help incorporating instruction in agriculture and the mechanic arts into his grand scheme. Declining an invitation to accompany Gilman on a visit to Ann Arbor, White stressed his eagerness to meet with Gilman to discuss the proposed college at length. White noted that Ezra Cornell had offered three hundred thousand dollars for the college to be located in Ithaca, which would bring the available funds to $1.1 million. Reiterating the resources available and the opportunity presented, White concluded: "it is in reference to this whole thing that I wish to talk with you. I hope to see a state university come out of it."[11] White asked if Gilman might come up to Syracuse sometime before the Christmas season. At their meeting, the two men not only laid out plans for a university in Ithaca; they also agreed that White should accept the challenge of heading the new institution.

White was optimistic. However, the approval of the Agricultural College's Board of Trustees was only the first step. In February 1865, Cornell introduced a bill for the founding of a new institution in Ithaca based on a proposal he and White had constructed. Realizing the challenge presented by the supporters of Peoples College and other higher education institutions, who attacked their proposed university as "godless," White and Cornell played what modern observers might describe as "hardball" politics. They used their powers as committee chairs to the fullest, with White holding bills for the construction of a new state capital until the Cornell University proposal was considered.[12]

Additionally, a well-timed gift from Cornell to Genessee College, a struggling Methodist institution with a number of friends in the state legislature, garnered key support when the vote was finally taken.[13] In May 1865, the state legislature approved Cornell's charter. White was elated and began to undertake plans for the new university.

> I did the most work and the hardest I have ever done in this fair office fighting rogues and dispelling the prejudices of honest men. I have been drawing up plans of buildings, schedules of professorships, etc., courses of study and though I have much aid from books, observation, experience and thought, I feel greatly the want of conference with men of strength.[14]

Attempting to build a research institution, White made creative and maximizing use of federal funds. Seeking the counsel of such men as Gilman, whose advice he sought in regard to the selection of faculty, the acquisition of books, and the building of laboratories, White also began the process of loosely coupled coordination among proponents of the research university. Such coordination would help define the specific usages of funds as well as the general parameters of institutional development.

White was most vociferously criticized by those who feared that New York's public institution would be too focused on agriculture and the mechanic arts. Responding to the *New York Tribune*'s criticism that the school would not offer a "classical education," White stressed that the institution was committed to providing education in all its forms.

> The act of the Congress, and the charter from the State of New York, which created the original endowment, while laying stress upon agriculture and the mechanic arts, are careful to name "other scientific and classical branches" and "military tactics" as subjects of study.
>
> Mr. Cornell in his endowment used these words "I would found an institution where any person can find instruction in any study." With such muniments as these, it will be seen at once that while the Trustees are bound to do all in their power to promote through special education in agriculture, the mechanic arts, etc., they are also bound to promote thorough general education; and certainly they are bound not to "discourage" any study whatever.[15]

For White, the Morrill Act provided an opportunity to create a university that provided the "liberty of choice." The act and Mr. Cornell's gift meant not only that the school could pursue multiple areas of study but, in keeping with White's ambition, that the school could pursue multiple areas of study in a detailed and thorough manner.

The Morrill Act did not create the ambition of such university builders as Cornell and White. However, as the tale of Cornell's founding represents, for institutional entrepreneurs, federal investment in the Morrill Act was well timed. The act encouraged and employed the nation's growing material wealth, as well as its young German-trained, research- and university-oriented scholars. It fostered partnerships between wealth and scholarship, creating Cornell; inspiring Johns Hopkins, the Massachusetts Institute of Technology, and other new institutions; and prodding Yale, Harvard, and other existing institutions to pursue a research-based model of higher education.

The Early Limits of Implementation: The Cases of
Yale and California

The politics surrounding the Morrill Act did more than just lead public institutions beyond the desire to instruct and train in agriculture and the mechanic arts. In some instances, the act also gave classically focused private institutions the opportunity to expand into the more applied areas of science and technology. Most notable among these institutions was Yale, whose Sheffield Scientific School served as the state of Connecticut's Morrill institution for more than thirty years.

Yale alumni held great sway in the state legislature at the time of the Morrill Act's passage. The Sheffield Scientific School was just beginning to take shape as an alternative to the classical curriculum of Yale College. While not readily accepted as an equal partner by some students and faculty, the Sheffield School was essential to the development of Yale as a true university, and Morrill funds were essential to the development of the Sheffield School. Not only did the state help fund the school's daily operations by giving the school interest on funds raised through the sale of land grants; it also provided scholarships for students who would not otherwise have attended.[16]

Eventually, the school's commitment to teach "principles rather than details" and to succeed "not so much by offering particular attractions to farmers as a class or to mechanics as a class, as by inviting students who wish to become scholars in science, well-trained in the higher departments of investigation, able to stand unabused by the side of scholars of letters,"[17] lost favor with the state's growing agricultural lobby. In 1887, an effort was made to rescind the grant; and by 1892, the proceeds of the original Morrill Act and of the second one, passed in 1890, were used to establish the new State Agricultural School in Storrs. Yale's loss of the grant is no more remarkable, however, than its receipt of it. Though the state's agriculture interests would later complain that it had cost twenty-five thousand dollars per student for the only six graduates of the agriculture program,[18] Yale admitted 241 state scholarship students. More important, it found a steady source of funding that allowed its fledgling and slightly embattled scientific school to weather the challenges and to become an integral part of the university by the end of the century.

Interaction between institutional entrepreneurship and political savvy were not unique to the East Coast. The University of California was born of similar circumstances to Cornell and Yale's Sheffield Scientific School: a struggling Presbyterian college's offer of acreage in the Berkeley hills and the crafty politicking of the governor and state legislature combined to establish the university. Higher education was a concern in California from that state's very acceptance into the Union. The state constitution of 1849 pledged to build a public university. By the time Congress passed the Morrill Act thirteen years later, this pledge remained unfulfilled. In drafting its constitution, California had borrowed heavily from Iowa's state constitution, adopting verbatim its provisions regarding education. California thus adopted the same Northwest Ordinance rhetoric that had helped found the University of Michigan and other midwestern state universities—regarding the necessity of education for the furtherance of religion and morality and the desire to establish a state-run "seminary of learning."

Higher education was only one of many public priorities in California, and for a number of years, a state university existed there only in rhetoric. In 1861, Governor Leland Stanford established a committee to advocate for a state university comparable to the finest in the country. The committee disappointed Stanford, however, by reporting that such ambition was futile because the state lacked the funds necessary to create "a University in the proper sense of the term, a worthy rival of the world-renowned European universities, placing California where she should be at the educational centre of the states bordering the Pacific."[19] Without sufficient funds or particular enthusiasm for any one plan, California remained without a state-run university.

When the Morrill Act was adopted in 1862, it not only provided additional funds; it also reinvigorated the debate over what type of higher learning institution the state of California should create. In the fall of 1864, the state legislature officially accepted the Morrill monies. The state did not, however, have an agreement on a plan for the institution to receive these funds. Acceptance of the Morrill grant meant that the state would need to establish a college within two years or forfeit the funds.

In March 1866, a little more than six months before the deadline, the state legislature smoothly passed legislation creating a college that would "carry out the provisions for maintaining an Agricultural and Mechanical Arts college." The bill pleased the large agricultural and mining interests, allowed for any location to vie for the campus, and left open the prospect of a broader curriculum. The only interests dissatisfied with the legislation were those from existing institutions, as the legislation required that the funds "not be united or connected with any other institution of higher learning in this state."[20]

The state's Republican governor Frederick Low was made chairman of the new institution's board, and by September of 1866, solicitation of lands for prospective sites began. The committee agreed that a college dedicated to agriculture, mining, and the mechanic arts would be built first, potentially followed by a campus dedicated to broader education. While spearheading the move to place the new state institution in Alameda county, Governor Low developed reservations about the limited scope of the project, after attending a June commencement address at the College of California by Yale professor and leading scientific scholar Benjamin Silliman. Low was struck by Silliman's criticism of the current plan as shortsighted and as a setback to efforts to create a true university in the state. In the late summer of 1867, after further discussion with Silliman and others, Low introduced a plan to revise the legislation creating the college. Low's plan called for a new college of agriculture, mining, and the mechanic arts to be augmented by a college of letters that would be formed from the existing College of California.

In October 1867, the College of California's board accepted Low's proposal and agreed to disband and turn over their campus to the new institution once it was established. In November 1867, the board planning the agriculture and mining college adopted a resolution accepting the College of California's offer of land in return for help in retiring its debt. With both parties in agreement, convincing the legislature was a relatively easy task, as the College of California offer was seen as a cheap addition that took nothing away from the proposed agricultural college.[21] State assemblyman John Dwindle, who was also a member of the board planning the agricultural college, drafted a new university bill formalizing the agreement, and in March 1868, the University of California was created.

Though building in Berkeley would be slow and though controversies over presidential leadership and local politics would hamper growth, the University of California originated in the politics and coordination surrounding the Morrill Act. The initial legislation simply called for an institution to instruct in agriculture and the mechanic arts, but the fight over such federal largesse demanded that greater constituencies be served and that broader ambitions be undertaken. The university would later establish a farm at Davis and eventually move all its agricultural teaching and training there; however, the Morrill Act gave birth to the diverse, research-based curriculum that the university attempted to undertake from its earliest stages.

The Morrill Act, Institutional Entrepreneurs, and the Origins of Coordination

The execution of the Morrill Act was not the first time the federal government had provided a source of revenue for education. Michigan, Iowa, and other states developed their flagship universities by using "seminary of learning" grants drawn from the Northwest Ordinance's provision that with "religion, morality, and knowledge being necessary to good government, and the happiness of mankind, schools and means of education shall forever be encouraged." In some ways, the Morrill Act can be seen as an extension of these early grants. Though formally geared toward higher education, the Morrill Act also represented an effort to universalize education.

The Morrill Act was more significant for how it looked forward than for how it reflected back. The act provided resources and allowed leeway for institutional entrepreneurs seeking to develop "true" research universities. White was not alone in seeing the Morrill Act as an opportunity to develop research universities. Daniel Coit Gilman (who served briefly as president at Berkeley), Benjamin Silliman (who served as dean of Yale's Sheffield Scientific School), and others sought to use Morrill funds to extend the application of scientific and rational principles to multiple fields of endeavor.

The infant nature of instruction in agriculture and the mechanic arts fostered early coordination between university leaders throughout the country. Educators at institutions that received Morrill funds and educators at those that did not corresponded with one another regarding the best faculty, courses, and research apparatuses for meeting the varied demands and expectations of the act. Additionally, educators sought to clarify their mission, define their relation to the national state, and develop standards for their institutions.

Of course, such informal coordination, built on personal and professional ties, was not unique to the Morrill Act. However, the political challenges the act posed, the material resources it provided, and the potential for institutional reforms it offered meant that university leaders sought advice and counsel from their peers. In the years right after the act's passage, coordination of leading institutions was driven by the entrepreneurial activities of Daniel Coit Gilman, who was among the founding faculty of Yale's Sheffield Scientific School and was a classmate and close friend of Cornell President Andrew Dickson White. Gilman proposed to undertake a survey of existing colleges to assess how Morrill funds were being spent. The U.S. commissioner of education agreed to fund Gilman's study. Visiting Berkeley in 1870, Gilman so impressed the faculty and regents that he was offered the presidency of the institution. Hopeful that he might replace the soon retiring Theodore Woolsley at Yale, Gilman declined. However, when he was passed over at Yale for the clergyman and academic traditionalist Noah Porter, Gilman accepted the California position.

From his time at Sheffield Scientific School and his survey of Morrill institutions, Gilman had developed the belief that in addition to including colleges dedicated to the study of agriculture and the mechanic arts, Morrill institutions should use the grants as seed money to pursue research in a variety of fields. Gilman actively promoted this position, and along with like-minded and similarly stationed men, such as White, he encouraged others to do the same.

Before even being formally inaugurated as the University of California's president, Gilman articulated his desire to develop in the distant West a full-fledged university with Morrill funds as its basis. Addressing the San Francisco Academy of Sciences at a September 1872 meeting honoring Professor Louis Aggasiz, Gilman stated:

> He [Aggasiz] has told you that the museum at Cambridge [Harvard] is distinguished as the museum of today. Should it not be so with the University? Should it not be the University for the wants of today? Should we not use it for the great problems which belong to this generation, for the great future that is opening upon us? Should we not all unite to gather up the best of the past experience of every nation, the accumulations of all men before us to bring them to bear upon our society, and upon, I will trust you will allow me to say it, our own State of California?[22]

Gilman continued these themes at his inauguration in November. Addressing his audience on the "building of the university," Gilman emphasized the larger relation between schools and society.

> Everywhere among civilized people, universities in their comprehensive scope are in this year of grace receiving impulses which are creditable to the spirit of the age as they are hopeful for years to come. Our state and national governments see that the questions of higher education must be met in the public councils, and in many places are vying with one another to devise wise schemes of educational development.[23]

Gilman went on to list a variety of programs in research and professional schools at other institutions around the country and ended this enumeration by stating that these represented fruitful "devises and arrangements to allure young men to higher attainment and to aid them in their onward steps." "Such," he maintained, "is the hopeful aspect of university education elsewhere."[24] Gilman recognized the promise of the university in its relation to the "spirit of the age," a spirit that valued the acquisition and dissemination of knowledge, as well as the application of knowledge to issues of society and governance.

In his inaugural address, Gilman pronounced more than the potential of the university in general. His emphasis was on the potential of the university he was to guide. Though it might have seemed a bit ambitious considering the age and location of the institution, Gilman stressed that Berkeley was as full of promise as any established university.

> First it is a "University," and not a high school, nor a college, nor an academy of sciences, nor an industrial school which we are charged to build. Some of the features may, indeed, be included in or developed with the University: but the University means more than any or all of them. The University is the most comprehensive term which can be employed to indicate a foundation for the promotion and diffusion of knowledge—a group of agencies organized to advance the arts and sciences of every sort, and to train young men as scholars for all the intellectual callings of life. . . . It is "of the people and for the people"—not in any low or unworthy sense, but in the highest and noblest relations to their intellectual and moral well being.[25]

The university was thus to serve the state by pursuing knowledge that was both useful to and elevating of its people. This knowledge, this expertise, was essential for educating students to serve.

Gilman's ambition was not enough to overcome a lack of support from the state legislature and the general public. Responding to Gilman's complaints about political meddling and a lack of public support, his friend Andrew Dickson White sympathized with his plight.

> Among the great branches of education in this country perhaps the greatest is the education of the people to the idea of their responsibility for public education in all its parts. It is hard at first but the idea will be developed in California as it has been in Michigan, so that the time will come, and that I think at no very distant day, when its state university will be safer in the control of the people than if it excluded them from any connection with it.[26]

In his expression of support, White articulated the often felt but rarely articulated belief that public universities were best off when safe from popular control. This idea was not only crucial in defining the development of the university's mission and tasks in the abstract but also fundamental to its selection of leadership, as we will soon encounter.

White hoped public support would benefit universities in "no very distant day," but he also acknowledged that such a day would still be too far off to help Gilman at Berkeley. He encouraged Gilman to consider the newly established Johns Hopkins University in Baltimore.

Writing Gilman in September 1874, White mentioned that the trustees of Johns Hopkins had just finished "a very thorough inspection" of Cornell, having previously been at Harvard and Yale, and were moving on to Michigan. White described them as "men of cultivation and gentlemen." He concluded by confiding in his good friend:

> Between ourselves, I think that you are to be called there, for I find that Eliot, Porter, and myself thoroughly agreed upon you as the man to organize the Institution for them. From the questions asked I judge that your organizing of faculty, your knowledge of educational matters at home and abroad, your catholicity in regards to all departments of knowledge and your liberal orthodoxy in religious matters gives them a great deal of confidence in you.[27]

The coordination between leading academics was as notable as White's lobbying. It was only natural that since Johns Hopkins was modeling itself on the "leading" institutions of higher education, it should ask for their guidance in selecting its leadership. This process helped lead, if not to uniformity, then to a consensus of opinion regarding the development of higher education. White continued to lobby his friend regarding the Johns Hopkins position, highlighting the opportunity it provided. Writing Gilman in December 1874, he stressed, "My general opinion is that the chance is a grand one—that there can be built up there a University in the highest sense—and I know of no one who can do it as well as yourself."[28]

Gilman's prominent role in developing coordination between institutions would continue and in fact increase as he became founding president of Johns Hopkins University. Endowed by the Clifton family that had made its fortune as a primary owner of the Baltimore and Ohio Railroad, Johns Hopkins might seem a peculiar institution to have a fundamental effect on the evolution of federally sponsored education in agriculture and the mechanic arts. It was private and did not possess an agricultural college. However, Gilman worked closely with White at Cornell, his successors at California, the faculty of Yale's Sheffield Scientific School, and James Burrill Angell at the University of Michigan (while Michigan was not a land-grant institution, Angell's influence would help shape all the universities of the developing Midwest and Pacific Coast) to expand the scope of the Morrill Act to focus on research and its application.

More important, the Morrill Act's influence lay not necessarily in the institutions it created as much as in the creative freedom it provided institutional entrepreneurs, such as White, to develop models of higher education and public service for other universities, both public and private. These institutions and those educated at them would define the parameters and expectations of research and its application, often supplying the first faculty of the post–Morrill era. By defining such parameters and expectations, these institutions—not the federal government—became primarily responsible for determining how the Morrill Act would be implemented and how its monies would be employed.

These loosely coupled institutions worked to define the role of expertise not for colleges of agriculture but for the federal government itself. The immediate place of emerging research universities in the implementation of the Morrill Act is fairly straightforward. They defined academic standards and approaches, trained faculty and researchers, and developed techniques and methods for these colleges. The long-term impact is less obvious but just as clear. As Daniel Carpenter notes, the development of scientific agriculture significantly altered the culture of the Department of Agriculture at the turn of the century.[29] Though instituted by agency head Jeremiah Rusk, this dedication to applied research was largely grounded in universities that had taken Morrill's legislation and independently extended its reach beyond his intentions.

It would be extreme, however, to suggest that universities simply grabbed Morrill monies and applied them as they wished. Programmatically, the Morrill Act fostered numerous partnerships. Among the most prominent partnerships stemming from the act were agricultural experiment stations. The state of Connecticut used Morrill funds to establish the first such station in Middletown in 1875. While the Connecticut station was not formally affiliated with an agricultural college, others soon followed at such institutions as Cornell and the University of California. Funded through Morrill grants and often staffed by professors and researchers from the Department of Agriculture, these stations were a creative attempt to maximize resources.

The Morrill Act did not require experiment stations. However, such stations were a means to address concerns about limited attendance that had plagued the colleges since their beginning and to develop an audience for the expertise such colleges could provide. In New York, Connecticut, and California, experiment stations proved such a successful adaptive use of Morrill funds that it inspired the Hatch Act of 1887, which provided funds for the establishment of an experiment station at every land-grant college. Reporting on the role of experiment stations in his annual report of 1882, the head of Berkeley's agriculture program since 1875, E. W. Hilgard, gave a sense of its creative use.

While the performance of the work of agricultural surveys and experiment stations by the colleges is not prescribed as a fundamental function by the Act, experience has shown it to be one of the most important means at their command for benefiting agriculture at the present, not only by the actual demonstration of the best methods of treating soils and crops under endlessly varying local conditions, but also in showing farmers the advantages to be derived from an intelligent observation of facts, and from application of scientific knowledge and principles to their pursuit, thus inducing fathers to give their sons the opportunity of acquiring such knowledge for themselves in the institutions created for that purpose.[30]

"Selling" the benefits of the Morrill Act to farmers was a basic responsibility of universities' partnerships with the federal government. More significantly, as Hilgard understood, the university was not only seeking to convince skeptical farmers of the value of the Morrill Act; it was attempting to show the value of expert knowledge and scientific techniques.

Buoyed by an entrepreneurial effort to establish multiple experiment stations and conduct multiple surveys, the University of California would have relative success in attracting farmers and their sons. However, though students from farming communities would take an agricultural course or two, they usually focused on other courses of study. For a school that had gained much of its initial funding from a grant designated for education in agriculture and the mechanic arts, the University of California had a strikingly low number of students enrolled in its agricultural college (see table 1). This pattern of enrollment did not eliminate the need for experiment stations. In fact, it simply enhanced the demands on the stations by the university, as they were seen not only as an effective tool for increasing opportunity and awareness of the institution but also as a means for pleasing the agricultural interests in the state.[31]

Like many major policy initiatives, the implementation of the Morrill Act was far more significant than its development, introduction, or adoption. Its impact was far from immediate. Five years after its passage, only twelve states had chartered schools to accept funds. Twenty-seven years after its passage, legislative squabbling or lack of initiative meant that some states had only limited collegiate education available in agriculture and the mechanic arts.[32] Such shortcomings as these led to the passage of the second Morrill Act in 1890. The second act supplemented the funds of the 1862 act and required that African Americans be granted access to such education. In the southern states, a policy of "separate but equal" education led to the creation of distinct land-grant

TABLE 1. Students at the University of California, 1884–95

	1884–85	1885–86	1886–87	1887–88	1888–89	1889–90	1890–91	1891–92	1892–93	1893–94	1894–95
Agricultural students	8	7	6	6	10	9	NA	NA	NA	17	17
Total students	241	250	288	306	363	401	NA	NA	NA	753	1,024

Note: Figures are not available for 1891–93. Owing to the university having no president at the time of submission, the university did not file a report between 1890 and 1892. However, even without these figures, the pattern seems quite clear.

institutions for African Americans. These schools formed the core of what today are known as historically black colleges and universities.

While the first Morrill Act of 1862 might not have provided for the universal education its author desired, the act was highly influential and helped facilitate a fundamental evolution in the nature and purpose of higher education. The act was so broad in scope and so open to interpretation that all potential for university relations with the national state were incorporated within it. Seeking to implement the act, university leaders often acted as institutional entrepreneurs, demonstrating the capacity of the university to coordinate policy and maximize resources as both active partner with and independent agent for the developing national state.

Defining Their Public: Universities and Presidential Selection

Universities were public institutions in their service and often in their funding. With the passage of the Morrill Act, the meaning of public service was being redefined. The development of a loosely coupled but highly coordinated group of academic elites meant that national standards for universities and expectations of service began to evolve. The selection of leaders for these developing research universities was instrumental to defining these standards and expectations. Considering the typical presidential selection processes at two institutions seeded with Morrill funds, Cornell and the University of California, we find that while universities might have seen themselves as partners with government in terms of serving the public good, their selection of leaders was a very closed and tightly controlled process in which the heads of national academic institutions would hold as much, if not more, influence than the heads of local political ones. Thus, in one of their most fundamental institutional functions—that of selecting leaders—even those institutions considered to be state schools were not publicly controlled.

Personality and Coordination: Presidential Selection at Cornell

While relatively successful in his efforts to build a university in Ithaca, White found battles with various critics—namely, state legislators and the populist newspapers—highly taxing. Similar to James Burrill Angell at the University of Michigan, White offered his resignation only to have it declined. As an alternative, White took various leaves of absence. For his first leave, in 1873, White sought to have Gilman serve as interim president. Upon his eventual departure twelve years later,

White arranged to have Charles Kendall Adams chosen as his successor. Both efforts represented a politicking reflective of the very close-
knit community of higher education in this era. White's lobbying was
not necessarily directed at the trustees who formally chose his replacement. His stature at the institution and the traditions of the time meant
he could essentially choose his successor. Rather, White's lobbying was
directed toward his colleagues and regarded his visions for the university in particular and for higher education in general.

In a lengthy letter to his best friend, dramatically tagged with the
word "Confidential" across each page, White complained about the toll
his work at Cornell had taken on his health and discussed the possibility of taking a leave from the post. He complained, "my repugnance to
office work, to traveling in cars, to discussing educational subjects, to
hearing statements made and passing judgment upon them, to selecting professors, etc., is rapidly becoming invincible." However, he also
spoke of how the university, in many ways, had succeeded "beyond his
dreams." White outlined what had been developed in Ithaca. He ended
by asking if Gilman would be willing to serve as acting president, with
the promise of his eventual placement.

> Now my dear friend you seem to be the best man to take over this work. You
> have just what is necessary to make a success of it. You enjoy educational
> work. You enter heavily into the grapple with public officials over educa-
> tional questions—the office work that is burdensome to me, you do with
> ease.[33]

Needless to say, White's complaints were the product of frustration. He
would remain at Cornell for another twelve years. White did not simply endure public grappling over educational questions; rather, he welcomed it. In his tenure at Cornell and beyond, White remained one of
the leading figures in American higher education, authoring numerous
speeches and articles on a wide array of issues.

White eventually found the administrative chores of the presidency
burdensome, and in 1885, he chose former pupil Charles Kendall
Adams to be his replacement and the next link in the legacy of academic leadership and institution building that White and Gilman had
defined. C. K. Adams, the first dean of Michigan's School of Political
Science, was a student of White's as an undergraduate at Michigan,
graduating in 1861. Remaining in Ann Arbor after graduation, Adams
did an additional year of study (earning a master's) and took charge of
White's courses while he took a leave of absence. When White left
Michigan to return to his native New York in 1865, Adams replaced

him on the Michigan faculty. A little over twenty years later, Adams would succeed White as president of Cornell. Only a few years younger than White and Gilman, Adams did his graduate work in Germany. However, as dean of Michigan's School of Political Science, he extended the influence of White and Gilman, working closely with Thomas Mortimer Cooley and Henry Carter Adams before their work for the Interstate Commerce Commission. C. K. Adams was White's seemingly natural successor.

Adams selection was not without its detractors, however. Early in his academic career, in 1875, Adams had been involved in a relatively minor controversy in which a letter in *The Nation* accused him of plagiarism. The letter claimed that Adams's *Democracy and Monarchy in France* had lifted certain passages from an earlier work. The letter's author gave his initials rather than his name. Adams's response and explanation of the similarity were more than adequate for his colleagues at Michigan as well as elsewhere. But upon the announcement of Adams's selection as president of Cornell, the issue was revisited by foes of White, mainly those with agrarian interests, who saw Cornell as too elitist. In a highly critical editorial, the *Brooklyn Eagle* asked, "Should a plagiarist professor be made a college president?" and the *Syracuse Standard* referred to Adams as "that literary thief."[34]

Adams was initially taken aback by the severity of the criticism. However, as others—such as the *New York Times*—came to his defense and as he received reassurances that Cornell's trustees and faculties supported him, Adams gladly accepted the offer. He wrote to James Burrill Angell:

> I find not the least evidence that the NY attacks have made any impression whatever in Ithaca, either on Trustees or Faculty or on the people. On this point the assurances are most gratifying and ample. Everybody seems to be enraged that the same knot of fellows which twice before had made gross assaults on White should now open their guns on me. I have been waiting to see what effect the election would have on them and I now infer that there is nothing to fear from them or from any influence they can exert. Tomorrow, therefore, I shall probably mail in my letter of acceptance.[35]

Ironically, as Angell would soon learn, Adams's selection was not as straightforward as all would believe.

Reflecting the close-knit nature of the academic community at the time, Angell would learn that Adams appointment was almost undone by a rumor of Angell's own selection. Moses Coit Tyler had taught at Michigan until 1881, when he was hired away by White to spearhead a course that combined history with political and social science and general jurisprudence. He was still friendly with Angell in 1885, and when he heard Angell might accept the Cornell presidency, he wrote immediately to express his surprise and explain that he had not been part of the effort to draft him for the position. Angell wrote back shocked at the suggestion that he might usurp his colleague Adams.

Chastised, Tyler sought to explain himself. In a confidential letter to Angell, Tyler explained that after nominating Adams on June 17, White came to Tyler on June 20 expressing doubts about the nomination. As Tyler described the meeting, White proposed withdrawing Adams's nomination, "then, drawing his chair close to mine, he said in a very confidential tone, 'What would you say, if on Monday morning, I should tell you that Angell could be had at the same terms as Adams?" Tyler expressed surprise, saying, "I have never thought that for any inducement which we could offer, Angell would leave Michigan." White insisted that it was true. Tyler decided to abstain out of loyalty to both candidates. He sought to avoid White but encountered a trustee who had been lobbying actively against Adams and who insisted that he "personally knows that Angell could be got and would like to come here." Believing the trustee and White to be correct and believing that White would announce Angell as his choice, Tyler "rushed off to write [Angell], a letter I now regret."[36] In the end, according to Tyler, White felt he could not in good conscience rescind the nomination.

All of this was news to Angell, for there is no indication that White even informally asked if he were interested in the position. Adams, as mentioned earlier, did accept and was inaugurated in November 1885. White had left for Europe almost immediately upon resigning the presidency and did not attend the ceremonies. However, when he finally received a copy of Adams's address, he was outraged. In his diary, White vented:

> This day came upon me one of 3 great disappointments in my life and in some respects the most cruel—Pres. Adams inaugural. It has plunged me in a sort of stupor—have I been dreaming 30 years?—ever since I began working for a university—or am I dreaming now? Not the slightest recognition of the Univ. or my work or Gilman and above all Mr. Cornell's name not mentioned and this is a man who owed his start in life to me—whom I made President of Cornell Univ. against fearful odds—defended him at cost of my health and reputation and the good will of friends—stood by him thro the worst of attacks and now! He praises unjustly the worst enemy of all my efforts [Charles Eliot] and ignores my work utterly—and solely to curry favor with Harvard University and the men who have lashed him to the Harvard set. There is no other explanation. They are living and active and can do him more harm—I am supposed to be declining in health and can do

him no more good. This is the hardest blow I have received. Yesterday my friend as I thought—today what? Yet I was warned by many.[37]

White's outrage was both surprising and in many ways unfounded. In Morris Bishop's *A History of Cornell*, White is criticized for being unreasonable: "He had complacently expected a glorification of his own work, which he could then gently, unconvincingly deprecate. Naturally, he was disappointed."[38]

Additionally, White's characterization of Harvard president Charles Eliot as his "worst enemy of all my efforts" strikes one as silly in light of their similar efforts to develop elective courses and encouraged specialization (all with an eye toward "public service"), their mutual friendship with Gilman, and their cordial communication. A rivalry no doubt existed between the two, but it did not deserve such an outburst. The relative merits of White's complaint are certainly debatable. However, White's outburst as well as the nature of his attempts to secure a successor highlight issues fundamental to our understanding of the university and its efforts to define its service to the public, the question of democratic participation in ostensibly public institutions, the nature of academic mentorship, and the relationship between mentorship and coordination.

Though Cornell was a public institution, its leadership and direction were not issues for democratic debate. White expected and received the privilege of anointing his successor. (This was not unusual; at Michigan, Angell was allowed to choose those who replaced him while he was on his various leaves.) Owing to the unique nature of its structure, once the New York state legislature had founded Cornell, its control over implementation of the Morrill Act and the use of public funds became minimal. The entrepreneur White had co-opted funds directed for education in agriculture and the mechanic arts and began a research university. In theory, the opportunity to select White's replacement might have allowed for a public assessment of the path he had taken. There was to be no such reflection.

White's entry also underscored the assumption, rarely articulated, of academic mentors in regard to their anointed successors. White assumed Adams would pursue a course of research and service similar to the one White had begun. Despite White's dismay at the text of Adams's inaugural address, the development of Cornell under Adams's leadership proceeded along the lines White had desired. This is not altogether surprising, the institution had developed schools and methods of operation that would have been difficult for Adams to radically alter even if he had desired to do so. However, the extent to which homage and compliance were expected by White strike one as remarkable and underscore the limited leeway allowed to those who succeeded leaders in the "golden age" of university presidents.

Politics and Coordination: Presidential Selection at Berkeley

Coordination among a select group of academics helped define the path universities would take. For public universities, such coordination not only allowed leading institutions to define standards; it also permitted circumvention and avoidance of obstacles presented by the meddling of local political officials. Cornell largely avoided such meddling through the force of White's esteem and acumen. The fledgling University of California did not immediately find a president whose commitment to their school and influence in the state could smooth the process; thus, it had to rely heavily on the guidance of leading academics elsewhere, with varying degrees of success.

Initially, California seemed to have selected a skillful institutional entrepreneur when Daniel Coit Gilman took the university's presidency, with great enthusiasm and expectation. But Gilman soon grew discouraged by California's geographic isolation, struggle for resources, and local political intrigue. With the coordinated help of colleagues in the East, he secured the presidency at Johns Hopkins.

With a vacuum at the top of the institution, the politicking that had discouraged Gilman only intensified. Grangers and others with agricultural interests expressed displeasure with the university's use of the Morrill grant and claimed that it was pursuing an elite agenda free from public control and oversight. Advocates for a first-rate research university argued that though the university was a public institution, it must be unfettered by the petty demands of politics and free to pursue knowledge and expertise.

It was hoped that an appointed board and a strong president would keep the university free from political meddling. This freedom from meddling would allow the university to pursue its multiple missions, including educating the citizenry in such a way as to "enable . . . graduates to formulate and defend, or combat with intelligence and force, new views affecting the public interest."[39] All elite universities desired to be relatively free from popular control. Initiating a standard that many other Progressive political institutions would follow, leaders and friends of the university argued that to best serve the public interest, the university needed to shield itself from the direct input of the people.

Appointed regents did not free Berkeley from political intrigue, however. Unlike Cornell University (which was able to bolster its resources through the generosity of its namesake) or the University of Michigan (which was constitutionally autonomous and, during Angell's tenure, was able to count on solid support from the state as well as a healthy income from the original "seminary of learning" grants), Berkeley did not garner much support from the state legislature in an effort to supplement its Morrill funds. The lack of resources and pitched battles with the state legislature hamstrung the university's presidents and frustrated their efforts to establish an elite institution on the West Coast.

President William Reid examined such difficulties at length in his report to the regents for 1882. He stressed: "the needs of the University are many and great. First among them, and including most of them, is the need of a large endowment." For Reid, endowing the university would not only help produce graduates concerned with the public interest; it would also further the development of the state itself.

> Indeed, I am of the opinion that, as a purely commercial enterprise, the ample endowment of the University would be a wise investment. We have only to add to our material advantages the best educational advantages to make the attractions of our state equal to those of any other state, in the eyes of people that we should most care to have settle among us. No material advantages compensate, in the eyes of a desirable population, for the loss of educational opportunities.[40]

An institutional entrepreneur seeking to secure support for his school, Reid linked the school's well-being to the state's ability to formulate effective and efficient policies and to recruit settlers from other regions. For Reid, the ability of the university to provide such public service and assistance in the growth of the state depended on politically detached, but financially extensive, support from the state.

> There must be withal a feeling of confidence in the stability and permanence of the institution; a feeling that whatever fluctuation of opinion there may be on matters of State policy or local interest, the University will always be the center of a common interest, and the common object of a hearty and liberal support.[41]

Yet Reid was unable to stir common interest or develop hearty support. Frustrated by the political bickering that undid his efforts to secure a steady source of income from a mill tax, he resigned in 1885.

Following Reid, in October 1885, the regents selected Edward Holden as both president of the university and director of the university's newly established Lick Observatory. A somewhat absentee president, Holden resigned at the end of the 1887 academic year, to devote his full attention to the observatory. In February of that year, through extensive lobbying efforts on the part of the regents, the university had secured from the state legislature a mill tax that nearly doubled the college's operating income. Believing that their concerns regarding finances and political intrigue had been basically solved, the regents desired a strong president to maximize the new resources available to the university. In this effort, the regents sought the counsel of academic leaders. These leaders in turn corresponded with one another in a coordinated response to select who would lead the nascent institution.

Former University of California and current Johns Hopkins president Daniel Coit Gilman was among the first the regents contacted. He soon turned to Michigan's Angell. Writing to ask if Angell would attend the Johns Hopkins commencement, he concluded by inquiring about the Berkeley position: "California is seeking a President in Holden's place, who will go? I suggested [Franklin] Carter of Williams College but he will not accept. Do you know any college President who would like a 'milder climate.' "[42] Gilman's tone does not suggest a discussion between two men simply offering advice to a fellow institution. As leaders of elite universities, Gilman, Angell, and others were often asked to pass judgment on the quality of fellow academics, not just for professorships, but for leadership positions as well. Thus, while not formally standardizing procedures and approaches, peer institutions helped define one another's development.

For the University of California, a developing western state institution, the University of Michigan was a model and aspiration. Michigan reciprocated by looking to California as a touchstone, comparing the development of academic programs or the nature of state support. Seeking advice on how to fill their presidency, Berkeley turned directly to Angell. John Swift, a member of the regents' search committee, wrote Angell in May 1887.

> We are very much in want of a President for our University and [are] engaged in seeking out one with the knowledge of the active members of the community. . . . Can you suggest anybody? In the first place would you entertain the position. It seems to be generally agreed that you would not; but still there can be no harm in asking you and I do it. Secondly, do you know a good man for the place. And if so who is he and where?[43]

Swift's bluntness illuminates the limits of loosely coupled coordination for those attempting to build elite universities. Without a formal organization to share information and define standards, such a university as Berkeley, which was somewhat isolated geographically and institutionally, did not readily know where to turn.

Building from the suggestions of Gilman, Charles Eliot (of Harvard), and others, Swift asked about various candidates, including the U.S. commissioner of education, William T. Harris; Williams College president Franklin Carter; and Angell's former colleague Moses Coit Tyler. Swift ended by stressing the benefits of the position: "You know pretty well what we have to offer. [The university is] . . . an institution now at last established and endowed with all the means that can be used advantageously. We feel that we are now in condition to offer to any man a reasonable opportunity."[44] For Swift, it was hoped that Angell and his fellow university presidents would tap someone to make the most of the opportunity.

Berkeley's search did not go smoothly. Angell and Gilman both recommended President Carter of Williams College. Swift and his fellow regents accepted this recommendation and pursued him. As the summer continued, the regents grew anxious. Swift wrote to Angell again, practically pleading for assistance.

> . . . as your university is like ours a state institution we would take your opinion before that of anybody. . . . But can't you find us a President. Can't you persuade Carter of Wlms. to come. Gilman has seconded him but I think I wrote you about that before. Harris can be had and possibly is good but you know how proud we are to think that what is only to be had is not worth having. . . . If you can think of anything in the way of a President don't fail to write and let us know as the time is approaching near when we shall surely be in need.[45]

California's desire to emulate Michigan, Angell's personal stature, and the need to rapidly fill the position meant that Angell could essentially choose Berkeley's next president.

The isolation of California and the uncertainties associated with a newly developing public institution led Angell's first recommendation, Carter, to politely decline inquiries made by Angell and Gilman. So, too, Angell's friend Tyler declined. Angell could appreciate their hesitancy, as he himself respectfully declined the offer to move west. Angell's friends in California still persisted in asking that he consider the opportunity to rescue the university from its many challenges or, at the very least, find them somebody who would. E. W. Hilgard wrote that while he was happily enjoying his time out west. He eventually hoped to "sell out to some bloated eastern capitalist and take that long desired trip East, and to Europe, and bid good bye to kantankerous

Regents and inquisitive grangers for a while." For Hilgard, the university needed strong leadership, but circumstances had driven qualified men from the presidency and left the university in its current state.

> That hornets nest, to which you predicted I was going, has turned out quite habitable for me, but seems to be hard on Presidents generally. Holden seems to be about as glad to get out his thorny chair as some others are anxious to get into it, and we who know all about it wonder who will try next. Gilman evidently has no leaning that way, having been there before. If you cannot be induced to change your mind and try to kill the hydra of 23 heads that threatens to swallow the U of Cal. from time to time cannot you suggest some other Hercules that will?[46]

Hilgard was not personally threatened by the hydra he described; his position as head of California's Agricultural College assured him relative autonomy. Yet he recognized that if the university were to develop overall, it needed a strong leader who would remain in office for a lengthy tenure.

Nearing the end of that summer, Swift became more anxious. The academic year was about to begin, and Berkeley still did not have a president. Disappointed that long-shot efforts to recruit back Gilman had failed, Swift wrote to Angell again.

> We are in not a little perplexity, as our president goes out with the academic year, and as yet we do not see much light ahead. We were somewhat in hopes that Mr. Gilman who has just paid us a visit and gone away to Alaska would or might be induced to stop with us and take hold again, but he went, and so that has to be given up.

Swift reiterated that anyone who received a stamp of approval from the leading university presidents would be offered the position.

> There is no sort of doubt that if you, for example, or indeed President Eliot, or President White, or any of you first rate men, could see your way to recommend any gentleman to us, as unqualifiedly and without reservation the man we are looking for, he would be upon the receipt of that certificate, as good as elected to the place, if he would allow us to think he would accept.[47]

Swift's anxiety provoked him to articulate the often unspoken influence of Angell, Gilman, White, and their colleagues. As the heads of the nation's leading universities, these men not only defined the development of their peer institutions; they also acted as gatekeepers, literally defining who would join their ranks.

Swift desired to have a president whose skills and expertise met with the approval of Angell and his colleagues and who could, as was the tradition of the time, be the face and voice not just for the university but for all public educational enterprises in the state.

> We want a good executive head, a man of "Savoir faire," some education, the more the better, with political and practical sense, capable above all things of making the general public believe that he is the right man for the place, and you know to do this he must not only have considerable ability but he must look like a president.[48]

Swift's desired leader would have to govern not solely on the basis of expertise and rationality but on the basis of charismatic appeal as well.

With the leading choices of Angell and others uninterested, Berkeley eventually looked internally and selected former congressman and Hastings College of Law faculty member Horace Davis to head the institution. A compromise selection, it was hoped that Davis could both appear and actually be "the right man for the place." Davis, however, was less interested in the university than in using it as his pulpit. He never moved from his home in San Francisco, across the bay; and after a year and a half, the university was again searching for someone to guide it.

Writing from his position as head of a preparatory school in Belmont, California, the university's former president William Reid sardonically bemoaned the difficulties faced by leaders of the institution.

> If you have an enemy who is in the line of promotion send him as Pres. to the Univ. of Cal—I wonder if I have a thicker skin than most other men. I held on for four years—my two successors lived only two years each. I thought that Davis would hold the place. I doubt now however whether any self respecting man who knows what an institution needs can secure the position.[49]

While Reid might have been overstating the case, his concerns regarding the fate of California's state university seemed justified. As an institution concerned with establishing itself free from the demands of local politics, Berkeley needed strong leadership of a lengthy tenure. As an institution interested in pursuing expertise and developing partnerships with the national state, Berkeley needed a president who was respected by and could work with the leaders of other elite institutions. Swift's letters to Angell reveal that these attributes were not mutually exclusive.

Berkeley would not find such leadership until 1899, when it secured the highly ambitious Benjamin Ide Wheeler from the Cornell faculty. In the context of the developing community of scholars, the 1887 search demonstrates clearly the limits to coordination. The leading academics of the day could not overcome Berkeley's perceived institutional deficiencies. Despite relying on assistance from peer institutions, Berkeley found itself with third- and fourth-choice candidates.

Implementing the Morrill Act:
Presidential Selection and Institutional Autonomy

When considering the development of the fledgling university, the process of leadership selection is just as significant as who was selected to lead. The emerging universities, even those that were privately funded, viewed themselves as public institutions, dedicated to serving their community and the nation. However, these institutions, even those run by the state, sought to choose their leaders in a very private fashion, by coordination among a small group of elites. Similar to the development of university-based expertise itself, presidential searches depended on a newly defined standard of knowledge and ability. The desired goal of these evolving public institutions was to serve the nation. Such service did not, however, mean responding to the whims of the people. University leaders had witnessed and still feared the inefficiency and corruption of the patronage state. These institutional entrepreneurs felt a need to protect their schools and their programs from the morass of electoral politics. Presidential selection was exceedingly significant, for it underscores the fundamental, but often unstated, belief that only through freedom from the popular masses could these institutions develop a national state and serve the public good.

The selection of university presidents possessed a subtle but major influence on relations between the university and the national state. No one would expect universities to allow the federal government to have a say in their leadership decisions. Additionally, state universities sought to avoid the partisan politics and bickering of local political influences by keeping the process closed to those outside the academic community. Yet the choice of university leader would define the relationship the institution pursued with the national state. University presidents were instrumental—often solely responsible—for choosing with which agencies their institution would work and for selecting the faculty who would teach at their institution. In selecting their presidents, universities established their public agenda and defined their role as potential partners with and agents of the national state. On the state level, university leaders were seen as de facto, if not de jure, heads of education. On all levels, they exerted a fundamental influence on the development of higher education.

As in their implementation of the Morrill Act, the institutional entrepreneurs who ran the nation's leading universities sought to define the development of their schools and mitigate the influence government would have in this process of definition. In seeking autonomy from government, universities depended on one another. While the heads of the nation's leading universities would not formalize relations between the leading higher education institutions until the establishment of the Association of American Universities in 1900, these leaders, by recommending scholars they had trained and mentored, were able to help establish standard expectations and parameters for universities and for their relationship to the developing national state.

4 Beyond the Morrill Act

Developing Partnerships in the "Loosely Coupled" Era

As the first major policy initiative to define relations between the developing American state and institutions of higher education, the Morrill Act offered a broad opportunity for universities and the institutional entrepreneurs who directed them. The act initiated fundamental changes in universities' notion of public service. Through universities' selection of leadership, implementation of the act, and related academic initiatives, a loosely coupled but relatively intimate group of academic leaders came to define universities' public service.

Supported by coordination between peer institutions, universities and the national state undertook reciprocal service in a variety of areas, ranging from public administration to military training. As the number of government agencies grew, so did the opportunities for institutional entrepreneurs to demonstrate their schools' societal contribution and utility. Not every effort at forging partnerships could be counted as a success. Nonetheless, they could be seen as evolving from an effort to develop and apply knowledge, skill, and expertise to the problems faced by the American state.

Early Partnerships: Individuals and Institutions in an Era of Transition

Keeping with the fragmentation inherent in America's developing national state, partnerships between universities and the national state were not driven by a systematic federal program as much as they evolved from the initiative of individual entrepreneurs bringing specialized knowledge to bear on problems of public concern. Neither Congress nor federal agencies had formulated anything resembling a formal research agenda. Instead, academic leaders applied themselves and their institutions to problems of public concern in an almost haphazard fashion, often based on their personal interest and institutional necessity.

These early years of expertise-based service and partnership saw individual ambition and occasional coordination laying the groundwork for the more systematic and far-reaching efforts that were to follow. Though offering an alternative method of governance, university-based expertise did not overnight or completely replace the influence of cronyism and personal connections. In fact, while seeking to promote their cause, proponents of expertise and efficiency sometimes resorted to similar tactics. This does not discredit their promotion of specialized knowledge as much as it highlights the difficulties they faced when attempting to institute reforms and the inherent overlap they encountered in seeking to spur a transition from a patronage model of governance to an expertise model.

Woodrow Wilson and the Politics of Personal Influence

Perhaps nothing better reflects the complications involved in such a transition than the early career ambitions of Woodrow Wilson. Having just been awarded his PhD at Johns Hopkins University and begun teaching at Bryn Mawr College, Wilson sought an appointment as assistant secretary of state. Pursuing appointment under Secretary Thomas Bayard, Wilson wrote to James Burrill Angell at the University of Michigan in November 1887. Wilson indicated he had heard from a "dear friend" that Bayard was having trouble filling the position. Wilson also noted that he understood "Mr. Bayard likes scholarly men rather than politicians as assistants." Wilson's friend had urged him to seek the position, suggesting that the young professor was "more favorably known—in Washington than anywhere else outside of university circles." Though helpful, Wilson's anonymous friend was not influential; thus, Wilson requested Angell's assistance. Wilson apologized for appearing forward, but he stressed: "there are men as young as I in high places in the Depts., and, if there really is any 'fighting' chance even for me, I am very loath indeed to miss it. And my reasons are such as I am sure you will think proper and honorable." He simply hoped Angell's "indulgent temper towards the ambitions of young men" would allow Angell to accept this inquiry.[1]

Among Wilson's reasons for seeking a position away from Bryn Mawr was his distaste for instructing women.

My teaching here this year lies altogether in the field of political economy, and in my own special field of public law: and I already feel that teaching such topics to women threatens to relax not a little my mental muscle—to exalt the function of commonplace rudiments in my treatment. Before I teach elsewhere I should like to mix with the rough practical things in which I was formerly at home—to recover the proper atmosphere of my studies.[2]

Though shocking to modern ears, Wilson's comments were unfortunately not uncommon sentiments for the time. Higher education for women had already taken hold at a number of coeducational institutions, such as the Universities of Michigan and California and Cornell University, as well as at a developing series of women's colleges committed to serious liberal arts education, including Bryn Mawr. However, while many approved of educating women, none of the leading academics advocated introducing them to systematic and scientific methods of inquiry or training them to be actively involved in the development of the new American state.

However, Wilson's interest in leaving Bryn Mawr was motivated by a great deal more than his dislike for teaching women. It was motivated by a desire to apply his academic expertise to actual action. Wilson recognized that there were other opportunities for a young man wishing to "mix with the rough practical things" of government and policy— notably, the developing civil service. He admitted to Angell:

I have sometimes thought of entering the Civil Service Examination for some govt. clerkship in order to see, if only in that way, the inside of the mechanism I am engaged in studying. I have been restrained, not only by the fact that a clerk's salary would not suffice for the support of my little family, but also by the consideration that such a view of the actual operations of the daily conduct of federal administration as I could obtain from a clerk's desk in one of the departments would be too imperfect to be of any real service to my thought.[3]

Aside from demonstrating an almost quaint concern for his domestic situation, Wilson articulated a very real concern for the particulars of practical experience.

Basic government experience would not help Wilson develop intellectually or, we can certainly imply, professionally. Wilson believed his knowledge would not be expanded or properly employed as a lowly civil servant. He desired a position of real authority and significance.

But I do want—and need—particularly, as it seems to me, at this juncture in my studies, a seat on the inside of government—a seat high enough to command views of the system. I acknowledge I dread becoming doctrinaire: I dread writing what will be of no practical usefulness—a mere elevated student's view of affairs. I want to handle the practical things of my subject for a time, with an official's diligence, and that is the reason I am tempted by the suggestion of my friend,—absurd as my candidacy may at first sight appear.[4]

Clearly, as Wilson himself admitted, personal and careerist concerns were partially motivating factors in his seeking an assistant secretaryship. From a broader perspective, his concern was the relation of knowledge to practice.

Wilson articulated a basic difficulty for a generation of scholars trained in the newly developing social sciences. Their expert knowledge was grounded in detached observation of and scientific training in politics and policy. New institutions of higher learning supported the development of such expertise. However, such expertise could not be self-sustaining or self-contained. Its validity needed to be tested, and its importance needed to be demonstrated. Wilson might have been trained in the most advanced theories of political economy and administrative law, but he was not familiar with the antiquated customs of the diplomatic service. With this and Wilson's young age in mind, Angell politely suggested that Wilson consider other options for government service.

Chastened, Wilson wrote back acknowledging the wisdom of Angell's rather stern advice.

I of course thought that the duties of the Asst. Secretaryship were such as one with a pretty thorough outside acquaintance with the public business might, with diligence, master; for I can of course pretend to no personal experience in affairs, much less to any acquaintance with the formal etiquette of the diplomatic service. I have already confessed that I wanted the office in order to learn, my only readiness being a trained understanding relative to such matters. Certainly, under the circumstances, the place ought to be filled from within the Department, by somebody drilled in its service. I must thank you very heartily for setting me right.

Perhaps out of contrition or perhaps out of a simple desire to explain himself further, Wilson expanded on his desire to link his expertise with application. For Wilson, application was essential for the development of his scholarship. Theories of administration needed to be tested in the laboratory of government. Studious detachment undermined not only the quality of expertise but its legitimacy as well.

Experience in affairs, I feel, is what I most imperatively need to vivify my chosen studies. A constructive imagination will but reach a little way; even a sympathetic instinct to know cannot complete instruction in practical affairs; and if I have heretofor [*sic*] studied Washington from a distance, it has been simply because I had no choice in the matter. It was a limitation to my work which I felt, but which I had no way of removing. The conscious- ness of it has, moreover, made me particularly impatient of studious isola- tion; leading me, perhaps, to magnify its present disadvantages. I love the stir of the world; that stir is what I chiefly desire to study and explain; and I know I cannot scarcely explain it from Teufelsdrocker's tower.[5]

These letters from Wilson to Angell demonstrate that to scholars of the historical and political sciences, the consequences of practical appli- cation were an integral aspect of their studies. As an extension of this interest, partnerships between universities and the expanding national state became almost inevitable. Government service was an inherent part of scholarship. Obviously, the idea of educated men working in positions of authority was not new. However, unlike previous concep- tions of service that were based on *noblese oblige* or patriotism, the ser- vice Wilson desired was based on a particular body of expert knowl- edge, and he wished to apply, test, and expand that knowledge. Despite this wish, Wilson remained in academia, securing a position at Wesleyan University in Middletown, Connecticut, in 1888. Two years later, he began his career as professor of jurisprudence and political economics at Princeton, where he became president in 1902. He would eventually have significant opportunities to apply his ideas to govern- ment, beginning with his election as governor of New Jersey in 1910.

Wilson's request of Angell reflected the difficulties in transitioning from a patronage- and connection-based conception of administrative appointment to a knowledge- and expertise-based conception. Wilson pursued a position in the State Department out of a desire to both expand and apply his knowledge. However, his appeal for a position was grounded in patronage and favoritism. Notable for its audacity as well its retrospective irony (a future president practically groveling for a midlevel bureaucratic appointment), Wilson's letter also represents a common tension in the pursuit of expertise. Educated individuals would often use personal connections or political favors to obtain posi- tions or pursue partnerships in which they might apply their expertise.

Remarkable as these letters from Wilson to Angell are, it is all the more interesting when we note that they were written in the same year in which his groundbreaking article "The Study of Administration" was published in *Political Science Quarterly*. Well received and widely read among scholars, Wilson's piece gained additional attention when his graduate school mentor Henry Baxter Adams invited him to return to Johns Hopkins University to deliver a regular series of lectures on the topic. The essay expanded on many of the sentiments expressed in his personal discussion with Angell. Wilson stressed the importance not only of educating the citizenry as to the advantages of expertise but also of having trained men ready to apply such expertise: "but is the whole duty of administrative study done when it has taught the people what sort of administration to desire and demand, and how to get what they demand? Ought it not go on to drill candidates for the public service?"[6]

Similar to his colleagues at leading universities throughout the country, Wilson did not look to the government for such training. Instead, he welcomed and championed the move to develop academic programs that would form the basis of such service: "there is an admirable movement towards universal political education now afoot in this country. The time will soon come when no college of respectability can afford to do without a well-filled chair of political science." However, as he had noted in his letter to Angell, Wilson again suggested that there were limits to what education alone could do.

> . . . the education thus imparted will go but a certain length. It will multiply the number of intelligent critics of government, but it will create no competent body of administrators. It will prepare the way for the development of a sure-footed understanding of the general principles of government, but it will not necessarily foster skill in conducting government.

For Wilson, the key to developing such a "competent body" was a partnership whereby officials would be better prepared to be the "apparatus of government." A thorough political education was the first step in such preparation. Second, administrators would need to be screened through an extensive process of examination and melded through practical experience into a "distinct, semi-corporate" organization.[7]

Wilson recognized that such a body of administrators might be derided as undemocratic, since it would be staffed by individuals trained at universities that were only vaguely responsible to the populous and that were organized beyond the boundaries of electoral concerns. In response to such critiques, he argued that administrative training in the United States needed to be uniquely attuned to public opinion; taking European models of efficiency and adopting them to American demands of participation. Wilson concluded his argument by stressing: "the principles on which to base a science of Administration of America must be principles which have the democratic policy very much at heart. The Cosmopolitan what-to-do, must always be commanded by the American how-to-do-it."[8]

As numerous critics have noted, Wilson's "The Study of Administration" does not necessarily detail how such sensitivity to public sentiment can be guaranteed, let alone developed. However, for Wilson and his contemporaries, advanced study was seen as much more open and democratic. In this spirit, new programs were introduced, such as Johns Hopkins's system of academic fellowships. As I will detail later in this chapter, these were among the first efforts to reward and encourage what was defined as merit. Wilson, for example, did not consider himself to be from a privileged background. Similar to the process of choosing university leaders, the study of administration was grounded in a fundamental belief that by picking the best men to apply expertise, the needs of all men would be met.

Expertise or Influence?

It might seem a bit churlish to criticize Wilson for not upholding his public pronouncements in private correspondence, but I would be negligent if I did not mention that in seeking the assistant secretaryship, he seemingly contradicts his own recommendations advocated in "The Study of Administration." In his letters to Angell, Wilson recognizes that he is not necessarily qualified or trained for the post, but he hopes to use it for his own "education." He does not wish to compete for a position in the civil service and instead asks Angell to secure him a position through influence. One might attribute Wilson's slight hypocrisy to pressures associated with the demands of domestic life and the unhappiness of his situation at Bryn Mawr.

However, the disjunction between Wilson's theorizing and his personal efforts reflect a paradoxical and difficult reality for advocates of the new American state. While advocating reforms of government and promoting expertise, these advocates often made inroads and secured positions through the very system of patronage and favoritism that they sought to replace. Wilson would eventually demonstrate ability and gain experience in the practical world of politics (though historians still debate whether he ever acquired diplomatic skills). Other Johns Hopkins fellowship recipients, such as Thomas Cooley and Henry Carter Adams (whom I will touch on more later), certainly were well qualified to serve the Interstate Commerce Commission. Yet their candidacies also were assisted by the fact that active University of Michigan alumnus and eventual Democratic Party chairman Don Dickinson was among those who recommended them to President Grover Cleveland.

It would be wrong, however, to assume that such actions simply reflected the extension of patronage. A new approach to training and a new definition of service emerged, and while it may not have been any

more open and democratic in terms of access, a loosely coupled con-
federation of universities—mostly autonomous, with tight control of
their own governance—began to redefine the American state. Beginning with the radical implementation of a federal initiative for practical
education and continuing with efforts to develop scientific political
training, university leaders started to develop partnerships that would
not only alter their institution's public role but redefine the public
sphere itself.

The Pursuit of Scientific Political Training

Among the most significant university initiatives dedicated to redefining higher education's public role was the push to develop programs
and schools in political science. The systematic study of politics and
administration had first been institutionalized in the United States with
Columbia's appointment of Frances Leiber as chair of History and
Political Science in 1858. Upon assuming the chair, Leiber outlined his
plans for the professorship. Among his primary goals was to expand
understanding of "the ends and reasons of political societies, the discussion of the means by which man endeavors to obtain the end or
ought to obtain it; in one word, to the science of government, and a
knowledge of governments which exist and have existed."[9]

Leiber's efforts laid the foundation for the development of American
political science. However, during his tenure, Columbia would never
offer more than a few courses on the subject. Attempts to establish a full
curriculum dedicated to scientific political training would still be a few
years in coming. Initiated by institutional entrepreneurs seeking to
establish societal relevance for their schools, these efforts stemmed
from a desire to apply specialized knowledge to issues of public concern and from a belief in the ability of universities to develop and disseminate this expertise. While not universally successful, these efforts
helped create structures and programs—such as advanced degrees and
fellowships—that would support the pursuit of advanced knowledge
across a variety of fields and domains.

White's Call, Gilman's Response

An expansive vision of the university pursuing particularized service
to the public emerged from a variety of sources and in a multitude of
forms. Among these, the platform provided by Johns Hopkins University's Commemoration Day celebration was unique in its influence.
Providing a national forum and publishing their remarks, Johns Hop-

kins's president Daniel Coit Gilman annually invited university leaders, such as Harvard's Charles Eliot and Cornell's Andrew Dickson White, to address the place of higher education in a rapidly changing society. Though their talks did not represent a formally coordinated vision, they were among the first efforts by university leaders to jointly address the university's response to an increasingly complex society.

For Andrew Dickson White, the challenge was to pursue knowledge for the sake of training men who could apply this knowledge to all questions and problems government faced. At Johns Hopkins' Commemoration Day in early 1879, White, speaking on "rearing a race of statesmen," addressed the proper provision for higher instruction. White's notion of statesmen and their education focused almost exclusively on expertise. He essentially ignored earlier conceptions of statesmanship and authority built on patrimonial inheritance or charismatic leadership.

According to White, statesmen did not simply come from great families or emerge as great men, they were educated to be great, by universities that pursued and disseminated expert knowledge of public affairs. During his speech at Johns Hopkins (an address also given to the Union League Club of New York in March of that year), White emphasized the need for universities as well as society to pursue expert approaches in all fields in which government endeavored to act.

> In a Republic like ours, the people are called on at the last to decide upon all fundamental questions, and to their proper discussion there must be two conditions—first, the education of the mass of citizens, and second, suitable instruction for the natural leaders rising from the masses. For their development there is at present in our higher education no adequate provision. With some training for better discussion of the political and social questions in the world, in the future we may begin to advance without paying the appalling cost of progress she has paid and is paying.
>
> Much has been said of our educated men keeping aloof from politics, but if scholarly young men are trained steadily in political questions from the outset, they will enter public life at such an advantage that this change will be brought to naught. American education is a case for exercise of American munificence.[10]

Notably, under White's leadership, Cornell University did not exercise such extensive munificence. Constraints on resources meant that Cornell did not found such a program until after White had left office.

White did not succeed in establishing the far-reaching school of public affairs he desired, but he did establish courses that focused on political economy, social science, the conditions of the poor, and the like. Addressing social problems rather than agricultural or mechanical ones, these courses grew from the Morrill Act's spirit of training students in how to apply expert knowledge in newly developing fields of study. These courses were justified not only on the basis of student interest but also, more important, on the basis of public service and the promotion of expertise. The university was bringing expertise to bear on an increasing variety of subjects. Such expertise was most valuable in its application. So if the university were to study political and social questions, it would also act as an active partner and directly train men for service in government.

Cornell was not the only university that sought to address problems of politics and governance by "rearing statesmen" through academic training. At Johns Hopkins, Daniel Coit Gilman actively pursued a prominent alumnus, University of Michigan legal and social scholar Thomas Cooley, in an effort to develop a program in public affairs.

Writing to offer a professorship of jurisprudence to Cooley in 1880, Gilman displayed his enthusiasm for a program dedicated to training men for service in politics and public life as well as for the legal profession. Gilman hoped that Cooley's lectures, coupled with courses in history and political science, would develop "so that the Johns Hopkins University may become a place of great usefulness in promoting among educated young men sound ideas of good government."[11] Gilman did not necessarily envision a whole particularized school of political science. He was, however, eager to expand the existing courses in the area. He stressed to Cooley that he would not be simply offering instruction to aspiring members of the bar. Johns Hopkins did not (and still does not) have a law school. Instead, Cooley would be helping provide expertise and train young men in the law while directing their focus to its broader social and political implications.

> You will perceive that we have in contemplation a scheme which differs both from the ordinary collegiate work, and from the technical training of an advocate; that we look to the liberal education of young men in subjects which will fit them to bear an honorable part in the discussion of public affairs whether or not they make Law their profession.[12]

In attempting to meet White's call for "American munificence," Gilman's plan continued the emerging approach of merging general instruction for all interested in a particular field with detailed study for specialists. Johns Hopkins's course in jurisprudence combined efforts to produce good citizens with efforts to develop experts who could solve the political and social problems that troubled these citizens.

Contemplating Gilman's offer, Cooley heard from Johns Hopkins trustee George Brown, who asked him to visit. In his invitation, Brown stressed the university's dedication to the program as well as to graduate work and research: "The growth of the university has not been rapid, but it has been healthful and vigorous. One half of the students are post-graduates. . . . No where in the country is so much original work done."[13] Brown acknowledged the infant nature of Johns Hopkins's programs but suggested that this would allow for freedom of approach and method. He emphasized to Cooley that the whole of the institution was committed to pursuing new and detailed knowledge in a variety of areas. He suggested that Cooley's career and reputation would benefit from strides made at this new institution.[14] Despite expressing a genuine interest in the post, Cooley would eventually decline the Johns Hopkins offer. Unable to find a suitable replacement for his position in Ann Arbor, he wrote Gilman saying that to accept would be to "do the University [of Michigan] a wrong."[15]

Initially remaining at Michigan, Cooley would not receive the Supreme Court nomination that Brown and many others expected and desired for him. He was, however, appointed as the first chairman of the Interstate Commerce Commission, in 1887. Though not achieving his ultimate ambition, Cooley embodied the fledgling partnerships between government agencies and university expertise. By attempting to recruit Cooley, the nation's first institution dedicated to graduate education sought a scholar who would oversee the federal government's first major attempt to exercise national regulatory power, an effort underscoring the embryonic partnership between developing universities and the evolving American state.

Even without Cooley, Johns Hopkins's program of advanced study in politics, history, and the law gradually developed. In addition to communicating with Gilman and his trustees, Cooley communicated with former colleagues on the Hopkins faculty, such as Herbert Baxter Adams, professor of historical and political science. Undertaking a more subtle recruiting effort, Adams wrote to Cooley that Johns Hopkins had "begun its fifth year very prosperously" and that the program in the history of local governments had fifteen graduate students and over twenty undergraduates.[16]

Adams's excitement was not limitless. By 1885, he was frustrated with his support from the institution and politely toying with the possibility of taking a position at the University of Michigan—to replace Charles Kendall Adams, who was leaving to succeed Andrew Dickson White as president of Cornell. Eventually, Herbert Baxter Adams would decline Michigan's offer. His explanation offers insight into his slight discontent with Johns Hopkins as well as his commitment to make a place for his scholarship there.

> [When offered the position] some weeks ago I was in a somewhat discontented state of mind, owing to the difficulties and obstructions encountered by my department. I felt a strong inclination to seek greater freedom in a broader field, where History and Political Science had already won their place. But today, amid the tranquil life of a New England town and surrounded by the steadfast hills, I am encouraged to stand by the work I have already begun in Baltimore. I am persuaded that it is better to clear my own field as did my own fathers before me.
>
> Professor C. K. Adams has opened a wide territory in the Northwest, but I am afraid that no other Adams could hold it with equal grip. He is so identified with the Michigan School of Political Science that, without him, the school cannot remain the same. On the other hand, my Baltimore work, circumscribed as it is, has a growth, a character, and surroundings all its own; it could not be successfully transplanted even to richer soil and made to fill an entirely different place.[17]

For Herbert Baxter Adams, the limits he felt at Johns Hopkins were less burdensome than the expectations he feared would come from being at Michigan. Despite his early concerns about the place of history and political science at Johns Hopkins, he would remain there until his death in 1901. First during his fellowship and later during his professorship, significant advanced work was undertaken and progressive training was done. This work and training was based in systematic class work and original investigations, approaches that are second nature today but were among the first of their kind at the time.

The success of these approaches that originated at Johns Hopkins can be seen in the fact that in the first years of the program (1877–91), the university granted twenty-five PhD's in historical and political science.[18] Among those who received training at Johns Hopkins were Herbert Baxter Adams himself; the university's first PhD recipient, economist Henry Carter Adams; sociologist Frederick Jackson Turner; and a South Carolina minister's son who had attended Davidson College before graduating from Princeton, Woodrow Wilson.

Michigan's School of Political Science: A Limited Partner

Thomas Cooley's decision to stay in Ann Arbor was not a slight of Johns Hopkins or of Gilman's proposed program as much as it was a reflection of Cooley's loyalty to the University of Michigan and its then president, James Burrill Angell. Additionally, Michigan was developing its own program in political science and public affairs to make use of Cooley's talents. In the summer of 1881, the University of Michigan announced plans to develop one of America's first schools of political science.[19] The school's first dean was Charles Kendall Adams, a protégé of Andrew Dickson White. Though formally on the law school faculty, Cooley also was among the new school's instructors.

In response to the founding of Michigan's School of Political Science and a proposed, similar, but less ambitious, program at Columbia, the *New York Times* detailed the prospects for scientific political training in a July 1881 editorial. The *Times* remarked that if "intelligently taught and faithfully studied," the program would produce "very accomplished scientific political thinkers." However, it also raised a skeptical objection to the application of such training. Noting that the school offered no course on how to run a caucus or how to be a party "boss," the *Times* worried whether graduates of the program would "know much about the history and theory of politics, and next to nothing about men."[20] The *Times* did not argue that such courses and schools were pointless. Rather, it simply articulated potential obstacles of applying the knowledge and principles developed in such courses and schools to the practical world of electoral politics.

The *Times* emphasized that its commentary should be taken not as criticism but as a realistic assessment of contemporary politics: "The existence of this untoward state of things, however, is no reason for decrying schools of political science. There is need enough of political education. Anybody can see that." However, while the *Times* expressed a positive interest in the prospects for such schools, it continued to be restrained from any heightened enthusiasm.

> It may be called an encouraging sign, therefore, that schools of political science are springing up at Ann Arbor, at Columbia College, and in other parts of the country. But these schools will not correct or remove the evils of our political system. . . . To cure these evils and make room for honest and competent men in political life we must destroy the spoils system. So long as bosses have the power to control the politics of a State by patronage they will take good care that no Doctors of Philosophy, political or otherwise, get into important office.

The *Times* did not devalue the prospective work being done at these schools. It did, however, express severe doubts about the number of political scientists who would be trained and about the impact they would have.

> Even under the most favorable conditions and with a reformed civil service, schools of political science would have no great influence in elevating and purifying our politics. It is possible they would be very slimly attended. The

American people are not in the habit of looking upon politics as a profession to be prepared for by special study.

With this in mind, the *Times* instead stressed the need for efforts to reach out to the voting public: "it is not by special departments of political science, but by giving the greatest possible amount of instruction of that kind in their ordinary colleges of study, that the colleges can make their influence most felt in our public life."[21]

Simple applications of expertise and partnerships with government were not enough to overcome the evils of patronage. For the *Times*, if these new schools were to make any substantial impact, they would need to foster a fundamental change in how citizens viewed politics and in what they demanded of their leaders. The *Times* did not dismiss the efforts of the institutional entrepreneurs who founded schools dedicated to scientific political training. Rather, it cautioned that the problems of late nineteenth-century politics were immediately greater than any solution offered by academic training. University-developed approaches to political and social problems were like university-developed approaches to agriculture or the mechanic arts; their value would be largely determined in the field—beyond the walls of academia and through efforts to work with government.

Michigan's new program in scientific political training faced an array of challenges beyond skepticism as to its utility. Similar to most fledgling academic programs, Michigan's ambitious program was dogged by questions regarding resources, staffing, and institutional commitment. At the same time the University of Michigan was seeking to lure Herbert Baxter Adams to its school of political science, Henry Carter Adams,[22] a former student and colleague of Henry Baxter Adams at Johns Hopkins, expressed to President Angell frustration with "the inadequacy of the present arrangement for the study of Political Economy in the University of Michigan."[23] From 1880 to 1887, Henry Carter Adams was splitting his time between the University of Michigan and Cornell. It was not, as the *Times* had predicted, a lack of student interest that frustrated him; rather, it was the lack of adequate faculty to handle all the students interested in political economy. Writing Angell, he raised his concerns:

under the present organization of the department, not more than 40% of those who begin the work carry it far enough to apply the principles which they learn to problems of practical interest. 80 students take the "elementary" course in Fall, the following Fall the number who continue drops to 20–40.[24]

To Adams, the lag meant that students wandered elsewhere in their studies and failed to receive adequate training to place their "elementary" knowledge into practice, making the course of little value. Adams felt overburdened and believed that all of his students, but especially those interested in "advanced work," suffered because of this.[25] After controversy at Cornell that I will discuss in more detail later, Adams ended his joint appointment and joined the Michigan faculty full-time as a professor in 1887. He was soon joined by F. A. Hicks as an assistant professor in 1888.[26]

The department of political economy would survive. Michigan's initial attempt to develop a full school of political science would not. Henry Carter Adams's assessment proved prescient. Once Charles Kendall Adams left for Cornell in 1885, the school suffered. Thomas Cooley was a more than able replacement intellectually but did not have the entrepreneurial skills necessary to grow the program. Therefore, when he left to become inaugural chairman of the Interstate Commerce Commission, the school formally ceased to offer its program, though courses in all the relevant subfields continued to be taught.[27]

The failure of Michigan's initial attempt to develop a school of political science should not be seen as demonstrating ambivalence or hostility toward university efforts to establish partnerships and share expertise. Even without an institutionalized school of political science, Michigan still offered instruction and graduate degrees in the relevant subfields that had comprised the school.[28] Rather, such failure simply underscores the fledgling nature of those efforts and their reliance on the entrepreneurial savvy of various leading academics. In these early years of the new American state, governmental need for specialized knowledge and expertise was not necessarily enough to sustain the more formalized programs that would provide it. As the idea of applying specialized knowledge to public problems was only beginning to take hold, the success of partnerships, both large and small, often depended on the actions and availability of a few individuals. Such relative scarcity of personnel would frequently drive development for such new programs but would also sometimes undermine their sustenance.

Scholars and Partnerships: Offering Early Expertise

The story of political science's early development is not just about efforts to institutionalize scientific political training in formal programs and schools. An emerging network of scholars would take leadership in developing the discipline, the university, and the national state. This leadership stemmed from a unique coordination based on extensive, lifelong correspondence and an entrepreneurial ability to maximize resources.

Andrew Dickson White and Daniel Coit Gilman were not political scientists themselves. Nonetheless, these two Yale classmates, who shared a passion for education, a commitment to the university ideal, and a desire to serve their country, developed institutions that would greatly influence the development of scientific political training, the university, and the national state. They also mentored scholars who would perpetuate their efforts in both academia and public affairs.

Among the most significant innovations implemented by Gilman at Johns Hopkins was a system of graduate fellowships modeled on those at the German universities. Gilman was not necessarily the first to consider such a scheme in the United States, but Johns Hopkins was the first to attempt it, in 1876. Typical of the loosely coupled coordination of this era, Johns Hopkins's fellowship program was highly dependent on its fellow elite universities. Gilman announced the program through a widely distributed circular and personally wrote to colleagues at Cornell, Yale, Princeton, Michigan, Harvard, Columbia, and Pennsylvania. Most of the fellows were nominated by the presidents of their undergraduate institutions. At this time, there were no formal disciplinary associations to oversee selection or standards within fields of study.[29] Instead, fellows were nominated regardless of field.

The opportunity to promote advanced study greatly excited Gilman's friend White. Writing to nominate two students of his for consideration, including one in political science, White concluded:

> These applications have set me at thinking more and more deeply than ever before regarding your system of Post-graduate courses and fellowships. If I see anything I see clearly that that is *the* thing in your organization [emphasis White's]. In that lies your greatest chance to do a great thing for this country. There are over three hundred institutions as you know ready to do the preparatory work; but this advanced work few are able to do at all and none to do it as it should be done. Were I in your place I would prize more deeply fifty advanced students than 500 undergraduates.[30]

With such sentiments, the efforts to build the modern research university began in earnest.

To perpetuate these efforts, White eagerly offered advice as to how Gilman should develop the program and strongly suggested that Johns Hopkins expand it.

I feel sure that you could not do a better thing than immediately to double the number of these fellowships. The great thing is to start with *a good nucleus of the best men from the various colleges* [emphasis White's]; and in this way you can be sure to get such a nucleus. Ten fellowships would much more than double the efficiency of the system. Twenty is, in this matter, considerably more than twice ten.

If your applications warrant the statement, and I have no doubt they do, why not at once issue another circular stating that this number of applications for fellowships leads the trustees to double the number and that up to the first of July you will receive the names of candidates for ten additional fellowships. Depend upon it a better use of five thousand dollars can not be made.

Of course, White was not the one who needed to raise the funds or issue the additional circular; but he was convinced that there would be more than enough prospective students to make such an effort worthwhile.

As I see these most thoughtful young men willing to give up larger pecuniary prospects for the place you offer securing them a bare support, but enabling them to push their studies, I see that, much as I hoped from the system of fellowships, I did not realize the force with which it appeals to the best young men. There are others here who would doubtless apply but that they suppose that with so few fellowships and two of our resident graduates in the field they would stand no chance.[31]

Encouraged by his friend, Gilman requested that the Johns Hopkins trustees expand the program to twenty fellowships, which they did. As mentioned earlier, this system of graduate fellowships and the reputation of Johns Hopkins's burgeoning program in historical and political science attracted many men who would greatly influence the development of the national state.

Forging Partnerships: Cooley, Adams, and the ICC

Among Johns Hopkins's initial graduate fellows were Henry Carter Adams, who, in 1878, received the first PhD ever granted by the institution, and Thomas McIntyre Cooley, who served as a teaching fellow, giving twenty lectures a year. The two would eventually reunite on the faculty of the University of Michigan. Soon after, in one of the earliest examples of direct partnership between the emerging university and the new American state, Adams and Cooley would help launch the Interstate Commerce Commission (ICC), in 1887. Cooley served as the ICC's chairman, and Adams served as its chief economist.

Before he was appointed to the professorate at Michigan and made chief economist for the ICC, Henry Carter Adams had served as president of the newly founded American Economic Association. In 1886, while on the faculty at Cornell, Adams encountered controversy. He had given a series of speeches that would evolve into his essay "The Relation of the State to Industrial Action." Focusing his attention on railroads, the largest industry of the day, Adams essentially argued against the simple application of laissez-faire and expressed concern about the industry's administration, especially in regards to capital and labor. For Adams, the solution lay in the application of expertise—in the form of guiding principles—to the economic challenges of the era.

> The collapse of faith in the sufficiency of the philosophy of laissez faire, has left the present generation without principles adequate for the guidance of public affairs. We are now passing through a period of interregnum in the authoritative control of economic and governmental principles. This is indeed cause for grave solicitude, for never were there more difficult problems demanding solution than at the present time, and never were men so poorly equipped for the accomplishment of such a task as are those upon whom these questions are being forced.[32]

Today, Adams's argument might seem a very reasonable call for limited regulation, and within a generation of his making the call, it became the operating assumption of the American state. Initially, however, his lectures and addresses, along with the expansion of his thoughts in published form, caused an uproar on the Cornell campus. He was branded a radical by the local press, and two prominent Cornell benefactors, Henry Sage and William Lago, advocated his removal. Adams vigorously defended himself against the charges but also recognized that he might do well to seek employment elsewhere.

Writing to James Burrill Angell at Michigan, he expressed doubts regarding the wisdom of staying at Cornell, since President Charles Kendall Adams "wanted to propose what would practically amount to an extension of my apprenticeship; because he feared friction, if he advocated anything else, on account of the misunderstandings of last year."[33] Henry Carter Adams boldly inquired if he might not be appointed to the Michigan faculty full time.

Angell was well aware of the controversy, as he corresponded regularly with both Henry Carter Adams and Cornell's president Charles Kendall Adams. In fact, a year earlier, when the controversy first erupted, Angell had expressed to Henry Carter Adams his concern that Adams supported a socialist agenda, and Angell had asked for a clarification of Adams's views. Agitated but feeling that his mentor and future employer deserved an explanation, Adams replied at length. In a frustrated tone, he explicitly spelled out his economic and social philosophy in a passage almost more detailed in its practical applications than his monograph.

> You ask to what extent I would advocate state socialism?
>
> I would maintain the post office under the control of the federal government and establish in connection with it a public telegraph and parcel post. I would maintain public education even to the University, under the control of the States and establish State forestry and State ownership of mines.
>
> I would extend largely the duties of cities, so as to give them control over gas works, water works, and street railways. They should also make the amusements and education of the citizens their care. I trust, on the basis of the above statement that I shall not be thought ignorant of the inefficiency of local governments *at the present time* [italics indicate words Adams added by hand].
>
> On the other hand, I would oppose anything like paternal government. Tenement houses at public expense, government insurance for working men, public eating houses and such proposals of mistaken charity, would be injurious to the class whom it was desired to assist for they would work like the old English poor law.[34]

It might seem remarkable that Adams, soon to be the economist of the first federal regulatory initiative of the new American state, would advocate for local control of various governmental activities. However, like his colleague Cooley, Adams recognized the constraints federalism would place on any efforts for reform. Most important, no matter what level of implementation reform efforts might reach, Adams's major concern was the application of knowledge and expertise. In fact, Adams believed that expertise provided a bulwark against socialism.

Adams concluded his articulation of beliefs by stressing, "it is my wish that our civilization may be saved from the sterility of what is commonly called socialism, and to that end I advocate a further development of proprietary rights and the science of government."[35] Adams ended the letter by expressing surprise at Angell's questions and by admitting his fear of being dropped from his position of teaching at Michigan one semester a year. He stated his hope that Angell recognized such action as unfair.

A year later, when Adams asked if he might join the Michigan faculty on a full-time basis, Angell again expressed concern about the economist's perceived socialism and the impact it would have on Angell's ability to make his appointment and on the regents' desire to approve it. Reflecting the intimacy of relationships between faculty and university presidents, Adams responded with a very direct challenge to Angell's inquiries: "you ask if I can help you see your way clear to my nomination. I don't see as I can except it to be to suggest that, in my opinion, your point of view in this matter is not the right one."[36]

Adams then proceeded with a rousing and spirited defense of the general principles of academic freedom.

> If you make a man's opinions the basis of his election to a professorship, you do, whether you intend it or not, place bonds upon the free movement of his intellect. It seems to me that a Board has two things to hold in view. First, is a man a scholar? Can he teach in a scholarly manner? Is he fair to all parties in the controversial questions which come before him? Second, is he intellectually honest? If these questions are answered in the affirmative his influence upon young men cannot be detrimental.[37]

Of course, Adams was not simply making his arguments in the abstract. He was fighting to retain his status in the academic community. Adams defended his own abilities and impartiality at length and concluded by summarizing both his teaching and personal philosophy: "my conscious teaching is two-fold. To portray social problems to men as they will find them to be when they leave the University." To Adams, the fundamental concern in all problems, social and economic, was "personal responsibility in the administration of all social power, no matter what shape that power may exist."[38] Articulating his teaching philosophy, Adams emphasized practicality and a desire to produce students who would see matters as they really are and recognize their own "personal responsibility."

Concerns about practicality and responsibility were common to Adams and others. Adams sought to bring newly developing knowledge and approaches to bear on problems of the day. Angell's concern did not lie in Adams's approach; Angell fully approved of efforts to tackle the social problems of the day. Angell's concern lie in his fear that Adams's approach was without a moral basis, as Adams's monograph largely disregarded the issue of morality. Eventually accepting Adams's defense and always recognizing Adams's talent, Angell proposed and Michigan's regents approved Adams's appointment as professor of political economy and finance in June 1887. Adams was relieved and, despite their earlier contentious exchanges, eager to join Angell's university full-time. In fact, during that summer, he expressed concern over rumors that Angell would be leaving Michigan, rumors Adams had heard at the American Economic Association meetings in Providence.[39]

These rumors proved unfounded, and Adams joined the faculty full-time in the fall. He also recognized that his trouble lie not with the university presidents as much as with their boards of trustees. Informing

Angell of intelligence from Cornell's Charles Kendall Adams that the main obstacle to Henry's promotion was a trustee who was expected to bequeath over one million dollars upon his death, Henry wrote that he believed he could win his place at Cornell if he fought but that he declined to fight because he did "not wish to place any obstacle to the prosperity of this institution merely to gratify my pride."[40] At both Michigan and Cornell, the battle over Henry Carter Adams's alleged radicalism was soon forgotten. He would serve a distinguished career as a member of the Michigan faculty, be welcomed at Cornell as a guest lecturer, and achieve renown for his work in developing the American Economic Association, which he had cofounded in 1885.

Adams's Michigan colleague Thomas Cooley had encountered a similar professional challenge in 1884. When aligning with the mugwump Republican movement, he lost his bid for reelection to a seat on the Michigan Supreme Court. Cooley remained on the University of Michigan's law faculty and would eventually serve a brief, if unremarkable, tenure as dean of the School of Political Science. Cooley's career took a dramatic turn when President Grover Cleveland appointed him as the first chairman of the Interstate Commerce Commission in 1888. Adams soon joined him as chief economist and statistician. Two men who only a few years before had found themselves at great odds with public sentiment were now defining the nation's regulatory policy. Adams would serve as the leading light of the commission in the 1890s, and Cooley would articulate the tenets of a new theory of law to fit an alternative mode of regulation for the new American state.[41]

The contributions of these two men would not have been possible if not for the support of universities. Adams and Cooley were among the first generation of scholars who would use their positions to examine social problems from a scientific and analytical perspective. For earlier scholars and institutional entrepreneurs, higher education institutions served the public through the production of moral, virtuous, and patriotic men. Such concerns were still of significance to developing universities. However, the ability to produce knowledge that would help the nation and to identify and solve social problems—be they in agriculture, railroad administration, or politics—was becoming an ever more important concern. This did not happen without some trauma, as Adams's struggles make clear. Yet overall, the university provided extensive and vital institutional support. When Adams and Cooley found themselves under attack, the university provided an intellectual home for both. When they served the commission, the university allowed them to keep their faculty appointments, offered them leaves of absence, and permitted them to appoint those who would serve as guest lecturers in their place. The university provided a network through which Adams and Cooley could develop and disseminate the ideas that they would put into practice regarding law and economic regulation. The university, in essence, subsidized their service to the national state as well as shaping the skills they brought to such service.

Beyond Politics: Partnerships, Service, and Coordination

Providing expertise in the realm of public administration was a natural partnership between universities and the national state. It was far from the only one. From foreign policy to international trade, geology to engineering, the emerging university provided individual and institutional support for the ever-specializing national state. Education and training had not been ignored in the era of the state of courts and parties, but it had not been prioritized. Additionally, in this previous era, college's education and training did not provide men with a particularized set of skills or knowledge as much as it socialized them to uphold standards of patriotism and morality. University development and provision of expertise did not stem from the simple expansion of government activity as much as it stemmed from government specialization. In providing service to the national state within these various realms of government activity, universities grew to be coordinated through the evolving network of loosely coupled academics and presidents.

Managing Growth: New Agencies and the Pendleton Act

Emerging universities did not simply develop programs dedicated to scientific political training; they also sought to provide basic manpower for the expanding array of agencies and departments that were developing as part of the growing national state. Not every agency formed extensive partnerships with universities. However, many developing agencies did offer an opportunity for universities to develop new programs and offer expertise. Sometimes, as with public administration and political science, universities developed general programs that would lead graduates to specific service. In other instances, university leaders sought to develop programs with more specific service in mind.

For both approaches, there were limits to the success of such partnerships. Political obstacles and limited resources sometimes hindered efforts at direct partnerships, and though university presidents were often well-connected and well-respected individuals, their loosely coupled lobbying efforts were only moderately effective. Both areas of specific technical expertise (e.g., meteorology and engineering) and areas of general expertise (e.g., civil service) offered opportunities for development of partnerships. Though not every opportunity was to be fully realized in the "loosely coupled" era, these efforts would lay the foundation for greater entrepreneurship in developing partnerships between universities and the national state.

The passage and signing of the Pendleton Act in 1883, with its establishment of a merit system and the national Civil Service Commission, represented a significant effort to recast governmental authority and operations toward a "professional, nonpartisan discipline."[42] Focusing on post offices and customhouses, the act led to moderate alterations in the federal patronage system. However, while university-based reformers were pleased with the appointment of their colleague John Gregory (the new president of the University of Illinois) to the commission, their enthusiasm waned.

Writing to his good friend James Burrill Angell, Andrew Dickson White sought to rally university men for a meeting with President Benjamin Harrison to encourage the expansion of the classified civil service. Frustrated with the moderate alterations made to the old system of patronage, White believed that the meeting was urgent: "it is now or never," he wrote. For White, a dangerous number of educators had abandoned the Republican Party, which he believed to be the party of reform.

> Among other points which we wish to impress upon him [Harrison] is the change in sentiment of educated men, especially in the Colleges and Universities, toward the Republican party, mainly on account of its non-fulfillment of the promise of reform made in its platform. As regards this institution, down to a recent period I can recall but two Democrats in its entire Faculty; now, with a Faculty of one hundred and six person, I can count all who vote the Republican ticket on the fingers of one hand.
>
> The number of College Presidents who still stand by the Republican Party is small, but if the names of Dwight and Angell and Carter and Gates are among them, they will carry weight, I am sure.[43]

Angell expressed support for White's efforts to promote civil service reform, saying "my heart is fully with you," but he confessed that he himself had not voted for Harrison.[44]

White and his fellow university presidents would continue to be frustrated as Harrison dismissively refused their call to expand the number of positions classified under the civil service. Describing a surprisingly enjoyable visit by Harrison when White was in Berlin a number of years later, White would recall Harrison as "rude and uncompromising" at the earlier meeting.[45] Policy failure and personal animosity aside, White's efforts reflected the growing coordination among university leaders to influence government policy.

Expanded Opportunities, Limited Results

In 1870, Congress directed the secretary of war to institutionalize meteorological observations at military stations across the country. With the congressional directive as their initiative, the army established the country's first school of meteorology at Fort Whipple, Virginia. In 1890, government meteorological activity was reorganized as a civilian enterprise, when the Weather Bureau was established as an agency within the Department of Agriculture. Michigan's James Burrill Angell and Cornell's Charles Kendall Adams attempted to use the transfer of the Weather Bureau to the Department of Agriculture as an entrepreneurial springboard for creating university-based schools of meteorology.

Writing jointly to Erwin Mecates, the assistant secretary of agriculture, Angell and Adams asked whether the department was considering the establishment of meteorological schools for the training of personnel to staff weather stations, and they offered their institutions as homes for such instruction. Mecates responded by telling the two that the transfer had been somewhat disruptive and that there were no funds immediately available for the creation of such schools. Additionally, Mecates noted, the Department of Agriculture was of two minds regarding the value of university-based research and expertise. While Mecates himself greatly valued the potential contribution offered by schools of meteorology and other similar programs of detailed investigation, he feared he was in the minority.

> We stand here in the Department of Agriculture between two forces, the most effectual and powerful is urged by those who believe in the practical, and who have no patience with the slow process of investigation which they claim is only remotely of benefit to agriculture; the other force which a few of us at least appreciate, is less influential in a measure.
>
> I stand in the department as its most strenuous representative; hence in the development of the work of the Weather Bureau, we are of necessity obliged to so conduct it as to accomplish obvious results, but we shall endeavor not to lose sight of the scientific investigation, and when we get fully engaged in the work, I am hopeful of a fair degree of research work.
>
> For the above reasons you will understand why at present, at least, we cannot consider the proposition of establishing a meteorological school at the University.[46]

While the second Morrill Act of 1890 permitted general land grants to be directed toward instruction in meteorology and other fields within the physical sciences, the Department of Agriculture never directly offered funds for such schooling. On the one hand, Mecates' frustration underscores the limits of partnership for proponents of expertise. The extension of government activities did not immediately or inherently lead to government sponsorship of programs directed toward advanced and specialized knowledge. On the other hand, a lack of direct federal sponsorship did not preclude universities from pursuing and providing expertise. Recognizing the expansion of the weather service would provide opportunities for men with advanced training, Michigan and Cornell would establish programs in meteorology by the end of the decade. While Angell and Adams were not able to secure direct federal dollars for their entrepreneurial enterprise, they did succeed in creating programs that would help with the growth of the Weather Bureau.

Just as universities helped with the growth of the federal state, the government helped with the growth of higher education institutions. This reciprocal arrangement was neatly reflected in the assignment of military officers to campuses as instructors. Formal relations between universities and the military began with the passage of the first Morrill Act. In addition to providing for instruction in agriculture and the mechanic arts, the act required that land-grant institutions offer military instruction. On such campuses as Cornell and Berkeley, an officer assigned to oversee military instruction drilled a rough assembly of students, often without proper uniforms and armaments. Despite the ramshackle nature of these college units and the general disinterest of students, many university leaders supported the military presence on campus. Cornell's Andrew Dickson White welcomed the discipline and routine such instruction brought. He also believed it was important for the nation to have "college men" ready to serve in response not only to foreign threats but to domestic ones as well. Writing in *Popular Science Monthly* on the value of "scientific and industrial education," White argued, "of all things fatal for a Republic, the most fatal is to have its educated men in various professions so educated that in any civil commotion they must cower in corners, and relinquish the control of the armed forces to communists and demagogues."[47]

White was not necessarily advocating military training at Cornell so that college men could protect themselves against those who were uneducated. Rather, he was replying to various critics who suggested that the military had better uses for its officers and who feared that a university education produced men so specialized and so detached as to be unable to serve their nation in times of crisis. For White, requiring all students to take some military instruction from an officer assigned by the government was a way to answer these critics, by providing manpower that could be of immediate service to the nation. Compulsory military instruction would eventually be eliminated, but the federal government would continue to assign an officer, and during World War I, the Reserve Officers Training Corps would develop from this program.

The military did not simply provide personnel for general instruction; it also provided specific personnel for advanced training. Beginning with the establishment of the Naval Engineering Corps in 1880, the navy detailed officers to universities to serve as instructors. University leaders welcomed the program as an opportunity to expand offerings and to extend partnerships with the national state. The first engineer assigned to the University of Michigan, Mortimer Cooley, would leave the service and develop the university's engineering department. The partnership between the two was not necessarily seamless. While leading universities were happy to incorporate naval officers into their faculty and naval engineering into their curriculum, the navy was often short of available men, and turnover was high. These difficulties often meant that universities were forced to coordinate their requests with both their fellow institutions and the prospective candidate.

In one notable instance, Presidents Adams of Cornell and Angell of Michigan both sought the services of the same engineer, Joseph Carnaga. However, rather than compete for his services or appeal to the government to arbitrate the dispute, the two men settled it between themselves. Adams was the first to call attention to their mutual desire for Carnaga's services. Writing Angell, he noted that Cornell had applied for Carnaga's services only to be informed that while Carnaga requested to work at Cornell, the department had already assigned him to Michigan. Adams asked if Angell might rescind his claim on Carnaga's services. Angell wrote back detailing the troubles he had had in finding a naval engineer and expressing fear that he would continue to be without one if he relinquished his claim on Carnaga. Adams recognized his friend's situation but hoped an agreement could be had.[48] With assurances from the navy that a replacement candidate for Carnaga could be found for Michigan, Angell granted Adams's request.

Beyond the actual partnership it displays between government and the university, the Carnaga case underscores the value of coordination and its usefulness in maximizing resources. If the navy had been working with each institution separately, a disgruntled officer would likely have served Michigan unhappy with his placement, and Cornell would have been assigned an officer possibly unfamiliar with the institution. Instead, the navy encouraged the universities to settle their disputed claims and, more generally, asked the institutions to judge the quality of the instruction offered. Notably, when the navy did assign an officer to Michigan a semester later, it asked Angell to thoroughly assess his abilities. The assigning officer stressed, "if it should turn out that he is not the right man please let us know and I will relieve you of him."[49] The partnership took on a reciprocal quality: the government would provide manpower for instruction, but it was incumbent upon universities to judge the quality and nature of the instructor's ability. Universities were testing grounds for naval expertise.

Such coordination did not necessarily assure that universities received government support. In keeping with the fledgling nature of these efforts, universities sometimes found themselves competing for resources with the government itself.[50] Though the partnership benefited universities, supplying faculty and expertise, it strained the navy. Ironically, this difficulty was in large part attributable to the lack of quality engineers coming from the U.S. Naval Academy.[51] In response, the head of the program, George Miller, had recommended to his superiors that "appointments be given to the graduates of the technical departments of such Universities as Ann Arbor."[52] Nothing came of Miller's proposal, and though many schools would continue to offer instruction by military personnel, the formal detailing of naval officers to institutions on demand was curtailed when the Naval Engineer Corps met the limit prescribed in legislation of 1882.[53]

As universities' experience with the Naval Engineer Corps reflected, not every partnership between universities and the state worked smoothly. Initially, the partnership between the universities and the navy provided manpower to universities and instructional opportunities for naval engineers. Eventually, however, the university and the navy found themselves disjointed. Uncertainties in staffing, difficulties in renewal, and competition for instructors limited program growth and frustrated academic entrepreneurs trying to develop engineering programs. Engineers were often assigned at midterm and withdrawn on short notice. Correspondingly, while the navy initially supported such details, the demands of its own fleet eventually became so great as to make the program a burden on the corps, and the formal program of details expired with the recall of all naval instructors in 1890.

Personal Partnership: James B. Angell and National Service

Providing basic manpower to a variety of agencies was a key, but not the only, component of universities' relations with the federal government. The service of high-profile university leaders was also a fundamental element of these partnerships. Among the most prominent and notable examples of individual service to the national state was the service of University of Michigan president James Burrill Angell. It might seem peculiar to think of one individual as forming a partnership with the national state, but Angell's three distinct tours of diplomatic service provide insight into university support for the federal state and into the developing community of peer institutions.

Appointed to Michigan's presidency in 1871 after serving for five years as president of the University of Vermont, Angell was already a relatively prominent public figure at the time of his first diplomatic appointment. In February 1880, President Rutherford Hayes's secretary of state, Daniel Evarts, asked Angell to head a diplomatic mission of three envoys to China. Angell was intrigued by the offer and set about informing the regents of his plans and his need to resign the presidency of the university. However, his friend and congressman J. H. McGowan suggested an alternative, a leave of absence. He told Angell, "I am satisfied that the people of Michigan would be proud indeed to have you called to such a work, and that the regents would surely upon reflection, if they did not at once, grant you such leave of absence as was necessary."[54]

McGowan's advice proved correct. The regents saw it "as quite a feather in the cap of the University to have its President chosen to fulfill so delicate a mission."[55] Angell's mission for the federal government was partially subsidized by the University of Michigan, a seemingly small price to pay. By granting Angell leave, the regents not only avoided having to replace their immensely popular and esteemed president; they also gained welcome publicity and praise for the university.

Informing Evarts that the regents would grant his leave with "generous spirit,"[56] Angell accepted the position. Angell's appointment was heralded by many as a welcome recognition of the skill and ability the academy could offer the state. Eli Blake, editor of the *Providence Journal*, summarized this view when he wrote about the appointment:

> It shows that when really serious matters are to be discussed it is still possible to go outside of the "machine"; and that real worth and ability has still a value even if not bolstered up by barroom politics.

It is a good omen for the future not only in politics but in education as tending to show that a wide liberal culture and study is not without its uses in the affairs of Government.[57]

In addition to gaining support from those outside academia who favored a move away from patronage and toward expertise, Angell's appointment was praised by many of his fellow academic leaders. Among the many to offer congratulations was Lerned Moss, president of Indiana University, who noted, "this worthy and admirable recognition of the 'scholar in politics' is gratifying to the scholars, whatever it may be to the politicians."[58] Provost Charles Stille of the University of Pennsylvania expanded on Moss's sentiment.

I am glad to find that among many good things which our worthy President does, he seems to have a proper appreciation of the value of College men in responsible public positions. You are a worthy representative of that club already distinguished by the work of such men as Sowell and White in the diplomatic service, and I am sure that we must all rejoice to know that these men are to have so worthy a colleague as yourself.[59]

Andrew Dickson White, writing from his position as diplomatic minister in Berlin echoed Stile's sentiment: "it is pleasing to see that college people are publicly recognized from time to time."[60] Angell responded to his friend with a self-awareness and recognition of what his appointment represented for higher education.

I agree with you that for the sake of "our guild" it is pleasant to have the recognition of it which this administration has made. I fear the President may find he has opened the gates for a new class of applicants for office. Mr. Evarts told me that since my appointment applications for appointments have been made on behalf of three college presidents.[61]

Angell concluded his letter by stating his plan was to return by the fall of 1881, with Henry Simmons Frieze carrying on matters while he was gone. In June, Angell, with the somewhat exalted title Minister Plenipotentiary and Envoy Extraordinary to China, left to serve the federal government. He was slightly mistaken in his prediction as to how long his mission would last and ended up in China through the winter of 1882, returning a little less than two years after he left.

While Frieze served as acting president, Angell, in many ways, guided the institution in absentia. Frieze would update Angell almost monthly on the status of the university's affairs. Typical of his dispatches was a letter at the beginning of the 1880–81 school year, in which he noted an increase in the size of the entering class and in the size of the various applicant pools, discussed the success of the law school's more stringent admissions requirements, and informed Angell of the local political news and gossip.[62] Angell stayed well informed of national politics through his friends in Ann Arbor as well but confessed that he found himself detached from such affairs. Writing to Henry Carter Adams, he noted:

> I suppose that you are in the full turmoil of the Presidential election today while I am sitting here in this scenic land. . . . I have so far caught the spirit of the people that I have hardly thought today of the election at all. But what can be expected of a man who has not heard a single campaign speech.[63]

Such sentiments might seem remarkable if one thinks of Angell as benefiting from patronage. However, he viewed his mission as an extension of his public service, outside the realm of electoral politics. The skill and knowledge required for the position did not change under the first three presidents Angell served (Rutherford Hayes, James Garfield, and Chester Arthur). His duty was to apply his diplomatic expertise for the benefit of the nation.

The relative success of Angell's tenure as minister to China—two treaties were signed, one involving immigration, the other involving trade—meant that he would be called on to negotiate on behalf of his country again. In 1887, he was appointed by President Cleveland to represent the United States in negotiations with the British over Canadian fishing rights. In 1896, Cleveland appointed him as chairman of the Deep Waterways Commission, which began discussions with the Canadians regarding an inland waterway that would become the Saint Lawrence Seaway. In 1897, Angell was appointed by Cleveland's successor, William McKinley, as minister to Turkey, for which position Angell was granted yet another leave of absence by the regents.

Angell's subsequent missions were not uniform successes. Nonetheless, on each assignment, he gave a good account of himself and the value of university men and their expertise. Discussing the appointment of Angell to head the Fisheries Commission, the *Manitoba Record* discussed his experience negotiating with China and praised him as "an able writer" who "has contributed to various views with exceeding success." The *Record* continued: "As a public speaker he is exceedingly attractive, fluent, easy and graceful. He is an amiable and affable man, popular with the students at Ann Arbor."[64]

Yet, as one of the first "university men" to serve in diplomatic circles, Angell was not immune from criticism. Reflecting a natural tension between proponents of experience and champions of expertise, Senator George Hoar of Massachusetts questioned Angell's appointment to the

Fisheries Commission during floor debate of its proposed treaty. Wondering if Angell "ever saw a mackrel until it came from the gridiron," he questioned if any of the commissioners "had had occasion to inform himself thoroughly in regard to the practical rights and interests of the vocation of the American fisherman."[65] Though Angell's fellow commissioner William Putnam, of Portland, Maine, assured Angell that the treaty was well received by fishermen in his region of the country,[66] Hoar's sentiment carried the day, and the treaty went down to defeat.

Not every opportunity for the application of expertise resulted in popular success. However, these opportunities were the leading edge in the development of partnerships between the university and the federal state. As Angell's son, James Rowland Angell, and Wilfred Shaw would recall in regard to the diplomatic service of Angell and others, such as Andrew Dickson White:[67]

> A new element in American public service was rising, a leaven destined to become increasingly important with the succeeding years. The peculiar fitness of university administrators and scholars for diplomatic service was becoming definitely recognized, and these appointments became the first of many similar calls upon university leaders, tributes to maturing American scholarship.
>
> The migration of scholars from the academic world into diplomacy not only foreshadowed a broader view of our relations abroad, based on experience in foreign ways and thought, but it also recognized the desirability in history, politics, and languages on the part of our diplomats. Moreover, it served to improve the standards of our foreign service at a time when too many of our representatives abroad were selected solely on the basis of political expediency and private income.[68]

James Rowland Angell himself would be intimately involved in the further maturation of relations between universities and the national state in the first decades of the twentieth century, serving as dean of the University of Chicago, founding chairman of the National Research Council, and president of Yale (succeeding Arthur Twining Hadley in 1920). As Rowland Angell underscored, the diplomatic service of such men as his father and Andrew Dickson White was not as significant for their work as individuals as it was for their work on behalf of universities as a class.

At this time, there was developing among universities a rising interest in service to the state as well as a growing awareness of the university as a distinct class of institution offering particularized skills, knowledge, and expertise. Reflecting such sentiment, James Burrill Angell wrote to White, regarding his own appointment to the Fisheries Commission:

I share your feeling of satisfaction that of late our government has shown some disposition to follow the old and well-established usage of European governments in looking to universities for some of the diplomatic representatives. Perhaps you and I may be supposed by the public not to be unbiased in this opinion, but we can speak to each other safely.[69]

As they were prominent and well-connected individuals, the appointments of White and Angell to diplomatic missions do not necessarily seem remarkable. However, the basis of their appointments—particularized knowledge and skills, rather than patronage (they served both Republican and Democratic presidents)—reflects a significant evolution in the partnerships between universities and the national state.

Developing a System of National Service: Partnerships in the "Loosely Coupled" Era

Early partnerships between universities and the national state encompassed a variety of activities. For purposes from weather forecasting to shipbuilding, the university sought to both provide and receive assistance from the federal government. Despite limited immediate success, the resulting partnerships helped foster growing coordination between institutions and helped lay the groundwork for universities to expand and explore the multitude of opportunities presented by the development of the national state. The creation of new government agencies meant opportunities to develop new academic programs and further relations with both established and developing agencies.

Frequently driven by individual efforts as well as institutional support, universities began to work in conjunction with the federal government. Universities still provided expert manpower for government agencies. The federal government occasionally provided expert instructors for university faculty. The support might have been reciprocal; the initiative was not. In both instances, it was university leaders, regularly coordinating efforts among their institutions, who drove the government to extend the reach of expertise. As an evolving effort, such partnerships were not always smoothly developed and formalized. Continuing from the implementation of the first Morrill Act through the turn of the century, university partnerships with the national state reflected what might best be described as growing pains. Notwithstanding occasional hurdles, institutional entrepreneurship and coordination laid the groundwork for a new service of expertise that would help define the development of the emerging national state.

5   Beyond Service

The Development of Universities as Independent Agents

In addition to working directly with government as a partner, universities began to work as its agent, helping establish national standards and define policy in a variety of arenas. The position of universities as agents stemmed in many ways from the loosely coupled regulation of education; from local elementary schools to advanced graduate and professional programs, universities helped define and nationalize the American educational system. This influence had implications far beyond educational policy itself, touching on most every domain into which the formative state would venture.

Universities' service as independent agent of the national state evolved from a variety of interconnected forces. Supported by institutional coordination and entrepreneurship, America's schools worked closely with one another and developed an informal national system of standardization. Though such efforts were not often undertaken in direct concert with federal, state, or local governments, they were often undertaken with these governments' informal support and occasional input. University leaders would share their plans and expectations with government officials, who would reciprocate with advice and interest as well as their implicit sanction. The federal Bureau of Education did not develop or enforce standards for secondary schools. However, its representatives worked with universities as they developed and enforced such standards.

Establishing Agency: Universities and Standards for Secondary Education

With the rise of compulsory elementary and secondary education, the expansion of opportunities in higher education, and the growth of graduate and professional education came a desire for uniform standards and expectations. The federal government's Bureau of Education was not equipped to or capable of pursuing such standardization. Similar to university presidents who shaped their institutions through lengthy tenures, William T. Harris shaped the bureau by serving as the commissioner of education in its formative years, from 1889 to 1906. Harris had achieved some renown as a public advocate of school reform during his tenure as superintendent of St. Louis public schools. Stressing the need for "directive intelligence" in an ever-specialized society, Harris championed the development of high schools as a means of ensuring that citizens had the basic skills and tools needed to nurture the expertise required to govern and lead.[1] Harris would continue to advocate reforms while commissioner, but he was limited by a federal agency that lacked resources and authority over local school districts. Harris's influence on national education policy was dependent on his personal connections and service in various national associations.[2] Instead of being driven by a federal agency, the development of a national system of public education relied on universities not only training teachers but also defining curriculum and establishing standards through accreditation and entrance requirements.

Like higher education, American secondary education could trace its origins to before the Revolutionary War. The Collegiate School of New York and the Roxbury Latin School of Massachusetts offered secondary education and preparatory assistance in the colonial era. During the nation's early years, college admissions were very particularized and localized. At those few schools where standards were firmly established and upheld, entrance exams were offered usually once a year. These exams were given on campus and administered by faculty. As a result, preparatory schools and private tutors were primarily located around collegiate campuses offering instruction and training for prospective students. Colleges would influence the nature of education and instruction through the detailed publication of exam topics and content and by the fact that many of the tutors were alumni. Overall, however, higher education institutions did little to directly shape the preparation of students for college work in the antebellum years. This began to change with the establishment of a system of admission by diploma at the University of Michigan in 1870.

Developing Agency: Admission by Diploma and the Roots of Regulation

Begun by James Burrill Angell's predecessor, interim president Henry Simmons Frieze,[3] admission by diploma was a system whereby graduates of accredited high schools who had completed the "college preparatory" course of study (high schools generally offered preparatory and nonpreparatory tracks) were admitted to the university without having to take entrance examinations. The university itself accredited high schools. Faculty from the university would spend two to three days visiting a particular school and assess the quality of its teachers, facilities, and curriculum. Initially, only high schools in the state of Michigan were allowed this privilege. Soon after taking the presidency in 1872, Angell expanded the program to include any and all high schools willing to participate, provided they paid for the faculty's travel and visit.

The program was a great success, beginning with five high schools in Detroit, Ann Arbor, Flint, Jackson, and Kalamazoo. A year later, four more high schools, in Pontiac, Coldwater, Grand Rapids, and Ypsilanti, were accredited. Growing consistently over the years, the program would encompass forty-five schools in 1886–87, fifty-eight in 1887–88, and seventy-one in the program's nineteenth year, 1888–89. Of these seventy-one, only forty-six were in Michigan itself, nineteen schools were in Illinois, three were in Minnesota, and there was one each in Ohio, Pennsylvania, and Indiana. By 1889–90, the program had developed to such an extent that a majority of students admitted to the university were accepted by diploma rather than by examination (164 to 131).[4]

While the university's accreditation program was successful, its policy of having out-of-state schools pay for faculty members' visits led to some complaints. In February 1891, the Chicago Board of Education responded to the university's announcement regarding accreditation by noting that "the Board of Education has no appropriation of money applicable to such expense." The board suggested that "in place of the proposed examination of our High Schools, the University of Michigan follow the custom of several of the Eastern universities and send a Committee to Chicago at a convenient time in the summer to examine applicants for admission to the same."[5]

Michigan traditionally had offered examinations during the summer in Chicago and other cities, such as Dubuque, Iowa, and Milwaukee, Wisconsin. The exams were not given at any particular school but, rather, were advertised in the local newspapers and administered at a local hotel. As admission by diploma expanded, these off-site examinations were discontinued in all cities but Chicago by 1891. As Angell wrote to Shatock Hartwell, principal of Kalamazoo High School, the exams in Chicago were an exception prompted by the need to maintain a presence in the city similar to that of the university's eastern peers:

"some years ago we did offer examinations at two or three cities remote from here, but we are holding such examination only at Chicago and would prefer to drop that if we could but as eastern colleges continue to hold examinations there we are compelled to do so at present."[6] Regardless of the existing examinations, Chicago's school board pressed the issue of faculty visitations, as they offered an opportunity for assessment and, if successful, an increase in stature.

In September of that year, Angell reported to the Board of Regents on the program's success, noting that its benefits had led the university "to assume the expense of sending committees of the Faculty to visit the schools in Michigan." For Angell, admission by diploma benefited the state as it attracted the highest caliber of students and reflected "the desire of the University to cultivate relations of the most cordial intimacy with [the high schools]."[7] Reflecting back on his twenty years as president of Michigan, Angell would conclude his discussion of the program by noting that the number of schools from which students were received "on diploma" had grown from an initial five to a remarkable eighty-two. Commenting on this growth, Angell suggested:

> If we consider either the effect on the schools or on the University it would probably be just to say that no act of the university has in the last twenty years been more serviceable than the careful development of the policy, by which it has brought itself into so close and fruitful relations with the preparatory schools in this State and some neighboring States.[8]

Michigan's service extended beyond facilitating admission and expanding opportunities for higher learning, to include improving secondary education for the state as well as its neighbors.

In addition to the simple numbers of students admitted and schools accredited, the regulatory influence of universities reached to the everyday operations of secondary education. Most notably, university accreditation led to changes and improvements in the curriculum. Typical of such a process was an exchange between Michigan alumnus and school examiner Dalbert Haff, Angell, and Kansas City High School principal James Buchanan. After inspecting the high school, Haff was effusive in his praise but believed instruction in English and science might be brought into greater concert with Michigan's requirements. He did not believe change would be difficult and wrote Angell, "I wish you would write a personal letter to Prof. Buchanan (Principal) making such suggestions as to the change of courses you would recommend." Angell did, and Buchanan soon responded that a visit would be "most welcome."[9]

The general sentiment of secondary school administrators was best synopsized by superintendent of Chicago public schools A. F. Nightingale: "we are gratified to learn that our high schools have been placed upon your accredited list, and we shall be glad at any and all times to receive suggestions concerning the betterment of our course of instruction and of the quality of our teaching."[10] The extent of Michigan's influence as accrediting agent is hard to overstate. Writing to Angell a few years later, Nightingale would highlight such influence when he wrote for the names of faculty the University of Michigan assessors had deemed inadequate.

> I have heard that one or two teachers were quite condemned by your visitors, and as I am obliged to report by May 1 my recommendations concerning the re-election of our teachers, this report will help me very much in the matter.
>
> I am sure that we do not wish to retain teachers that the U. of Michigan does not approve of, and, therefore would like to know the opinions of your experts.[11]

The ability of the university to act as an agent of the state rested on its position at the head of the educational system and in secondary schools' acceptance of its authority and belief in its expertise regarding the educational process.

Michigan was the first, but not the only, institution to adopt such a system. The University of California soon followed suit, adopting a similar system in March 1884. Representing the unique coordination between these two western institutions, Berkeley essentially adopted Michigan's exact system. A committee of the university's faculty would visit public high schools at the request of the principal, and if their report was favorable, the school's students could be admitted without examination. Previously, examinations had been given to applicants at Berkeley, in San Francisco, and in the outlying areas of Los Angeles and Marysville.

In a section of his 1884 annual report to the governor, entitled "Want of Preparatory Schools," University of California president William T. Reid stressed the importance of good high schools and bemoaned the condition of such education in California.

> The most serious drawback to the University is the want of suitable preparatory schools throughout the State, in fact, the entire absence of them in many portions of it, and to this cause may, doubtless, be attributed the slight representation of many counties in the University. The standard of admission to the University has, within a few years advanced; while, under the discouragements of the new Constitution, the establishment of high schools has been retarded.

> It must always be difficult to bring a people to prize the higher education, if they are not accustomed to the encouragement and support of the intermediate.[12]

For Reid, the visitation and accreditation of high schools by the university's faculty was a great method for developing such support. Two schools, Berkeley and San Francisco, were initially accredited, and twenty-seven of their graduates were admitted in 1884, constituting 31 percent of all admitted.[13] Four years later, in 1888, the program had grown to include four additional schools (Alameda, Oakland, Sacramento, and Stockton) and forty-three students, 33 percent of all those admitted. The program, mirroring the rapid explosion of the state itself, grew to such an extent that for the class entering in the fall of 1899, 434 students, 83 percent of all those admitted, were accepted "on diploma."

Michigan and California recognized the value of accreditation not only in developing their universities and raising their stature nationally but also for improving educational standards throughout the state and the West. While the two institutions did not jointly accredit high schools, Reid sought to emulate Michigan's program. Such imitation would evolve into a systematic and loosely coordinated effort to regulate secondary schools in the West.

For Reid, Berkeley's program of admission by diploma was "an important step toward establishing relations between our higher grade public schools and the University, and a heartier cooperation between them." He was confident this program would accomplish such a step in light of Michigan's success: "there can be no doubt, I presume, that the excellence of the public school system in Michigan has been greatly promoted, if indeed, it is not greatly due, to this cooperation between the University and the secondary schools."[14] Explaining the program to the regents and the governor, Reid stressed that the university was closely intertwined with the quality of education.

> The University must always react upon the secondary schools, to their great benefit. Parents can have no warrant that the public school of the community in which they live offers as good educational opportunities as are offered in other communities, unless the scholarship is measured by the same standard applied to other like schools throughout the commonwealth.[15]

Regulation of secondary schools was thus an explicit function of universities and the system of "admission by diploma." Reid granted that such regulation and assessment might not be popular with local school districts, but he believed that it was necessary not only for the benefit of the university but also for the benefit of secondary schools throughout the state. In assessing high schools, the university sought to improve education not only for the best students in the state but for all students in the public schools.

During the assessment process, schools were judged on the preparedness of their students for admission to higher education, as well as on their overall curriculum, facilities, and faculty. Reid cited Michigan as an example of the advantages of such an approach: "the result of giving to the University of Michigan the power to set the standard of education in the secondary schools throughout the State is, perhaps, the most evenly balanced system of public schools in the United States." As well as simply improving the general quality of the system, university-based accreditation also directly influenced the faculty and administrators of secondary schools.

> A further result of this coordination in the school system is an active spirit of cooperation between the teachers in the secondary schools and those in the University. While the Faculty of the college, indicates what, in the temper of the community and in the quality and capabilities of the teachers is possible. The tendency of the University is constantly upward, and this upward tendency reacts powerfully upon the schools in the desire of the teachers to meet every new requirement made by the University; and this healthy stimulus is felt, not only by the teacher, but by the community. It becomes the ambition, not only of the teacher to see his school made a diploma school, but of the community as well.

This community ambition became so influential, according to Reid's sources, that "the principal of a high school in Michigan cannot feel at all secure in his position if he fails within a reasonable time to get his school on the list of diploma schools."[16]

Reid hoped such ambition would result from Berkeley's adoption of the system, and preliminary indications were that it might. Reid ended his report on the system by noting, "the effect of the regulation has thus far unquestionably been favorable to higher aims and higher scholarship in the preparatory schools, and it therefore promises to be highly beneficial to the University."[17] Reid's words proved prescient: diploma admissions would quickly grow to be the standard means by which students entered the university not only at Berkeley but also at other institutions in the West, such as the universities of Indiana, Iowa, Minnesota, Missouri, Ohio, and Wisconsin.

At this time, there existed no formal coordination among the western universities in regard to accreditation. There was, however, a loose affiliation based in the university presidents' relationship with Angell and in Angell's awareness of the unique position Michigan held as the model for other universities in the West. Discussing a related debate over whether improvement of secondary education and the growth of graduate and professional education might lead the university to shorten the course for a bachelor's degree, Angell stressed that Michigan could not undertake such a decision without appreciating the full influence of its decision.

> We cannot neglect to consider what would be the effect of such action on education in the west. Without assuming too much for ourselves, we can hardly doubt that if we made the proposed change, our example would compel the smaller colleges in this region and probably tend to bring all the State universities in the west to make the change also.[18]

Angell and Michigan chose not to adopt the proposed "short course," so we are left unable to judge the exact extent of their influence on this matter. We can, however, see in Angell's comments a growing awareness of Michigan's role as a linchpin in an emerging system that was national in its orientation.

In terms of high school accreditation, it is clear that Michigan was the model. Writing to Angell about his school's efforts to undertake admission by diploma, S. S. Lows, president of the University of Missouri, wrote: "you are in advance of us in the arrangements for preparation work in cooperative schools, and for the curriculum prescribed and optional work. Our growth within the last 10 years has been such as to encourage us to feel our way to a more advanced stage of organization."[19] Angell and Michigan did not simply develop a model program that others would imitate. Michigan's standards were often other western school's standards or, if not their immediate standards, their aspiration. Hence, a simple program for accepting students in Michigan evolved into a system of regulation for secondary schools throughout the West.

The informal coordination at the heart of this system extended to secondary school administrators, such as William Reid, who instituted the "diploma system" as president of the University of California and then left to become headmaster at Belmont Academy. Not having the resources to bring faculty out for a visit, Reid asked to have his school join Michigan's accreditation list on the basis of its accreditation by the University of California.[20] Reid's story reflects the depth of coordination but also alludes to the limits of entrepreneurship in creating a national (or at least western) system for secondary education. While Reid successfully brought admission by diploma to Berkeley and later gained "diploma" status for his preparatory school, such efforts were driven primarily by an individual belief that they would improve the quality of education.

No incentives or sanctions existed to encourage or maintain membership in this system of admission by diploma. So some states and some schools lacking initiative or sufficient resources failed to participate. Owing to informal adoption, such standards were not implemented in the most uniform or methodical way. Nevertheless, the broader popularity of admission by diploma did further a move toward national standards. The quasi-government apparatuses of the new American state were like the federal government itself—developing, but not fully formed.

The Limits of Agency: Admissions Standards and the Committee of Ten

Unlike schools in the West, eastern and southern universities still relied primarily on examinations to determine admission. Drawing primarily from private high schools, academies, and tutors, these schools did not directly regulate individual schools. Beginning in this era, however, they did seek to reasonably coordinate their admissions requirements so as to develop standards and expectations. The initial step in this process was the introduction, in the post–Civil War era, of admission by certificate, whereby universities and colleges would accept students on the basis of having passed another institution's exam rather than requiring them to take their own. This process was still marked by vagueness, so various efforts at more formal coordination were attempted. The most ambitious of these undertakings was spearheaded by Harvard University president Charles Eliot in 1891. Under the organizational umbrella of the National Education Association, which at the time incorporated both secondary and higher education institutions, Eliot directed establishment of the Committee on Secondary School Studies, also known as the Committee of Ten because of the number of its members.

Among the ten that Eliot tapped, the first he asked was Michigan's Angell. Angell had been highly involved in drafting a preliminary report to the National Council of Education, a branch of the National Education Association (NEA), "on the general subject of uniformity in school programmes and in requirements for admission to college." The committee sought to develop detailed standards for admissions to colleges and universities and a general guideline for high school curricula. To accomplish this, the committee arranged conferences of the leading instructors in the principal subjects tested for admission, including mathematics, history, classics, and the like. Writing to thank Angell for agreeing to continue on with his service, Eliot stressed: "the selection of these specialists will be the most difficult work of our committee. The members of the conferences ought to be not only good teachers, but also reasonable men who can enter into a wise and influential agreement." Eliot also expressed hope that the conferences might "represent fairly the different parts of the country."[21] Despite his intentions, the initial Committee of Ten did not include any members representing states west of Colorado or south of Missouri.[22]

The committee and its conferences were well supported by the NEA, who appropriated twenty-five hundred dollars and secured discount rail passage for its work. Eliot, as was his habit, ran over budget, but he managed to secure funds to offset the additional costs. Financial concerns were the least of Eliot's worries. Eliot initially encountered some delay obtaining component reports, but he wrote Angell to reiterate that he felt "sure our Committee will be able to contribute to the improvement of American Secondary schools."[23]

Unfortunately for Eliot, a simmering conflict undermined the ability of the committee to present uniform standards to the association and its schools and universities. In addition to the usual petty squabbles that mark any committee process, a significant series of objections were raised by James Baker, president of the University of the Colorado. The rift was so significant that Baker shared his initial concerns with the whole of the sponsoring council rather than simply with the Committee of Ten itself. In his letter, Baker emphasized that he was in complete support of the committee's aims but that he wished to raise objections to aspects of the committee's work.

The report of the committee had stressed flexibility in the application of its recommendations. Baker took issue with such an approach, arguing that the committee's recommendations were "based upon the theory that, for the purposes of general education, one study is as good as another,—a theory which appears to me to ignore Philosophy, Psychology, and Science of Education."[24] For Baker, breadth of study was admirable, but prescription was necessary. Baker felt that a broad but detailed and prescribed curriculum could be developed from the various subject committee reports.[25] Baker's dissent underscored the difficulty of informal coordination. Ironically, by attempting to offer flexibility and achieve the greatest consensus possible among the general membership, the Committee of Ten had undermined its own consensus.

Angell and Eliot wrote to Baker asking him to withdraw his statements offering only qualified support, but to no avail. Eliot and Angell agreed that the committee's recommendations were "but tentative" and would "doubtless be modified by different schools to meet their various circumstances." Unfortunately, Baker was not of the same mind. His objection exasperated Eliot, who wrote to his friend Angell:

> I saw in my first interaction with him, nearly two years ago, he believed it possible to invent a uniform high school program for the entire country. The idea that he still clings to—indeed, he thinks he can write that programme himself, and that it would closely resemble his programme in the Denver High School. That is the real reason why he advocates a continuation of the work of our Committee, or of some committee. I need not say that I agree with you in thinking that the National Council had better not continue our Committee. Public discussion of our work is the next thing in order, and I should think two or three years a short time to allow for that discussion.[26]

Eliot did convince the NEA's executive board to approve the committee's report and forward it to the full membership. Additionally, the report received the sanction of the national state, thanks to the support of committee member and commissioner of education William T. Harris. The federal government subsidized and distributed thirty thousand copies of the committee's report throughout the country, under the auspices of its Bureau of Education.

While the Committee of Ten's broad and flexible recommendations were generally well received, specific pockets of acrimony would continue to obstruct effective coordination between academic leaders and, correspondingly, nationwide implementation of the report's recommendations. Following the Committee of Ten report, the first major meeting of secondary school leaders and other academics was the annual conference of the association's department of superintendence. Returning from this meeting of leading academics, Columbia's president Nicholas Murray Butler wrote to Eliot that the committee's report had generated enthusiasm. Describing its work as "a prominent feature in the intellectual landscape," he added, "I am sure you will be glad to hear that it was received with almost unqualified admiration and with substantial approval be the large body of serious minded public school men."[27]

Significantly, however, support for the committee's work was not universal. Butler continued:

> one or two others, notably Supt. Greenwood of Kansas City, showed a disposition to find fault with matters of minute detail; and one or two others, notably Mr. Nightingale of Chicago, apparently unacquainted with the

courtesies of life, endeavored to substitute a malicious attack of the committee for the criticism of their report.

Though annoyed by Nightingale's manner, Butler was generally unconcerned about Greenwood and his objections. Saying their complaints were "strongly reprehended by the leading men present," Butler believed that "on the whole you would have been very well satisfied at seeing and hearing the impression that the report has made."[28] Eliot said that he had never had any dealings with Nightingale and thus assumed that his issues with the committee were "impersonal." Overall, Eliot was "content" with the reception the report had received, believed it was "having a very thorough and useful discussion in this part of the country."[29]

Effective coordination in the "loosely coupled" era was contingent on close working and personal relationships between leading academics. When tensions arose, it often undermined not just short-term efforts at coordination but the long-term attempts to develop and implement policy as an independent agent. As with admission by diploma, though reputational concerns and peer influence could encourage systemization, no formal organization or agency of consequence yet existed to maintain uniformity and stability when the relations between institutions became strained.

Toward a National System of Regulation: Coordinating Diplomas and Certificates

Though not immediately succeeding in their efforts to establish general standards for high school curriculum, the Committee of Ten did succeed in laying the groundwork for the development for minimum standards for college admission at the nation's elite universities. These curricular standards would be in many aspects formalized by the related College Entrance Examination Board and the Association of American Universities a little over ten years later. The report was widely distributed and widely read. It was not necessarily widely implemented. Limited by faculty and curricular resources, some schools could not meet all the standards. Systematic distinctions still existed. Western schools generally admitted students "on diploma," while schools of the South and Northeast continued to require examinations. In developing shared expectations for accreditation, the western schools coordinated with one another through correspondence and through James Burrill Angell's informal oversight as the dean of western university presidents. Eastern and southern schools began to develop informal coordination through an emerging system of admission by certificate and gradually undertook efforts to move toward more formal relations between schools.[30]

The certificate and diploma systems shared similarities. Some schools, most notably the University of Michigan, functioned in both. As Michigan's president, Angell would help draft the Committee of Ten report that was criticized by western school principals, such as Greenwood and Nightingale, as elitist and unreasonable in its expectations. Nonetheless, he would also be praised by Nightingale, who wrote:

> Your influence in advancing the cause of higher education—East as well as West—will never be fully weighed. Your advocacy of a broader spirit in courses of study, of individual rather than class development, and of placing greater confidence in the honest work of secondary schools, has been of untold benefit to all of the country.[31]

Angell's relationship with Nightingale underscores both the limits and the successes of efforts to establish standardized admissions requirements. On the one hand, many school principals sought freedom to develop particularized programs of instruction and recognized that not all of their students would necessarily be attending college. On the other hand, such principals were interested in furthering the cause of education and saw the emerging universities as a natural and forceful ally.

Universities did not necessarily wish to prescribe a curriculum for all levels of education but did feel a responsibility to increase the number of students interested in higher education as well as to improve the quality of students it did admit. To do this, universities developed both admission by diploma and admission by examination. While individual universities would develop their own standards through informal communications and more formal committees and organizations, these informal standards would develop into standardized quasi-regulatory systems. As Angell noted in writing his son, James Rowland Angell, upon the former's return from presiding at a session of college and secondary school leaders at the University of Chicago, "there is a laudable effort all over the country for the colleges and school men to work on educational problems."[32]

These systems developed to the point where universities would oversee many high schools' curricula. Yet there were limits to its reach. First, high school participation was essentially voluntary. High schools were not required—by anything other than public sentiment or the demands

of benefactors and prospective students—to meet university requirements. Even the state of Michigan, whose university was at the forefront
of the accreditation movement, did not require high schools to have
accreditation visits or to offer curriculum in keeping with the university's entrance requirements. Second, before the turn of the century, no
truly national system of regulating high schools arose. Instead, two distinct but occasionally overlapping methods of oversight drove American education, admission by diploma and admission by examination.

Nonetheless, it would be fair to say that a loosely coupled national
system regulating secondary schools began to develop in this era. Not
every high school participated, and those that did were not all judged
on the same criteria. However, from the beginning of the system of
admission by diploma in 1870 to the end of the century, a dramatic shift
had taken place. The institution of the American high school had gone
from being solely local to being influenced by national standards—
standards developed not by the federal government but by universities
acting as independent agents on behalf of the national state. Such initiatives were often local or, at most, regional in their origin; yet they
were greatly influenced by national forces. Coordination among the
heads of leading universities and their shared "nationalist" agenda
devoted to the pursuit and application of expertise, as well as the fluid
interaction between these academics and representatives of the federal
government, underwrote agency. Though not enforced by the federal
government, national standards for secondary schools supported the
development of a national state.

Taken on its own, universities' regulation of schools might seem
detached from their efforts to build a new American state. However,
when we consider universities' active partnership with the federal government and their overall efforts to develop and enforce standards
across a variety of domains, we find that in regulating secondary
schools, universities worked on behalf of the emerging national state.
The limited reach of the Bureau of Education and the local nature of
school governance meant that America did not have a government-run
system of education, but thanks to the work of the nation's leading universities, it was developing a national system based on shared standards and expectations.

Extending Agency: Defining Higher Education

In attempting to define and standardize admissions standards, the
nation's elite universities not only influenced the development of sec-

ondary education but also shaped the evolution of their peers. The formal organizational umbrella of the AAU would not be established until the first years of the twentieth century. Nonetheless, loosely coupled coordination between institutions had enabled colleges and universities to outline national standards for higher education and to define expectations of agency and service to the developing national state.

Unlike today, no formal accrediting body with governmental sanction held sway over the nation's early institutions of higher learning. In the late nineteenth and early twentieth centuries, almost any institution could call itself a college or university, and many did. However, closely linked leadership and competitive pressures did enable the leading universities to regulate one another, laying the groundwork for later formal standardization through the development of the AAU. Coordination would lead to an eventual standardization of credentials and degrees, especially in the professions. For the story of American political development, it is essential to appreciate that the movement to ensure certain competencies, skills, and expertise among teachers, lawyers, doctors, and others was not initiated and institutionalized by the state; rather, it was initiated and institutionalized by this emerging system of national universities.

Defining Expansion: From College to University

The decades following the end of the Civil War witnessed exceptional expansion and advancement in the fields of knowledge and courses of study housed in America's leading universities. Attempting to give shape to their new functions and missions, established eastern colleges—such as Columbia (1883), Yale (1887), Harvard (1890), and Princeton (1896)—retitled themselves as universities.[33] These actions represented more than simply the renaming of an institution. They symbolized the desire of schools to move beyond their traditional role with a commitment to pursue research, extend knowledge, and define expertise. They also reflected a collective effort to give general definition to such a desire. In simplest terms, by taking the title *university*, the more established institutions of higher learning (e.g., Columbia, Yale, Harvard, and Princeton) could help legitimately direct the course of the emerging higher education institutions that took the title *university* from their founding (e.g., Michigan, California, Virginia, Cornell, and Johns Hopkins).

By taking the name *university*, these schools pronounced their belief in the promise of expertise and the potential that it held for the American state. Justifying Yale's name change, which had faced some opposition from the more conservative elements of its faculty and governing corporation, Timothy Dwight stressed the need for Yale to include the graduate and professional schools and their pursuit of expert knowledge as "essential parts of the university, without which its life cannot, by any means, be complete."[34] The development of Yale University, he argued in his inaugural address, "bears in it the promise of the coming era."[35]

Yale was not alone in changing its name to incorporate and reflect a belief in the "promise of the coming era." This promise meant both new curricular initiatives and new notions of service—and, to some extent, new identities. Publicizing the changing of Columbia's name and pronouncing the potential of expertise that accompanied it, the *New York Times* editorialized:

> The President and Trustees of Columbia College have announced their purpose to build up in this City "a university of the highest order. . . . They have set forth the country's and the city's need of such a university and . . . hope it shall draw students from every part of this country, and from other countries, and shall furnish here upon our own soil that post-collegiate education which American students must now seek abroad. This latter fact is reason enough for establishing such a university.

The *Times* not only saw potential in the institution's ability to keep students from having to go abroad for advanced study; it saw promise in the defined expertise an advanced university would pursue.

> But to the city and the Nation a well-endowed university would also supply a new and more fully equipped class of workers in the sciences and mechanic arts. Aside from the honor which men of creative minds and great attainments conferred upon the countries of their birth and training there are considerations of the highest practical utility connected with opening up of a university for professional and scientific training.

After listing a variety of potential areas for the university's attention (e.g., engineering, electricity, botany, geology, geography, biology, physiology, astronomy, archaeology, and disease, pollution, and sewage), the *Times* stressed the universality of subjects that these newly titled institutions could pursue: "there are ample fields which American scholars are more and more eager to cultivate. They should be fitted for work here."[36]

Obviously, name changes and pursuit of an increasing variety of subjects were not the only criteria by which universities came to define themselves. In this period, universities began to more actively pursue collective definition as well. At the core of these efforts for collective definition were attempts by universities to pursue similar policies, structures, and courses of study for bachelor's, graduate, and professional degrees. No government agency or outside accrediting body drove such collectivity, nor was it undertaken by the associations of universities that were being developed prior to the AAU. Among the first of these, the Association of American Agricultural Colleges and Experiment Stations (AAACES) was founded in 1887, and the National Association of State Universities (NASU) was founded in 1890; neither counted among its members the leading public universities—California, Michigan, and Wisconsin. Rather, the close working relationships between academic leaders and the uncertainty their new institutions faced led universities to turn to one another for direction and guidance. Such institutional isomorphism meant not only the creation of similar policies, structures, and courses but also the development of a loosely coordinated and increasingly prominent national system of higher education.

The nation's elite universities were self-defined institutions, regulating themselves. In this "loosely coupled" era, no formal organization existed to define their ranks; but the leading universities shared a collective search for definition. This search for definition impacted higher education itself and would also come to define and regulate such professions as education, medicine, and law. Universities, serving as agents of the national state, proscribed the skills and knowledge that would be seen as necessary for members of these professions and institutionalized formal programs of study and credentials that would encapsulate such expertise. By sharing their best and most useful approaches with one another, the institutional entrepreneurs who ran universities began to develop standards and establish expectations.

The development of state administrative capacities relied heavily on an intellectual cadre, developing professions, and standards of expertise. However, unlike in nations with strong ministries of education or strong national universities, the development of such capacities in the American state relied on the support of a self-regulating group of universities. In defining themselves, leading universities were also defining the nature and reach of the expertise that supplemented bureaucratic development. University leaders were not in conflict with federal officials; they were simply better positioned. By taking responsibility for the development of advanced knowledge (a task that could have fallen to the national state itself), universities acted as independent agents of the national state—serving and defining its goals, but essentially free from its authority.

Before the Civil War, colleges were largely autonomous, taking little counsel from one another. After the war, when faced with challenges presented by increasing societal complexity and popular demands, developing universities looked to one another, with select institutions leading the way. Not every university was newly founded, but every university was an institution in search of a new definition. Gradually, mutual oversight and regulation would lead to standard expectations for and approaches to higher learning. The leading universities looked to one another—and were also looked to by their less-established peers—for insight into their administration, internal affairs, external relations, and credentials.

Loosely coupled through personal and professional relationships, the elite universities essentially functioned as a national regulatory agency, not only broadly shaping the lower tiers and their relationship with institutions of higher learning, but shaping their peers in higher education as well. Such regulatory activity had a dual effect on the university's role as independent agent. First, it meant universities would be self-regulating. Through loosely coupled coordination, universities themselves, not the federal Bureau of Education, would begin to define standard shape and structure for the new institutions emerging from federal, state, and private support. Second, by regulating themselves, universities sought to standardize not only their internal operations but their role as agents of the state, through oversight of degrees and credentials. This reliance between peers evolved into a system whereby more established universities and more senior presidents took the lead in guiding new institutions and newer leaders.

Throughout the later years of the nineteenth century, the meaning of the title *university* continued to be of interest to educators. Appealing to the Maryland state legislature for funds in 1898, John Hopkins University president Daniel Coit Gilman echoed his sentiments from California many years earlier.

> The question is often asked in these days, when so many institutions great and small, good and bad claim the title of a University—what is a real true University? One of the best answers is this, that it is an assembly of superior teachers and advanced scholars who are engaged in the acquisition and advancement of knowledge. It is a place where the best agencies that the world has are employed in the instruction of youth, and where the lamp of science is carried onwards into regions hitherto obscure. The training of youth and the promotion of knowledge are its essential functions.[37]

The institutional entrepreneurs who guided leading institutions were very concerned with protecting and defining their good name.

Defining Peers: Administration, Staffing, and Competition

For university-based expertise to possess political authority and societal value, universities needed to ensure that institutions bearing the name *university* shared similar definition. Therefore, the leading universities looked to and guided one another in regard to a multitude of issues. The institutional entrepreneurs who shaped the modern university tapped the shared wisdom of their peers, frequently addressing concerns that included but were not limited to the overall administrative and academic structure of the university, relations with faculty, sources of funding, and the discipline of students.

To the older, established institutions of the East, competitive pressures would lead to institutional similarities. Such institutions as Yale and Harvard would occasionally survey one another as to how best to approach curricular and structural initiatives, but they also looked at one another with occasional jealously. The nature of such competition was clearly evident to many, as is attested by a later anonymous gift of ten thousand dollars from a Harvard alumnus to Yale to "promote good relations between the universities."[38]

Despite their competitive nature, eastern universities still communicated regularly and took interest in their peers' success. Writing to Gilman in 1890, Charles Eliot remarked about his peers Cornell and Columbia: "President Adams of Cornell is having a horrid time, and it looks as if he won't stay long.[39] Low begins extremely well at Columbia, and it is a thoroughly cheerful subject to contemplate."[40] Such interinstitutional concern would become formalized with the establishment of the AAU, but its roots lie in the developing awareness of peer institutions.

As the leading public institutions in their region, Virginia and Michigan served as model institutions for other developing schools of higher learning. Since its founding by Jefferson in 1819, the University of Virginia had been a benchmark institution for schools of the South. In writing "The Influence of the University of Virginia upon Southern Life and Thought" in 1888, William Trent would note (in apologizing for his own usage), "the University of Virginia is known throughout the South as 'the University' and this is my excuse for using an expression otherwise indefensible."[41] Defensible or not, Virginia's influence grew as southern institutions of higher learning pursued courses of study more in keeping with the title *university*. Virginia brought many aspects of the university system to the South—most notably, the elective system. As Charles Smith noted in the October 1884 edition of the *Atlantic*

Monthly, "at least thirty-five southern colleges and universities have adopted this system, following the example of the University of Virginia."[42] For a number of southern schools, however, limited resources and facilities meant that other aspects of the university, such as graduate education and research, were not necessarily prominent. Virginia had granted the region's first PhD, in 1885, but still lacked a system of fellowships and a culture of original research. Even though it was somewhat behind its northern and western peers in pursuing a graduate curriculum and adopting a research model, Virginia's role as the leading institution in the South was secure and would continue into the twentieth century. The school was the first southern institution to join the Association of American Universities, in 1904.

Another prominent public university, the University of Michigan, found its influence covering a great expanse, primarily rooted in its relations with the state universities of the West. Reflecting Michigan's role as a model, James Bryce, upon receiving an honorary degree, noted that he took special pride in such an honor: "knowing what an eminent place the University of Michigan holds and how much it has done and continues to do for education and culture in the great Northwest, I feel special pleasure in being thus connected with it."[43] Michigan's influence was best seen in its extremely close ties with its sister institution, the University of California, but it would also influence schools across the West.

During the eight years between 1887 and 1895, for example, the newly founded or newly defined state universities of Washington, South Dakota, Illinois, Indiana, Missouri, Idaho, and Utah all requested curricular and administrative guidance, referring to Michigan as their aspiration. In part because of James Burrill Angell's lengthy tenure and in part because of its own location at a geographic "crossroads," Michigan would in many ways serve as a model for institutions across the country. Upon taking office as president of Rutgers, the state university of New Jersey, Martin Scott wrote (to Angell) that among his "first duties will be to aid in the development of the relations of our college to the state" and that Michigan would be an "exemplar" in this effort.[44]

Michigan and Angell's standard did not only influence public institutions, however. Writing to Angell, Charles Kendall Adams's successor as Cornell president, James Schurman, predicted a large move toward public support for universities in the eastern states.

> In my opinion the support of higher education by the State is likely to become universal with the future progress of our democratic civilisation. But the people of the older states, especially in New England, have not yet

overcome that suspicion of government which they inherited from their struggle with the British despots over a hundred years ago.

Praising Michigan and Angell's contribution to the development of public higher education, Schurman continued:

> It is a blessed circumstance that in the West men have been forced to trust themselves. Of course, they have had many wise leaders, and I may here say that it was the example of what you had done in Michigan, and what other States had followed Michigan in doing, that first convinced me, not indeed of the wisdom, but of the feasibility of the public support of higher education.[45]

Schurman was in some ways mistaken, as new sources of capital and the pressures of expansion meant that even public institutions soon pursued private support. However, while incorrect in the particulars—state support for public universities of the East would remain behind western counterparts—he was correct in recognizing that while being public concerns, universities were increasingly becoming governmental ones as well.

In keeping with Schurman's sentiments, newer private institutions often looked to more established institutions, be it Michigan or the private schools of the East, when developing academic and administrative structures. However, such interaction was not unidirectional. Increasingly, more established institutions examined and at times considered themselves threatened by newer institutions and their exceptional resources—most notably, Leland Stanford's university in Palo Alto (founded in 1885 and opened in 1891) and John Rockefeller's university in Chicago (established in 1891).

Soon after announcing the founding of a new university as a memorial to his late son, Stanford wrote President Edward Holden of Berkeley, seeking to assure him that Stanford University was not a threat. Stanford stressed that his university's goal was to "do all the good which is possible" and that "to attain this it will have to work in unison with other like institutions." Stanford concluded, "I trust therefore that the State University and the Leland Stanford Jr., University will not only be able to work in harmony but will prove a mutual support."[46] Holden replied that Stanford's desire for coordination was a welcome and important one, not only for the individual institutions, but for the "the whole pacific coast."[47] This initial spirit of cooperation did not lead to meaningful coordination. Soon, Holden and his colleagues would bemoan the challenge presented by the riches of Stanford on the Pacific Coast and Rockefeller in the Midwest.

Bluntly summarizing some of the anxiety and anger these institutions initially caused other institutional entrepreneurs, Cornell's Charles Kendall Adams wrote Angell regarding a mutual fear of "faculty raids."

> At present it is still uncertain as to what depredations Chicago and Palo Alto will make upon our forces. Wheeler, Hull, and White[48] have all been taken up to the summit of the mountain and shown all the kingdoms of the west; but as yet no one of them has either succumbed or spoken the decisive word, "get thee behind me." My chief reliance in hoping to keep them here is the uncertain financial condition of the Chicago enterprise.[49]

While Chicago and Stanford did succeed in luring some faculty away, Adams's fear of wholesale defections proved unfounded. Rather than a threat, these newest of institutions soon became part of the loosely coupled system. Stanford hired David Starr Jordan as its first president on Andrew Dickson White's recommendation. Chicago's first president, William Rainey Harper, quickly developed close ties with his colleagues at Michigan, Wisconsin, and California.

More than simply encouraging institutional similarities, relations among elite universities fostered a coordination that was fundamental for universities' development as agents of the state. In a fashion not unlike the regulation of secondary education, universities guided one another. For example, when Angell considered raising faculty salaries at Michigan in 1892, he polled his peers at such places as Wisconsin, Harvard, Yale, California, Columbia, Johns Hopkins, and Cornell. When Martin Kellogg wished to construct new dormitories at Berkeley in 1897, he polled a similar group of schools as to the ideal structure for students' residential life. Through such internal definition, universities developed a collective identity and an external role in relation to the state and society. In other words, universities acted as a regulating agent for the national state by supervising themselves.

Defining Standards: Organizing Basic Knowledge

Credentials were essential to universities' collectivity and external influence. Universities needed to do more than simply produce degrees. They also needed to standardize and codify the knowledge such degrees represented, to give them value and authority. Harvard president Charles Eliot's campaign to shorten the time for a bachelor's degree from four to three years underscored the collective nature of this process and highlighted the fact that even the most prestigious and established of institutions would not radically alter the nature of its credentials without peer support. In keeping with his efforts at preparatory reform, Eliot sought to alter the bachelor's degree. Seeking Angell's support, Eliot bemoaned the inefficiencies of the current system.

> Our Freshmen now average nineteen at entrance, and as we have increased the term of professional education, the age at which a young graduate is first able to earn his living has become absurd. It seems to me that two remedies should be applied; one the saving of time in schools, and the other the reduction of the course for the AB.[50]

Angell wrote back that he understood Eliot's frustration but believed that students lacked maturity as it was and that shortening the time of preparatory and collegiate work would only heighten such difficulties.[51]

Writing to Adams, Angell alluded to "rumors that the Harvard men are thinking of trying a 3 yr. scheme for Bachelor's or something similar," and he questioned the wisdom of such a plan.[51] Discouraged by such colleagues as Angell and Daniel Coit Gilman and daunted by the inflexibility of his own faculty, Eliot abandoned his plan. However, Eliot's failed efforts say more about the growing dependency between elite institutions than about his own ineffectualness. As elite universities began to see themselves as a collective body, academic reforms, especially in regard to degrees and credentials, were no longer undertaken individually; they were done with the advice and consent of peers.

It would be almost fifteen years until a committee of the AAU would formally define uniform standards for degrees. Nonetheless, universities were already working informally to systematize the production of such credentials. This coordination and regulation would have a dual purpose, highlighted not only by universities development of academic standards in collegiate and graduate education but also by the development of professional standards in such fields as education and law. These efforts enhanced universities' societal usefulness as well as their effectiveness as agents of the national state itself.

The contribution of universities also built on their evolution as national institutions. In this era, the leading universities increasingly began to draw in students from across the country and to send graduates out far and wide. By the 1895–96 academic year, Yale could boast of having students from each of the forty-five states. The West's model university, Michigan, had students from forty-one different states. Even the fledgling University of California had students from twenty-six states. Perhaps reflecting unhealed wounds of the Civil War, the University of Virginia only counted students from seventeen states.

Nationwide recruitment of students and disbursement of graduates helped foster the national influence of institutions, especially in regard to the professions. In 1893, for example, the large number of Michigan graduates residing in the state of California prompted the state legislature to include Michigan, along with Berkeley and Stanford, among schools whose graduates were entitled to certificates allowing them to teach high school. Interestingly, Michigan first learned of the legislature's action from an educational journalist who praised the move. May Cheney wrote Angell with word of the plan and May's own approval: "as some of our best material comes from Mich., this is a step which all friends of education on the coast heartily approve. We have some excellent workers already in the field and we hope to introduce many more."[53] The news was confirmed by J. W. Anderson, the state's superintendent of public instruction, who laid out the details of the plan. Michigan soon joined California's major universities as the only institutions whose graduates could be recommended to teach high school. This placed Michigan in unique company, for as Anderson noted, "no Board shall consider the application of any party who is not a graduate of the pedagogical department of an institution that has been recommended by the State Board of Education in this state."[54] In other words, the University of Michigan would be one of only three institutions defining the skills, knowledge, and expertise deemed necessary for California's teachers.

Michigan did place a number of teachers in California schools. However, geographic distance and statutory vagueness meant that the university's work as a regulatory agent was occasionally muddled. Elmer Brown, the University of California's professor of pedagogy, wrote Angell to inform him of difficulties with the statute. As it was written, to be eligible for certification, a prospective teacher needed to have graduated from a pedagogical program. However, Michigan would not dedicate instruction to the "science and art of teaching" until 1889.[55] At Berkeley, Brown taught a number of Michigan alumni who either graduated before the pedagogy program started or had failed to take the proper series of courses while in Ann Arbor. Brown noted that under the wording of the statute, Michigan was required to certify both types of students. He acknowledged that there should eventually be "some settled policy in the matter" and expressed hope that Angell would pass along the records of such students in the meantime. Brown stressed that he did not mean for Michigan to grant official state certification to such students; rather, he simply asked Michigan to inform the state of California that particular pedagogical requirements had been met.[56]

Angell replied that he feared Brown's suggestion might appear to "disguise" the facts in particular cases. Brown worried that he had not made himself understood, and he continued to stress the difficulties presented by the current law. In one of the American state's first instances of bureaucratic red tape associated with credentialing, the law did not provide for cases in which the academic work had been taken at one institution and the pedagogical work had been done at another. Brown argued that the solution he offered would meet the spirit of law and not violate its letter. He maintained that training done at California obviously met "the requirement that professional pedagogical training be equivalent of the University of California." He again apologized for the "awkwardness" of the law and expressed hope that it would be amended soon.[57]

Angell soon heard from a student in the predicament Brown described. Louis Webb of Los Angeles, who had graduated from Ann Arbor in 1878, wrote directly to Angell to ask for the University of Michigan's assistance. Webb explained that he had been a teacher in Michigan immediately after graduation, eventually becoming principal of Flint High School, but that he had later moved to California and gone into the insurance business. He now wished to return to teaching, and the Los Angeles County Board of Education had suggested that he write to the University of Michigan requesting that the school certify him based on his previous experience.[58] Realizing the slightly unique nature of his request, Webb soon wrote Angell again. Apologizing for again writing Angell before the university president could reply to his first letter, he said he felt that he needed to clarify his request and to underscore Michigan's ability to grant a certificate. In order to do so, he attached a letter from Brown, who, by virtue of his position as head of Berkeley's pedagogy program, was a member of the state's Board of Education. Webb stressed Brown's interpretation that universities were free to use whatever standard they saw fit in determining what the statute described as "equivalent pedagogical work." He noted that it was not uncommon for the California universities "to grant certificates based on professional training rather than formal pedagogical work."[59] After further correspondence between himself, Angell, and Brown, Webb would eventually receive the necessary certificate.

More significant than the individual certification of an alumnus, Webb's experience underscores the fundamental role of universities as independent agents not only accrediting schools but also defining the profession of teaching. Interestingly, while the Los Angeles County Board of Education oversaw teacher credentials, they relied on the universities to determine the particular skills and knowledge necessary to become a teacher. No one on the county board questioned the value of Webb's experience. Webb's difficulties stemmed from the need to demonstrate expertise in the form of an appropriate certificate.[60] Such troubles demonstrate that while states relied on universities as independent agents, their support was not without complexities. Difficulties occasionally arose, but the developing network of loosely coupled universities would work to overcome them and would begin formal definition of professional standards and expectations for secondary education.

Defining Advanced Work: Standardizing University Degrees

As the nineteenth century drew to a close, universities not only oversaw standardization of the credentials required to teach in secondary schools; they attempted to standardize their own advanced degrees as well. Over forty-eight institutions would grant PhD's by the end of the century, but uncertainty existed as to the place of graduate education and advanced degrees at American universities. In response to the common practice of using undergraduate work as criteria for graduate degrees, T. C. Chamberlin, head of the University of Chicago's Geology Department and, later, dean at the University of Wisconsin, suggested taking the quality of work into greater account. Writing to Wisconsin president Charles Van Hise and Michigan's James Burrill Angell, Chamberlin expressed a wish "that in all our institutions the master's and doctor's degrees could be made to stand upon their own bases and be more independent of the—at present—dominating influence of undergraduate and preparatory work." For graduate education to be valued, there needed to be standards and distinctions. Chamberlin rhetorically asked his compatriots, "if the master's and doctor's degrees are differentiated, why should not the differentiation be based upon the work for these degrees, and not undergraduate and preparatory work?"[61]

Chamberlin was far from the only educator concerned with the development of uniform standards for the pursuit and awarding of graduate degrees. In one striking instance, W. W. Campbell of Berkeley's Astronomy Department wrote of a colleague who had received an honorary MS degree from Michigan in recognition of his work at the Detroit Observatory but had found that "it actually injured his standing with many profs., students, and high university officials." Because Berkeley bestowed the MS for only one year of postgraduate work, it was considered quite commonplace, especially since all of the man's colleagues had received doctorate degrees for similar work.[62]

Academic leaders wanted to grow their graduate programs but worried that proliferation of degrees might devalue the credentials. In addition to awarding many of the nation's first doctorates, Johns Hopkins also offered the first fellowships. However, as Harvard's Charles Eliot reported, once this practice spread, leading academics grew concerned over the dangers of competition between universities for graduate students. Writing to Angell after having visited Baltimore, Eliot stated:

> In my opinion the business of hiring students to pursue advanced studies by offering them free tuition, board, and lodging, is likely to be decidedly overdone. I was much pleased to hear Pres. Gilman and Profs. Ramsey and Gildersleeve of the JHU say that that was their opinion. The John Hopkins University began the method in this country for reasons which were good at the time; but it is already clear that the policy if carried on a large scale by several universities will have just the same effect on graduate schools that [university-affiliated seminary] education of ministers has had on the ministry.[63]

For Eliot, Gilman, and others, the question was whether too many fellowships would weaken the overall quality of graduate schools by broadly dispersing talented students between the various universities as competition rose over prospective students. Additionally, Eliot and others expressed concern about the resources required to fund not only fellowships but the apparatuses (libraries, laboratories, etc.) of advanced scholarship. Some academics and public officials even suggested maximizing resources by encouraging disciplinary specialization between institutions.

Despite such talk, the leading universities continued to build their graduate programs with recent graduates. With some exceptions, the common practice was for students to attend graduate school at their undergraduate alma mater. This custom minimized competition, but it did little to foster quality, as students did not always find themselves studying under those best suited to guide their research. Writing to Angell in regard to this "matter of inter-scholastic courtesy," Provost Charles Harrison of the University of Pennsylvania acknowledged the custom but suggested:

> Does it not seem desirable, however, that the Graduate students of our American Universities should be encouraged to move freely from Univer-

sity to University, much as is done in the Universities of Germany? That the
need of some such system is becoming felt among the students themselves
is sufficiently evinced by the publication of the Graduate Handbook, which
has been recently undertaken by the Federation of Graduate Clubs.[64]

Harrison's long-term ambitions for cooperation were large, but his
immediate plans were limited. He ended his note to Angell by simply
asking if he might send along Pennsylvania's graduate catalog and if
Michigan would send its catalog in return.

Angell agreed with Harrison's suggestion, and an exchange of cata-
logs was begun. Angell had discussed the need for improvement in and
coordination of graduate education a few years earlier. Writing to
Michigan's Board of Regents in his 1885–86 annual report, Angell
emphasized the need to increase standards in order to give graduate
degrees value.

> In thus establishing a high standard of work for the attainment of the Doc-
> torate, we are acting on harmony with the better American Universities,
> which are aiming to give significance and value to that degree. . . . It is cer-
> tainly one of the functions of a university like this to furnish the higher train-
> ing which our graduate school is attempting to provide.[65]

It would still be almost a decade before the American Association of
Universities would discuss formal agreement on various aspects of
graduate education, such as standards for degrees, the nature of fellowships, and intercollegiate exchanges. Nonetheless, the discourse
between leading academics reflected concern over not only the quality
of graduate education but the significance of such education to greater
society. As the sole regulators of these newly developing advanced
pursuits, universities could largely define society's expectations for
and demands of graduate education as well as the nature of their peers.

At this time, universities also began to exert nationwide influence
over a number of professional domains, such as law and medicine.
Unlike today, professional school was most often an alternative to,
rather than an extension of, undergraduate education. No law school
required college education for admission until those of Harvard and
Columbia did so in 1903. Requirements for medical school were similar. The first medical schools to require college education, those at Harvard and Johns Hopkins, did not do so until 1901. While the number of
students attending professional schools increased in the decades following the Civil War, the relative percentage of college graduates
attending professional schools at such elite institutions as Yale did not
increase (see table 2). Additionally, while the percentage of college

graduates in law and medicine remained small, the percentage of college graduates pursuing divinity degrees remained high.

For the most part, professional education in law and medicine would not undergo significant reform until the first decades of the twentieth century. In the last half of the nineteenth century, university leaders motivated by and associated with concern over the quality of graduate education began discussing and seeking ways to improve the quality and stature of professional degrees overall and their own professional schools in particular.

At Yale, for example, Arthur Twining Hadley complained in an 1895 address that Yale was losing many potential professional students to Harvard and Columbia because of the allure of Boston's and New York's courts and hospitals.[66] Despite this handicap, Yale sought to emulate the courses of study offered by its more urbane colleagues. Beginning in 1896, after lengthy and sometimes contentious debate, Yale finally extended its law course from two to three years and its medical course from three to four years, in keeping with the practice of its peer institutions.

Similarly, Cornell sought to develop professional programs. In keeping with the institution's avowed mission of offering instruction in all fields and endeavors, Andrew Dickson White had attempted to establish both law and medical schools at the outset of the university's development, but a lack of funds and concerns over the perceived elitism of professional education had thwarted his efforts. Stressing the need to offer courses and programs comparable to other institutions, White's successor, Charles Kendall Adams, was able to found a law school at Cornell in 1887. The law school's fortunes were significantly boosted in 1891, when the university won a suit with the state of New

TABLE 2.   Yale Professional School Enrollments

Year	Law		Medicine		Divinity	
1871	5/23	23%	6/33	18%	40/53	76%
1876	25/75	33%	12/42	29%	84/97	87%
1881	31/58	53%	6/25	24%	65/86	76%
1886	21/52	40%	10/25	40%	78/98	80%
1891	47/111	42%	22/62	35%	107/119	89%
1896	69/186	33%	31/119	26%	73/87	84%

Source: George Pierson, *A Yale Book of Numbers: Historical Statistics of the College and University, 1701–1976* (New Haven: Yale University, 1983).

Note: Numbers reflect the ratio of college graduates in Yale's professional schools. For example, only 23 percent of law students in 1871 had a college degree.

York over ninety thousand dollars in interest from sales of Morrill land grants. A portion of these funds went to build classroom facilities and a library for the law school; another portion was used as seed money for Cornell's medical college, which admitted students beginning in 1898. The use of Morrill funds for the study of law and medicine certainly was removed from the Morrill Act's original fields of agriculture and the mechanic arts. However, this use was not distant from the original entrepreneurial spirit that had fueled Cornell's initial development.

The push toward development and standardization of law schools was driven by the move toward a national system of universities and by the rising influence of the American Bar Association, founded in 1878. However, law schools' efforts to create national standards were undertaken with awareness of the need to negotiate state and local politics. In the process of hiring the first dean of Cornell's law school, Charles Kendall Adams recognized this need and expressed frustration over being unable to find a suitable candidate: "we have been trying to find a man for the Deanship of our Law School who unites the proper knowledge and experience to a familiarity with New York law and New York lawyers."[67] Such local concern was not always welcome, however. As mentioned earlier, before the emergence of the American Bar Association and the reform of statewide exams, legal education and credentialing were conducted by an array of apprenticeships and clerkships. The move to systematize accreditation of attorneys through statewide bar exams would eventually rely heavily on law schools with the requirement that all who sit for the exam graduate from a bar-accredited law school.

Michigan was one of the first states to consider requiring graduates of its law school to take examinations for admission to the bar. The university's president, James Burrill Angell, moderately supported such efforts. His primary concern was a desire to raise the standards of the law school, which in turn would elevate the standards of the profession.[68] Angell proposed working with state bar examiners in this effort. However, some university officials objected to what they saw as an unnecessary and unwarranted intrusion. The hostility and disregard felt by some for the bar examiners could be seen in the objections of Henry Wade Rogers, dean of Michigan's law school, to two potential faculty candidates on the basis of their having served on the local board of examiners. Writing Angell, Rogers noted: "those examinations, as is well known, have been farcical—absurdly loose. The fact may well be kept in mind in reaching a conclusion as to whether Mr. Knowlton or

Mr. Cramer would seek a high standard and force the students up to it."[69] Rogers's immediate concern was the qualifications of those administering the exam; his deeper concern lie in the relationship of the bar exam to the law school.

Rogers and others feared that a scheme requiring bar examinations would undermine the law school's authority. However, Angell justified such efforts as supporting the movement toward national standards of legal expertise. Angell stressed that the school would maintain its share of autonomy but would also work with bar examiners in developing a more thorough system of exams. He reiterated his desire to improve the standards of the school as well the need for greater specialization. In the following year's annual report to the regents, Angell noted that the "experiment of grading the course" had been "successful in a gratifying degree." He explained: "Both teachers and students heartily approve of it. More, thorough, systematic, and efficient work is secured by it."[70] Angell also praised plans to improve instruction by calling on nonresident lecturers from across the country to share their expertise in particular specialties. In the following year, Angell reported to the regents that coupling more stringent examination with more specialized course offerings had "materially raised" the school's standard of work.[71]

Angell had satisfied the critics of the bar and those who sought to improve the standards of the law school. Yet he still harbored concerns regarding the school's national reputation and the quality and reputation of the bar itself. In keeping with the demands of developing western communities, Michigan's law course was only two years. But Angell acknowledged, "the fact that some of the leading schools in the country have extended their course to three years forces on us the inquiry how long can we afford to ask less work than they." While Angell complained about the need for such advanced work to "be more completely organized and provided for,"[72] by the next year, the law school had begun offering an optional third year of courses, for which fifteen students enrolled.

Within a couple years, owing to the law school's efforts at expanding the curriculum and to Angell's own relationship with leading academics across the country, Angell would express satisfaction with the national position of the law school. Nonetheless, he continued to harbor doubts regarding the standards set by the bar. Reflecting Michigan's position as both a national institution and a regional leader, Angell assessed the school's position.

> It must be admitted that the question of what policy to adopt in fixing the requirements for admission and the requirements for graduation is not so simple as it might first seem. In Michigan and several other western States students are admitted to the bar on so easy conditions [that] if a law school sets up very high standards the great mass of students may go to the bar after brief and perfunctory study in the offices and very little systematic training.

The woeful standard set by many of the region's state bars dismayed Angell. However, recognizing the university's position as an agent of reform and coordination, he stressed the far-reaching impact of and institutional responsibility for raising the law school's standards.

> We profess and aim to be an institution of higher learning. We have already a reputation which gives weight and influence to our example. If we courageously, but not too rapidly elevate our standards, we can hold as many students to them as we care to have. The attainments and the mental discipline of the men we graduate will commend our work to all men of proper aspirations. By sending men of good general, as well as professional, education through all the west, we shall most effectively do our part in creating a sentiment in the profession which will insist on substantial requirements for admission to the bar.[73]

In setting standards for professions such as law, the authority of universities was still relatively diffuse in the later years of the nineteenth century. As loosely coupled independent agents of a gradually evolving national state, universities did not always possess formal control over professional standards and expectations. Yet as Angell and others articulated, the development and expansion of professional programs offered an opportunity to systematically train students and to provide a new form of knowledge and expertise within the university. Additionally, such development and expansion also offered an opportunity to reshape existing local practices into a more unified, efficient, and national system.

New Professions, New Authority, a New State

The push to apply new and more systematic approaches to issues outside of academia did not end with the traditional "learned professions" of divinity, law, and medicine. Driven by societal expectations and the efforts of their peers, universities expanded their reach into such areas as engineering and commerce/business. At Berkeley, Dean Carl Plehn, reporting on the reasons for the College of Commerce's establishment, stressed:

Modern life requires of many people a higher training than was required in the past. And that requisite for success is being sought in the Universities. An increase in the number of those seeking a college education so vastly in excess of the increase of population can but signify that there are new spheres in life in which it is hoped to apply the learning of the schools.[74]

For Plehn, the establishment of such a college was the "the natural and logical outcome of the economic development of the country." Plehn hoped that the program would be a "forerunner of many similar courses in different parts of the United States," but he also noted that other elite institutions, such as the University of Chicago, Columbia University, and the University of Pennsylvania, had already begun or were beginning similar schools.[75] In Plehn's explanation, just as in Angell's, we find university leaders seeking to serve societal demands as well as match the initiatives of their peers.

Coordination meant that national standards for doctors, lawyers, businesspeople, and engineers were not set by the federal government or a consortium of state and local leaders. Instead, such standards and related reforms were primarily initiated and overseen by a broad cadre of universities acting as agents of a developing national state. Examination of this public service highlights the prominence of institutional entrepreneurship in establishing and enforcing professional standards through courses and credentials. Such efforts provided the institutional entrepreneurs who ran institutions of higher learning with a highly visible purpose, as well as solidifying relations with the developing professional class on whom universities would rely for support.

Of course, as both the emerging university and the American state were in their formative years, the process was not flawless. Acceptance of standards and implementation of reforms were by no means universal. It would take the formal creation of the Association of the American Universities and the final failed efforts of John Hoyt to create a federally sponsored university to fully coalesce the influence of universities over the emerging professions and their relation to the national state. Nonetheless, in the years before the complete actualization of their influence, universities helped shape professions that were both a reflection of and an expansion on the reforms that defined the expanded federal government and the new American state.

6 The Origins of Formal Alignment

The National University Movement and the Creation of the AAU

By the turn of the twentieth century, academic leaders recognized the need to build on the dramatic institutional restructuring and expansion that had taken place in the years since the Civil War. Loosely coupled coordination had encouraged a variety of initiatives. However, its limitations had become apparent to a number of leading academics. Out of such concern emerged two approaches: (1) the reinvigoration of the movement to found a national university and (2) the reinvigoration and establishment of formal associations. For the development of the American state, the most prominent example of the latter approach was the creation of Association of American Universities, a formal collection of the nation's leading institutions for graduate and professional education. Some institutional entrepreneurs would lend their support to both causes, but for the most part, leaders of the elite institutions that comprised the AAU generally frowned on and lobbied against efforts to establish a federal institution of higher education. More than simply further defining and clarifying the relationship of colleges and universities to one another, these efforts were instrumental in structuring universities' relationships to the federal government and their roles as active partners and independent agents of the national state.

Prior to this period, formal coordination was sporadic, driven by individual initiative and institutional need. With the challenge of a federally sponsored university and the creation of the AAU, partnership and agency became more clearly defined. The potential alternative of a national university forced universities to examine and promote their efforts with and on behalf of the American state, while the establishment of the AAU created a regular forum for coordination and clarification in pursuit of such efforts.

The failed efforts to establish a national university and the successful creation of the AAU helped forge formal alliances that furthered the role of schools as partners and agents. The movement to found a national university originated in the desire to establish a center of learning in the nation's capital during the Revolutionary era. John Hoyt, the most vigorous proponent of this cause, had been actively lobbying educators and politicians since the late 1860s. For almost forty years, Hoyt proclaimed both the necessity and the benefit of a federally supported institution of higher learning. Having achieved some success lobbying Congress in 1891, Hoyt stepped up his efforts in the last years of the twentieth century, attempting to create a capstone institution formally overseeing the loosely coupled system of universities that were beginning to pursue research and advanced degrees in earnest.

Simultaneous to Hoyt's efforts, the heads of America's leading universities developed an interest in further formalizing the structure and nature of graduate education. Spurred by the Berkeley chapter of the Federation of Graduate Clubs, University of California president Benjamin Ide Wheeler proposed a meeting of university heads in 1899 to discuss the treatment of American degrees by European universities. Wheeler's peers agreed, and as discussions in anticipation of the meeting continued, the agenda for the first session soon expanded beyond the leading American universities simply sharing thoughts on their relations with foreign schools, to concrete consideration and formalization of their relationships with one another. From these initial meetings developed a coordinating organization that extended the ties and reach of the loosely coupled institutions that had shaped higher education in the later half of the nineteenth century.

Both Hoyt's attempts to establish a national university and the formal organization of America's leading universities are important for our understanding of the development of higher education in the United States. Just as important, these two related efforts are crucial for understanding the process by which university-based expertise grew to be central in the development of the national state. While not necessarily stemming from an "organized anarchy," the rise of expertise did stem from a somewhat chaotic and haphazard process driven by the actions of entrepreneurs and their specification of alternatives.

Since, as I have stated earlier in this book, there was nothing inevitable about the extent and nature of the rise in university support for the national state, detailing the process that led to formal organization of the universities requires consideration of Hoyt's significant alternative and the response it initiated. In considering Hoyt's failure and the AAU's formation, the powerful position of established universities certainly must be acknowledged. However, one should also recognize that in addition to possessing influence, the institutional entrepreneurs who ran the country's leading schools were able to make a compelling case for how and why the nation's pursuit of specialized knowledge and other related interests would be best advanced by a series of coordinated institutions, rather than through a centralized federal university.

The Persistent Entrepreneur: John Hoyt and the National University Movement

Numerous efforts to found a national university had been undertaken since before the Revolutionary War. Presidents Washington, Adams, Jefferson, Madison, Monroe, and Quincy Adams all expressed a desire for the federal government to found a federally sponsored institution of higher learning in the nation's capital. Presidential commitment to such a university varied. Washington was arguably the idea's strongest proponent. He continued to lobby on its behalf after he had left office, and his will even bequeathed Potomac Company stock (which proved to be worthless) for the establishment of a federally run university. While Washington's successors did not necessarily offer their own resources and were not as particularly detailed in their proposals, they all, in one form or another, called on the Congress to found—and on the "General Government" to oversee—a "university or institution for the communication of knowledge in the various departments of literature and science."[1] Despite this presidential support, a national university was never established. By the 1830s, the election of Andrew Jackson, the rise of spoils-driven "Jacksonian democracy," and the correspondent decline of the "patrician" presidency meant that grand plans for a national seminary of learning lay dormant.

The effort to found a national university at the turn of century was spearheaded by western educator and political activist John Hoyt. Hoyt's interest and efforts spanned over forty years. From the late 1860s onward, Hoyt served as the most prominent advocate of and organizer for the national university cause. A graduate of Ohio Wesleyan University, Hoyt began his career in education as a professor at Antioch College in Ohio. Among his many positions, his most notable employment was as founding president of the University of Wyoming, where he served from 1887 to 1890. Modern sensibilities might characterize Hoyt as a self-promoter. He was an unceasing advocate for his idea. He worked almost perpetually to fulfill what he characterized as "Washington's vision."[2] To better understand the nature of Hoyt's efforts at the turn of the century, we need to examine his first attempts at institutional entrepreneurship years before.

One Union, One University: Hoyt's Early Efforts

With the end of the Civil War and the beginnings of the industrial age, which were marked by a rise in societal complexity and a correspondent evolution of expertise, plans for a national university were rekindled. An early Republican organizer, Hoyt was appointed secretary of the Wisconsin State Board of Agriculture in 1857. In this position, he was an early supporter of the Morrill Act and was actively involved in the development of the state's university. Having attended the London International Exhibition of 1862 as a state commissioner, he was appointed as a U.S. commissioner to the Paris Universal Exposition of 1867. In addition to serving as a representative to the exhibition, Hoyt was asked by Secretary of State William Seward to tour and report on educational institutions and systems throughout Europe and to make a comparative study of the United States. In the course of these tours, Hoyt concluded that the United States was lacking and severely needed a national university dedicated to postgraduate studies. Upon returning from Europe, Hoyt submitted to the secretary of state a report in which he articulated the need for a newly founded national university to address the challenges of the modern era.[3]

Hoyt built his plan from observation of schools, gymnasiums, and universities throughout Europe. However, he stressed that no system and no country was sufficiently advanced to serve as a model. In proposing what he suggested would be the world's first "true" university, Hoyt sought to draw on the breadth of the European and American experiences to establish a new type of educational institution. Hoyt's university would be dedicated not only to the advancement of knowledge but, more significantly, to the application of that knowledge on behalf of progress and of the nation.

Having spelled out his ambitions, Hoyt immediately set about trying to put his plan into action. In 1869, at the annual meeting of the National Education Association in Trenton, New Jersey, he gave a speech entitled "University Progress," in which he offered his proposal for a national university in Washington, D.C. He maintained that the university would focus on postgraduate work and utilize the vast facilities for literary and scientific culture afforded by the several departments of the government, with the hope of making "the National Capital the most important intellectual centre in the world." Hoyt's suggestion was generally well received. The association passed a resolution supporting the idea in principal—suggesting that "a great American university is the leading want of American education"—and established a committee, with Hoyt as chairman, to report on the proposal at the next year's meeting.[4]

In addition to overseeing the preparation of the committee's report, Hoyt used his chairmanship to call on many of the nation's leading educators, seeking to gain their support. Among those who expressed sympathy with Hoyt's plan was the commissioner of the federal Bureau of Education, General John Easton, Jr., who praised Hoyt's efforts while speaking before the NEA in August 1870.[5] Those assembled agreed with Easton's sentiment. Hoyt's committee's report was unanimously adopted, and the committee was instructed to continue its work on behalf of the national university cause. The committee's second report, presented at the NEA's annual meeting in St. Louis in 1871, further specified the mission and scope of a national university. In addition to embracing "every department of science, literature, and the arts, and every real profession" and offering fellowships, laboratories, and the "best known facilities" for advanced study, the report suggested the university should be "established as to command the hearty support of the American people, regardless of section, party, or creed."[6] Coming less than half a decade after the end of the Civil War, the proposal touted the national university as a unifying institution. Hoyt and his fellow supporters believed it would provide not only advanced knowledge but also a structure to help overcome the nation's sectional, partisan, and denominational differences.

Beyond its role in advancing knowledge and unifying the nation, Hoyt's proposed university would also serve as a standard-bearer for educational institutions throughout the country. Though Hoyt's proposal did not suggest formal coordination, it did state that a national university

> should be so coordinated in plan with the other institutions of the country so as to not in any way conflict with them, but on the contrary, to become at once a potent agency for their improvement and the means of creating a complete, harmonious, and efficient system of American education.[7]

In Hoyt's conception, a national university supported by the federal government was to be instrumental in establishing standards and expectations for all of higher education. The committee's report was well received by the full assembly. Its recommendations were adopted, and a permanent committee to further pursue the issue was established.[8]

Having mobilized a number of leading academics and gained the support of the NEA, Hoyt turned his attentions to Capitol Hill and securing legislation for the establishment of a national university that would serve the nation and promote expertise. In January 1872, Hoyt's committee submitted a draft of a bill to members of Congress asking for "criticisms and suggestions." With significant assistance from Senators Charles Sumner of California and Timothy Howe of Wisconsin, the committee drafted a bill (S 859) that Howe introduced in March. The Howe bill initiated discussion on the topic, but no report was made. However, a subsequent version of the bill, presented in May by Senator Frederick Sawyer of Massachusetts (S 1128) and Representative Legrand Perce of Mississippi (HR 2389), was referred to committee. These initial bills would serve as templates on which all later efforts would be heavily based.

A little less than a year later, in March 1873, the House Committee on Education and Labor, which was chaired by Perce, reported back unanimously in favor of the bill. The committee report stressed the ever-increasing need for expertise and the value a university based in Washington, D.C., would have in producing such expertise for the nation and the federal state. In addition to detailing the structure of the university, its postgraduate nature, and its connection with various government departments, the bill offered a university endowment plan that the committee called "simple, definite, and secure." The federal government would in perpetuity pay the national university 5 percent interest on a "registered, unassignable, certificate" of twenty million dollars to provide for the purchase of grounds, the erection of buildings, the acquisition of equipment, and so forth. It was expected that private donors and tuition would help supplement this income.

Despite the unanimous support of the committee, the bill never reached the floor for consideration before Congress adjourned. Undaunted by their failure to get the bill to the floor and buoyed by their support in committee, proponents of the national university sought to rally support. By the NEA's annual meeting in 1874, the national university movement had gained two prominent supporters, Cornell president Andrew Dickson White and Missouri educator and, later, commissioner of education William T. Harris. Both men addressed the convention on behalf of Hoyt's cause. Reflecting on his travels throughout Europe and his experience as an educator, White stressed:

the history of all civilized nations and especially our own, shows that the thoughtful statesmanship of each generation should provide for the primary, secondary, and advanced education of each.

Accepting this principle the immediate care should evidently be to strengthen by public action the best foundations for advanced education which we already have; and . . . should it create one or more new ones worthy of the nation placing one of them at the national capital, where vast libraries, museums, and laboratories of various sorts now existing may be made of use for advanced instruction, and where the university could act directly and powerfully for good in sending graduates admirably prepared into the very heart and center of our national civil service, to elevate and strengthen it, I believe in spite of pessimists and doctrinaires that the result would be vastly for good upon the whole country.[9]

White did not embrace the specifics of Hoyt's plan, but White's general support for the national university movement brought added national attention. Following his speech, which received coverage in the *New York Times,* he actively promoted the idea in lectures and editorials for more than twenty years. White would soon leave academia to join the diplomatic corps, but even from across the Atlantic, his advocacy would continue.

In a lengthy speech, Harris also praised Hoyt's efforts, stressing that his proposed institution addressed the nation's greatest unmet need, knowledge applied on behalf of educated governance.

> All the evils which we suffer politically may be traced to the existence in our midst of an immense mass of ignorant, illiterate, or semi-educated people who assist in governing the country, while they possess no insight into the nature of the issues which they attempt to decide. . . . Our colleges, as at present constituted, do not fully answer the needs of this country at this time. The problems of sociology and statesmanship, the philosophy of science, of literature, of history, of jurisprudence, these demand the concentrated labor of a large corps of salaried professors provided for at well-endowed colleges and universities.
>
> It is in this respect that the National University, founded by the American state and endowed munificently, would prove of the greatest value to the country.

Harris ended his address by articulating the rationale that would drive the national university movement for decades to come. Hoyt, Perce, White, and others had all suggested the importance a national university would have in providing advanced knowledge to both the governed and the governing. Harris built on and clarified such sentiments when he stated (in terms that, though somewhat lengthy, are absolutely fundamental to our consideration):

It is a trite lament of our time that our Government needs purifying; that it should be surrounded by elevating influences. It is the mistake of certain abstract political theorists in this country, who would attempt to purify the Government by divorcing it from its concrete relation to civil society, that has prevented the growth of a science of statesmanship here and has caused the humiliating spectacle of acts of corruption done through sheer ignorance of the proprieties of statesmanship.

When we consider the great advantages that would ensue from the connection that a national university would have with the several bureaus of our General Government, and of the digested results that would proceed from the investigation of the statistical data there collected from the various phases of our social political life; when we consider the effect of collecting, by means of a vast endowment, the best educated intelligence of the time in a university faculty, and the resulting study of our institutions by free disinterested investigation, elevated above the atmosphere of strife wherein the practical everyday world is immersed, the importance of this movement to found a national university is fully apparent. Its advent will correct and prevent wrong tendencies in the direction of common schools, and likewise of colleges and private schools. It will be the source of supply for teachers and professors who shall take up the work of secondary education in the several states. From its lecture rooms will emanate the science that will solve our political and social problems, and furnish the philosophy of true statesmanship.[10]

Harris's comments reflect the breadth of the movement's support. Hoyt believed it was necessary to have the support of educators from all levels, not just university leaders, and he actively courted prominent secondary educators, such as Harris. More significantly, Harris's comments represent one of the clearest articulations of the movement's belief that a federally sponsored university was essential not only for the promotion of quality education but also for the promotion of good government itself.

Despite such rhetoric and mobilization, Hoyt and his supporters could not convince Congress to take action on the Perce-Sawyer bill. The movement's most vocal critics denounced the idea as elitist and questioned the feasibility of the funding mechanism. Others wondered how well represented all the nation's regional and denominational interests would be and worried that such an institution would become an instrument for, rather than a relief from, corruption and politicking. The bill languished, inactive.

In 1876, Hoyt attempted the first of many efforts to revive the national university legislation. However, his initial effort at revival was, as he described, "thwarted by the excitement growing out of the electoral contest and by other factors occasioning a further postponement."[11] Though the contest over Rutherford B. Hayes's election to the presidency might have dampened Hoyt's efforts at revival in 1876, it did provide the movement with a vocal proponent in the White House. In his annual message to Congress, delivered in December 1877, Hayes pronounced support for a national university serving as a capstone and benchmark for the American educational system.

> The intelligent judgment of the country goes still further, regarding as both constitutional and expedient for the General Government to extend to technical and higher education such aid as is deemed essential to the general welfare and to our due prominence among the enlightened and cultivated nations of the world.
>
> It is encouraging to observe in connection with the growth of fraternal feeling in those states in which slavery formerly existed evidence of increasing interest in universal education; and I shall be glad to give my approval to any appropriate measure which may be enacted by Congress for the purpose of supplementing with national aid the local systems of education in those states and in all states; I here add that I believe it is desirable . . . to the great and lasting benefit of the entire country, that this system should be crowned by a university in all respects in keeping with the national capital and thereby realize the cherished hopes of Washington on this subject.[12]

Unfortunately for Hoyt and the national university's proponents, Hayes was not able to lend much more than rhetorical support. Hayes reiterated his recommendations for a more active federal education policy in his address the following year, but the movement still could not garner enough support or clout to generate movement in Congress.

A New Institution for a New Century: Hoyt's Later Efforts

Hoyt's efforts in the 1870s would be far from his only attempt to create a national university before the turn of the century. Over the next twenty years, he would continue his activities as an institutional entrepreneur. Eventually transforming the NEA's permanent committee into an organization called the Committee for the Establishment of the University of the United States, Hoyt continually promoted his cause in speeches, editorials, and letters to prominent university officials. Hoyt was able to generate public expressions of support from such educational policymakers as Grover Cleveland's secretary of the interior, L. Q. C. Lamar (who oversaw the Bureau of Education), and such university educators as Andrew Dickson White, Charles Kendall Adams, and Herbert Baxter Adams. However, he was frustrated in his efforts to gain the full support of the higher education community and the Washington establishment. From the very outset, Hoyt attempted to promote a federally sponsored university not only as a solution to the problem of developing and maintaining educational standards, systems, and institutions across the country but also as a unifying force bridging the nation's sectarian and regional divides. While few disputed the need to address such concerns, many questioned the viability of Hoyt's plan and its ability to meet the challenges he had identified.

Despite these setbacks, Hoyt persisted. Even though he had moved further west, to Wyoming (where he took the territorial governorship from 1878 to 1882 and to which he returned as founding president of the University of Wyoming in 1887), Hoyt kept an active presence in Washington, D.C., and remained vigilant in his efforts. At the beginning of the 1890s, he began again to mobilize support in earnest. Hoyt found a willing ally in Senator George Edmunds of Vermont, who introduced a bill in May 1890 for the establishment of the "University of the United States." Edmunds's bill (S 3822) was modeled extensively on the movement's previous efforts and called for a onetime appropriation of five hundred thousand dollars and for the establishment in the Treasury of a perpetual fund of five million dollars from which an interest of 4 percent would be derived annually and put toward operating expenses.

Similar to earlier efforts, Edmunds's bill never reached a floor vote. Having introduced the bill at the end of the session, Edmunds secured the formation of the Senate Select Committee to Establish the University of the United States. The committee, with Edmunds's fellow Vermonter Redfield Proctor as chairman, worked through the recess and actively cooperated with Hoyt's committee in modifying the legislation and securing support. In 1892, Hoyt presented to the Senate his *Memorial in Regard to a National University*. In addition to providing arguments for establishing such a university and for placing such a university in Washington, Hoyt's memorial contained a lengthy historical summary of all previous efforts and expressions of support for the concept, from George Washington onward. The Senate not only received Hoyt's report but authorized the printing and distribution of five thousand additional copies by the Government Printing Office, a not insubstantial expense at the time.

The Senate's action provided the movement with its broadest audience yet. However, Hoyt and his supporters were unable to capitalize. Further committee reports on the Edmunds bill were issued in 1893 and 1894, with Senator Eppa Hunton of Virginia serving as the new chair, but no legislative action was taken before the end of the session. Reconstructing why these committee reports never reached the Senate floor is difficult. Legislative history simply records that no further action was taken after committee reception of Hoyt's reports.

In a 1902 report to Congress, Hoyt summarized the arguments offered by various opponents to the national university over the past quarter century: (1) the nation had no need for an exclusively post-graduate university; (2) the trend of educational thought in Europe was for the state to create multiple campuses rather than a singular central-ized one; (3) higher education was a luxury, more appropriately left to private and denominational benefactors; (4) improved graduate facili-ties were needed but should not be established by the national govern-ment for fear of political interference; (5) existing colleges would be "overshadowed, minified, stripped of their professors and students and reduced to nothingness by the competing Central institution"; and—perhaps the most extreme suggestion—(6) "it is no proper func-tion of the Government to care for interests of education."[13] These objections were raised by a variety of opponents to the national univer-sity, ranging from the heads of four leading universities,[14] who criti-cized it as unnecessary; to the president of the Methodist-run American University (which had been recently established in Washington, D.C.), who criticized it as "godless"; to a leading radical populist, who criti-cized it as "elitist." Such disparate forces did not necessarily unify the opposition to Hoyt's proposed university, but collectively they pre-sented significant obstacles.

Seeking to overcome such obstacles, Hoyt sought to mobilize other leading academics whose reputations carried influence and respect. Writing to University of Michigan president James Burrill Angell, Hoyt explained the difficulties the movement had encountered in getting the bill out of committee during the Fifty-third Congress. Hoyt hoped to broaden his movement's support, as he and his colleagues were plan-ning a campaign to introduce legislation at the very beginning of the Fifty-fourth Congress and were seeking "most distinguished of Ameri-can(s)" to join a "Committee of 100" to promote his legislation.[15]

While not providing specifics, Hoyt, in an entrepreneurial attempt to cultivate Angell's membership, suggested that prospective private backing was in the offing. Recognizing Angell's position as the "elder statesman" of university presidents and leader of the flagship univer-sity in the West, Hoyt continually sought Angell's guidance and sup-port. In pursuing Angell's membership on his committee, Hoyt also not very subtly articulated his desire that its members would be willing to exert their influence: "Demands for money will be made upon no member of the Committee; but we shall confidently expect their friendly advice and hope for their personal influence at all convenient times."[16] Angell was willing to lend Hoyt a sympathetic ear. He would also offer general words of encouragement and suggestions as to how the university ought to be structured and legislation drafted. Angell's polite encouragement, however, was not the equivalent of his support.

Some colleagues of Angell's, such as the president of Hamilton College, E. P. Powell, actively endorsed the proposal. Writing to Angell about efforts to make his college a part of the State University of New York, Powell stressed the need for a national system of higher education: "It seems to me very desirable to work up and lay before the people the idea of completed state systems and to urge immediate incorporation of a federalist National University at Washington."[17]

Angell remained skeptical of Hoyt's plan but saw some wisdom in it. Because Senator Edmunds was an old acquaintance of his from Vermont, Angell would not dismiss the legislation out of hand. Edmunds wrote Angell at the beginning of 1896, seeking his strong support. Edmunds wrote of the need for an institution "which shall coordinate and bring the cooperation of all institutions of learning to the work of still higher learning," and he stressed that there was still much to be attained by a properly equipped institution—of "which we, even in this country of wonder, can have little conception."[18] Despite the lobbying of such friends as Edmunds, Angell refrained from joining the "Committee of 100." However, because of Hoyt's persistent correspondence and Angell's position among his peers, Angell would remain a distant observer of the movement. Other leading academics, including Stanford's David Starr Jordan and Mississippi's Robert Fulton, would join the "Committee of 100."

Though garnering active support from various university presidents, Hoyt's efforts in the Fifty-fourth Congress failed. A number of forces contributed to the bill never reaching the floor, including the protracted absence of the education committee's chairman, John Kyle. Most significant was highly influential oppositional lobbying by such prominent university presidents as Yale's Timothy Dwight, Harvard's Charles Eliot, Columbia's Seth Low, and Penn's Charles Harrison. Beyond writing members of Congress, the four presidents spoke publicly and wrote openly against the proposal. Charles Eliot's argument in the magazine *Critic* was perhaps the most influential such piece. The elite universities certainly did not object to the goals of the national university, nor did they necessarily object to the prospective of greater federal involvement in higher education. They did, however, object to the breadth of Hoyt's plan. Despite having organized his most effective and broad-reaching network of support to date with the "Committee of 100," Hoyt was not able to overcome the challenge presented by such prestigious forces and other scattered sources of opposition.

A remarkably persistent policy and institutional entrepreneur, Hoyt pressed on with the issue. Attempting to use the dawn of the twentieth century as a call for action as well a springboard for attention, Hoyt managed to arrange for Senate committee hearings in January 1899. As Hoyt noted in his letters to Angell, the legislation he offered was little changed from that which he had originally introduced in the 1870s. Over the last decade, Hoyt and his allies had begun to frame their argument around the need for a coordinating institution that would maximize the research and resources of the federal government. Therefore, in addition to mobilizing the support of academic leaders, Hoyt enlisted the support of various federal officials, including Charles Walcott of the Geological Survey and William J. McGee of the Smithsonian Institute.

During his earlier efforts, Hoyt had called on the commissioner of education and the secretary of the interior, the two federal officials most responsible for overseeing national education policy. Their support had not been enough, and Hoyt looked to broaden his base of agency support. In addition to highlighting the coordinating function of such an institution, Wolcott and McGee's testimony in Senate hearings underscored the importance of partnerships that a national university could pursue with existing agencies.

Wolcott spoke of the need for a postgraduate institution in Washington, D.C. Citing the fact that 30 percent of his current staff had done their graduate study abroad, he stressed that Hoyt's proposed institution "would afford American students in Geology the advantages at home for which they must now at present go abroad" and that "what is true of the Geological Survey is true also of many of the other scientific bureaus of the Government." Among the other bureaus Wolcott envisioned as active partners of the national university were the Fish Commission, the National Zoo, the Coast and Geodetic Survey, and the weather, botanical, biological, and entymological bureaus of the Department of Agriculture. He ended his testimony with a strong endorsement of the plan.

> I think that the national university would exert an educational influence of the highest type that would be felt in the remotest portions of the country. It should set a standard toward which all persons seeking higher education could look as to an ideal, a standard which would meet the approval of all

our colleges and universities and which would not interfere with the work they are doing.[19]

Aware of the basic criticisms of Hoyt's university, Wolcott emphasized its place as a needed supplement rather than an unnecessary substitute.

McGee echoed and extended Wolcott's sentiments. For McGee, the primary justifications for a national university lay in the great resources available in Washington, D.C., and the need for the nation to maximize them.

> The National Government, like most of the State governments, has found it expedient to investigate various natural conditions and resources for the public benefit; and thereby experts in different lines of knowledge have been employed and trained. In the national capital this has resulted in the development of . . . [bureaus and departments] engaged in researches and surveys relating to the country and its resources. Thus a corps of scientific and technical experts has grown up, of such magnitude as to render Washington the leading scientific center, not only of the country but of the world.
> While we thus have in the United States a superb system of public education, beginning in the common schools and rising well toward the higher grades through State institutions, and while the system is effectively coordinated by the Federal Bureau of Education, we have not yet sufficient provision, or, indeed, any suitable provision, for the highest grades of education in accordance with American principles and standards. Accordingly, there is a need for a Federal educational agency of such sort as to crown and perfect our public school system, to give American citizens the benefit of the highest education, and to fit our men and women to extend the noble career of the nation of which they are constituent parts.[20]

As Walcott and McGee both represented, supporters of the national university argued that such an institution was necessary to maximize the opportunities for partnerships between academics and the federal government and for a corresponding development of expertise.

Building on these hearings, Hoyt and others rallied supporters over the next few years with letters, speeches, and articles. With the formation of the "Committee of 100," the resurgent support of the National Education Association, and the continued cooperation of such notables as Andrew Dickson White, David Starr Jordan, Robert Fulton, and R. P. Barringer (faculty chairman of the University of Virginia), Hoyt believed he had mobilized his broadest support yet. Michigan's Angell, while still not an active supporter, was intrigued by the latest proposal, and on the request of the NEA, he surveyed various western university presidents to gain their opinion of it.

The responses of those at the most prestigious and powerful institutions reflect an overall difficulty Hoyt encountered: his support might have been broad, but it was not necessarily deep. Many of the leading academics did not consider such an institution to be an urgent necessity, especially in light of the expansion of graduate education at existing institutions, and thus were less than intense in their support. Charles Kendall Adams, who was now president at the University of Wisconsin, summarized such sentiment. Writing his old colleague Angell, Adams noted that he had been frequently asked to join his mentor White on Hoyt's committee and once had been "ardently" in favor of a national university, but he admitted that "now that graduate studies have been so earnestly and successfully prosecuted in most of the universities, I have had somewhat less enthusiasm." Despite such ambivalence, Adams also stressed that "we are never likely to have too much higher education." Adams had no hesitation in regard to Hoyt's proposal and felt that a national university could be successfully managed "if the incorporaters see that it is kept out of the hands of the politicians and guarded in such a way that scholars of the country will be in control of it." He concluded by saying that if such management could be accomplished, "it would be of inestimable advantage to make the various departments at Washington available for advanced studies," and he expressed a feeling that his opinions were in keeping with the general sentiments of the Madison campus.[21]

President Wheeler of the University of California expressed similar sentiments. Emphasizing that he could not speak for others on campus, Wheeler stated, "we do not want another university which shall duplicate, imitate, or even better any existing institutions." Yet Wheeler conceded:

> a university organization located at Washington, which shall bring into cooperation all the academic forces now present in that city and supplement these with help from the various universities of the country, would be a very great help to us and our cause. I think of a national university as a means for cooperation among the existing university elements than as a new and distinct institution.

Wheeler suggested that research and publication, rather than teaching, should be a national university's aim. For Wheeler, the Smithsonian provided a "proper nucleus," and different government bureaus, such as the Coast and Geodetic Survey, would "furnish a means for widening the org[anization]."[22] Wheeler's comments came at the same time as he was beginning to take the first steps toward helping create the American Association of Universities. Regardless of the organizational form, Wheeler wished to extend the existing trend toward both coordination and partnership.

Besides lacking intense support from leading academics, Hoyt also faced ambivalence from leaders of denominationally affiliated schools. In the previous decade, the Catholics had founded the Catholic University of America, and the Methodists had founded the American University in Washington, D.C. Thus, presidents of religiously affiliated universities, such as Northwestern's Henry Wade Rogers, found themselves in an awkward position. Responding to Angell's inquiries, the former University of Michigan law professor said that he had often been asked to express his support but had declined because "I dislike to appear publicly out of sympathy with Bishop Hurst in his proposal for an American university under the control of the Methodist church." Rogers continued:

> I will say to you that I have no sympathy whatever with Bishop Hurst in his proposed American university and think the effort an unwise one for the Methodist church, . . . but since our leadership has endorsed the idea at their Central Conference I do not feel free to speak against it.
>
> Personally, I sympathize with the movement for a national university at Washington and wish to see one established under the auspices of the government of the United States.[23]

Rogers noted his impression that his university's trustees also had "no sympathy" with Hurst's scheme for a Methodist-sponsored institution but that they were indifferent as to Hoyt's federal university.

In addition to slight ambivalence and questionable urgency from tepid supporters, Hoyt also encountered increasingly active opposition from elite northeastern institutions. Dismissed by many of them as foolhardy and unrealistic, Hoyt's earlier efforts had largely been ignored by the leaders of the older, eastern universities. As Hoyt persisted and more members of Congress became supportive, ambivalence changed to active opposition.

Hoyt earnestly attempted to bring these older, eastern institutions into the fold at the turn of the century. To help do this, Hoyt called on Angell, asking him to lend the cause his name and formal support, rather than just his usual sympathetic ear. Aware of scheduled meetings regarding the formation of the Association of American Universities, Hoyt asked if Angell could influence those there to support the proposal, pleading, "The scale may turn upon your influence and vote."[24] Hoyt's proposal was never formally discussed at the AAU meetings, but he pressed forward in seeking to gain the support of—or, at the very least, to minimize opposition from—the leaders of the oldest and most established universities. He wrote Harvard's Charles Eliot and the newly appointed Arthur Twining Hadley of Yale and Nicholas

Murray Butler of Columbia, providing each with a copy of the draft legislation he hoped to introduce as well as his memorial that Congress had published in 1892. Hoyt believed his new legislation to be "simpler in plan, more explicit as to offices to be filled, and mak[ing] a wider geographical distribution of members of the sole governing body than the legislation of 1896 to which they had objected."[25] Hoyt expressed his hope that his latest draft overcame concerns various opponents had regarding partisan, sectarian, and regional interference, and he asked for comments and critique as well as expressions of support.

Eliot and Butler responded to Hoyt with little more than detached advice regarding the university's governing structure. However, Eliot, while polite in his correspondence with Hoyt, had little actual tolerance for Hoyt's entrepreneurial enterprise. A few years earlier, when Eliot and other leaders of eastern universities first expressed their formal opposition to the plan, Eliot wrote to Johns Hopkins University's Daniel Coit Gilman:

> Will you kindly tell me what your view is of Mr. J. W. Hoyt's present proposal about the "University of the United States"? He has been at this job for more than twenty years, and has introduced bill after bill into Congress. He now seems to have obtained a considerable backing if I may infer from the "authorized" list of members of the "National University Committee." I see your name on the committee. The actual bill seems to me to propose a thoroughly impracticable plan. Neither the Board of Regents nor the University Council can possibly be a suitable working Board for the government of a university. I remember when Mr. Hoyt was engineering this scheme twenty years ago he used eminent names in support of the project without the least authority. Has he been doing that again? I see various inaccuracies in the list. He puts people in places and offices where they do not belong.[26]

Gilman responded that while he had not been actively involved in the plan, he did generally support the sentiment, if not the particulars, of Hoyt's bill.

> I have only glanced at the last "bill" and am not entirely in accord [as I have informed him] with the plans of Dr. Hoyt, but as I believe Washington must have something better than what it now has in the way of an organization for the engagement of science and letters, I have contented myself with pointing out what have seemed to me errors or defects in successive schemes that have been proposed.[27]

Reflecting the importance of personal credibility for policy entrepreneurs, Hoyt's apparent (to Eliot at least) tendency to overstate the breadth and depth of his support not only clouded Eliot's opinion of the man but solidified Eliot's inclination to oppose the proposed institution. Ironically, a list of supporters meant to encourage greater support had backfired, as it served to stoke the fires of a significantly influential opposition.

Unlike Eliot, who chose to keep a disdainful but courteous distance and not to engage in substantive discussion with Hoyt, Yale's Arthur Twining Hadley responded to Hoyt's inquires regarding his effort of 1900 by expressing, in no uncertain terms, his extensive concerns regarding the national university plan. Hadley began his response to Hoyt by stating that if the goal was the establishment of a national university to more fully organize collections at Washington and give better facilities for instruction, then he was "in full sympathy" with its purpose. However, Hadley stressed:

> If it [the National University plan] means the establishment of a central body "to represent the sum of human knowledge," I fear that it will do harm rather than good. This system is most fully carried out in China, and we see the consequences. It is to some degree carried out in France, and I believe that the general testimony of educators is that it has been harmful in that country also. I believe the tendency of the organization of a body which claims a dominant position in the intellectual world, based on any act of incorporation, contains more evil than good. Perhaps I do your plan injustice; but it seems to me to attempt to substitute the principle of intellectual authority for that of intellectual liberty, and to do it in a form so plausible as to commit people in the wrong direction before they really know where they are going.[28]

As well as questioning the general principle of Hoyt's plan, Hadley questioned Hoyt's analysis of European systems, on which many of the arguments in favor of a national university were based. Hadley offered a list of specific questions—based on Hoyt's 1892 memorial—that he felt needed to be answered.

> 1) What instance can be cited of a national university in any country which has met the demands of higher education as well as a group of local universities, acting independently? 2) Has not the influence of national universities upon government service been habitually bad, instead of good? 3) Is not their work in coordination pursued to such an extent that it deadens inspiration instead of augmenting it? and 4) Is not the contact with a centralized institution of learning a thing which habitually does harm to those fundamental ideas of liberty which are the basis of a American system of government?
>
> Pardon me if I seem to put things strongly. I believe the danger to be a real one and a great one; and I have not yet seen in any of the memorials in favor of a national university a single paragraph that shows that the writers have ever attended one, or know what it is like, or that they recognize the dangers with which such institutions have been habitually attended in their practical workings.[29]

Hoyt reassured Hadley that the proposed university sought to supplement, rather than supplant, existing institutions of higher education. For Hoyt, a federal university would not restrain existing institutions but, rather, assist in their development, through its coordination of programs and its facilitation of partnerships.[30]

Hadley responded to Hoyt's defense by apologizing to Hoyt for portions of his correspondence that might have seemed "scornful" and by praising Hoyt's 1892 *Memorial* as one of the "most compact and forcible presentations of the reasons for such a university" that he had seen. However, he reiterated his skepticism, referring to the controversy between *Ecole Libre* and the university in France and noting that "none of the advocates of the National University, as far as I know, have seen the workings of national university life from the inside."[31]

Hoyt's efforts to gain the support of older, eastern universities had failed, and by the time he provided arguments on behalf of his legislation to Congress in 1902, he dismissed their opposition as representing an antiquated and provincial view. Submitting yet another lengthy report in support of legislation submitted to the Senate by Senator Edmunds, Hoyt summarized the opposition of Harvard, Yale, and other older institutions. Stressing that even these institutions looked elsewhere for advanced degrees and expertise, Hoyt remarked:

> There has also been active opposition from a very few of the great and non-sectarian universities—all of them at the northeast and priding themselves quite as much on age as on real worth. The most of their students have always been mere college boys, and many of their graduates hasten to finish their studies abroad.[32]

Highlighting the national appeal of the proposed university, Hoyt contrasted the established schools of the northeast with elsewhere: "The noble University of Virginia and all the more important institutions at the South and West have always been staunch supporters of the National University measure."[33]

For Hoyt, the opposition of the most established institutions represented anachronistic fear and jealously rather than progressive analysis and ideals.

> The opposition of the four older institutions is well understood. For more than a century they have struggled to gain and to hold a foremost place in the university ranks, and have accomplished so much that neither they nor their friends find it easy to yield any point that may look to the establishment of an institution which, because of its centrality, its supreme standards, its national functions and its international relations, would, in the

nature of the case, secure to it a foremost place among the universities of the world. They simply misunderstand the situation, and it has not been possible for the present leaders in these universities to see how truly the University of the United States, when duly established, would become a mighty force for their advancement, confining its general work to fields beyond those of the other universities, and for the most part limiting itself to special fields and those of research and investigation.[34]

Hoyt did not envision a federal university as an institution competing with other schools. Rather, he saw it as the national defining source of specialized and advanced knowledge, the caretaker of expertise.

Introducing the 1902 version of his legislation, Hoyt believed that despite the opposition of some leading academics, all legitimate objections to his proposal were answered in its most recent version. In the report accompanying the 1902 version of the bill, Hoyt concluded:

The pending bill avoids every objection ever raised, wisely regards the welfare of all other educational institutions, looks to the best interests of the Government, and to such work in the field of research as will clearly make of Washington both the educational and scientific center of the world. . . . [The Congress] can not hesitate, and will not when satisfied that the pending bill looks purely to the interests of the whole country and gives such control as will best protect the proposed university from all meddling influences, whether individual, local, denominational, or political.[35]

Believing he had addressed all significant organizational and policy concerns, Hoyt felt emboldened by his ability to fully mobilize many of the nation's smaller universities and normal schools. Their support was summarized in a resolution passed by the Association of American Agricultural Colleges and Experiment Stations stating that the AAACES "would welcome with satisfaction the development and organization of a national university devoted exclusively to advanced and graduate research."[36]

Hoyt's optimism was misplaced. He could accurately claim to have offered his most workable and realistic proposal that had garnered the movement's broadest and most established support to date. However, the 1902 legislation failed to move out of committee. Hoyt and his supporters had raised awareness, but they failed to be the defining force in shaping higher education's relationship with the national state. Their efforts did make some impact. Many who criticized graduate education as elitist had come to recognize the need for advanced education and national standard-bearing institutions. The NEA, the AAACES, and the National Teachers Association also expressed unqualified support. Nevertheless, a federally administered university still remained elusive, as the leading research universities actively lobbied against the concept, suggesting that they presented a more viable and appropriate alternative. Such pluralist arguments, supported by elitist connections, would eventually win out. Hoyt briefly attempted to rekindle his proposal again in 1908, but to no avail. By then, the elite universities had formalized and institutionalized their roles as standard-bearers and capstone institutions, clearly establishing themselves as the preferred alternative.

Hoyt's failed effort to establish a national university highlights the fact that there was nothing inevitable about the evolution of elite colleges into leading universities that would define standards not only for their self-selected peers but also for all of higher education. Proponents of a national university had hoped that their institution would be the next step in an effort begun by fledgling universities across the country to raise national standards and define American expertise. Hoyt and his supporters were among the first to advocate formal coordination among universities to define parameters and expectations for advanced degrees. They were not to reap the idea's general acceptance. Without adequate political support or funding, Hoyt's entrepreneurship fell short, and established institutions would fill a widely recognized void.

Specifying Alternatives: The Formation of the AAU and the Origins of Formal Alignment

Founded in 1900, the Association of American Universities would emerge as an alternative model to a federally sponsored national university. The initial concern of the AAU's founders was the reception of American degrees at foreign universities. In October 1899, prompted by a report detailing the difficulties of students abroad and a request for action from the Berkeley chapter of the Federation of Graduate Clubs, University of California president Benjamin Ide Wheeler wrote his colleagues at Columbia, Chicago, Harvard, and John Hopkins. He inquired how their graduates and advanced degree recipients had been treated when studying in Europe and what formal policies their own institutions had established regarding foreign degrees. Strikingly, Wheeler's concern did not rest solely with how such degrees were seen abroad; rather, his primary interest lay in more formal alignment and standardization of degrees among the nation's universities.

Writing to his colleagues, Wheeler stressed, "it is believed that the time has arrived when the leading American universities should make a combined effort to induce the authorities of foreign universities to establish more uniform regulations with reference to the admission of American students to the examinations for the higher degrees." Wheeler believed that such a combined effort would help facilitate negotiations with foreign universities, and he assured all that such negotiations would be undertaken

> with a view of securing proper credit, where it is not already given, for advanced work done at home at a university of high standing, and for the purpose of protecting the dignity of the degrees of Ph.D., etc., by discouraging foreign universities from conferring the doctor's degree on such American students as are not prepared to take the degree at home at a university of high standing.

Wheeler believed that this objective could easily be attained through discussions with the German Ministers of Education, as long as it came in the form of a joint request by the "leading American universities."

> But the German universities would then undoubtedly desire such information as would enable them to rate our American students in accordance with their actual attainments, when they apply to them for a doctor's degree. At present no adequate uniformity exists in the requirements for admission to the various schools of our own country, nor in the standard of graduate work which lead to the higher degrees.

To remedy this situation, Wheeler suggested a "conference of representatives" at the earliest possible date.[37]

Wheeler wrote Charles Eliot of Harvard, Daniel Coit Gilman of Hopkins, William Rainey Harper of Chicago, and Seth Low of Columbia to facilitate the planning and to establish the agenda for such an initial conference. Noting that Germany was not the only country for which such issues were a concern, Wheeler hoped that such a meeting not only would help systematize relations between American institutions and those in Europe but would be a major step toward uniformity in graduate and undergraduate standards and programs.

Wheeler's letter was well received by all recipients, and within three months, a formal letter was sent by Eliot, Gilman, Harper, Low, and Wheeler to nine of their colleagues at the nation's leading institutions.[38] Reflecting the geographic reach of university education at the time, these original members of the movement were primarily concentrated in the eastern and northern regions of the nation. Summarizing Wheeler's earlier arguments, the letter began:

> On behalf of the Universities which we represent, we, the undersigned, beg to suggest that the time has arrived when the leading American Universities

may properly consider the means of representing to foreign Universities the importance of revising their regulations governing the admission of American students to the examinations for the higher degrees.[39]

The authors stressed that in addition to securing due credit in foreign universities, such a conference would help higher education at home as well. By developing greater uniformity among elite universities, Wheeler and others also hoped to facilitate migration between institutions from undergraduate to graduate school and sought to raise standards at colleges and universities of all types across the country. The invitation also noted that in the interest of coordination, the U.S. commissioner of education and a delegate from the Federation of Graduate Clubs would be asked to attend the meeting.

The signatories, representing California, Chicago, Columbia, Harvard, and Johns Hopkins, were active supporters. Yet not all invitees were initially enthusiastic. Some—most notably, newly appointed Yale president Arthur Twining Hadley—questioned the necessity of such an organization. Responding to his colleagues' invitation, Hadley respectfully expressed his skepticism. Noting that the meetings were scheduled during exams, an inconvenient time for Yale and its faculty, Hadley suggested that it was unlikely they could send a representative. Additionally, Hadley asked for further clarification of the meeting's goals and purposes as well as examples of the difficulties suggested.

> We are most desirous to cooperate in all matters of common interest. . . . we should not hesitate to do so did we clearly understand the objects which you have in view in response to difficulties with foreign universities as reason for meeting. . . . It is a surprise to us to know that such credit is not given at present, we have had occasion to be grateful for the courtesy with which all such work has been recognized by foreign universities. To put ourselves in a position of complaint concerning evils of whose existence we have no evidence would be unjustifiable from our own standpoint and from that of foreign universities.[40]

Hadley was not opposed to cooperative efforts and often asked his colleagues for advice regarding various aspects of university activity and educational policy. He did not necessarily object to moving from loosely coupled relations to more formally aligned ones. Hadley did, however, question the rationale and urgency of such a meeting.

Writing somewhat more candidly to his colleagues Eliot of Harvard and Harper of Chicago, Hadley detailed his concerns. In correspondence with Eliot, Hadley enclosed a copy of his reply to Wheeler. Saying he was a tad puzzled by the invitation and stressing his desire to cooperate with other institutions, Hadley asked Eliot for his advice.

I can readily understand how the many students and the few professors who conceive of the Doctorate of Philosophy as a sort of inflated Mastership of Arts, for whom attainment of a certain quantity of work can be prescribed, should feel that they have grounds of complaint, and should be glad to identify themselves with a movement of this kind, But I am somewhat at a loss to understand how Harvard, with its traditions concerning the Doctor's degree, comes to be identified with the movement in question.

Perhaps I am making a great deal out of a rather unimportant matter; but I have for so many years been occupied in contending for a qualitative rather than a quantitative conception of the Doctor's degree, and have relied so much on the support of Harvard in this matter, that I am quite unwilling to proceed in any direction without taking counsel with you.[41]

Eliot replied by stressing the need for a more formally systematic and coordinated relationship between institutions of higher learning and by highlighting the opportunities for exchange that such a conference would provide.

Hadley still remained unconvinced of the meeting's urgency, especially since it fell during Yale's examination period. He explained his situation to the meeting's host, Harper of Chicago.

I wish I saw my way clear toward attending Pres. Wheeler's proposed conference in Chicago on Feb. 27th. It comes at entirely the wrong time for us at Yale and we have not suffered from the particular difficulties which are alleged as a reason for calling a conference. On the other hand, the advantages of such a meeting and interchange of ideas would be very great indeed.[42]

As the meeting drew closer and Hadley learned that other leading institutions would indeed be sending representatives, he felt the need to express his opinions on the subject even if absent from the conference. He offered regrets for the inability of himself or anyone from Yale to come to Chicago for the meeting, as no one had "leisure at this especially busy season." Hadley "doubly" regretted this fact "as much cooperation and free interchange of thought between the heads of different universities is at present desirable." He concluded, "I shall hope to have the opportunity to address a letter to the conference dealing with the points included in the call."[43]

Hadley took the opportunity he desired and authored a lengthy statement of Yale's position, addressed to all of the meeting's attendees. Hadley prefaced his statement by attaching a brief note to Wheeler, the conference's organizer:

It [Yale's position] is stated with a definiteness which may sound rather abrupt. I am sure that you will understand that this does not spring from any want of the spirit of cooperation, but that it is solely the result of our desire to leave no doubt as to our position on the points in question.[44]

Hadley's definitiveness was clear. In addressing the conference attendees, Hadley stressed, as he had in private correspondence, Yale's desire to "cooperate in matters of common interest." However, he also wished to offer questions in regard to the purposes for calling the meeting. First, he stated that he found it

> difficult to believe that [quoting from the conference announcement] "the time has arrived when the leading American universities may properly consider the means of representing to foreign universities the importance of revising their regulations governing the admission of American students to the examination for higher degrees."

"Such a step," Hadley argued, "unless very carefully considered, and based on irrefutable evidence of its need, might readily be regarded, and perhaps properly regarded, as an intrusion."[45]

The request of foreign universities to revise their standards was only a portion of Hadley's concern. He also questioned the primary issue on the conference's agenda—securing "such credit as is legitimately due to the advanced work done in our own universities of high standing." Building on his first point of concern, Hadley worried that American universities might offend their European counterparts, especially if the group acted on what he saw as unsupported allegations. He not only took issue with the conference's approach to foreign universities; he also expressed doubts regarding the specifics of any systemization geared toward allowing migration of students from one university to another. Questioning the invitation's stated desire to "secure uniformity" among the leading universities, Hadley stated:

> If by this is meant that our universities should adopt rules stating that a student who has already studied a certain number of years, or taken a certain number of majors and minors, in one university can presumably get his degree in a certain specified length of time at some other university, the authorities at Yale would be compelled to question the wisdom of this proposal; inasmuch as it would mean a departure from the qualitative standard, and a reversion to the quantitative one against which they have for forty years protested.[46]

Hadley reiterated that he did not object to formalized coordination. Rather, speaking for the faculty of Yale as well as himself, Hadley concluded that he simply wished to urge caution and to warn against hasty decisions.

Despite specific concerns, Hadley and Yale did not object to the overall purpose or general principles of the conference. Therefore, when formal invitations to AAU membership were extended after the first Chicago conference, Hadley accepted on behalf of Yale "with great pleasure." He did, however, note that since the annual meeting date was set once again for the same time of year, it would be difficult for he or a Yale representative to attend. He politely requested that an alternative date be considered in the future.[47]

Wheeler's 1899 call for a conference had quickly evolved into a formally aligned organization comprised of the leading universities from across the country. All of the invitees aside from Yale, Cornell, and Wisconsin attended the 1900 meeting, and all accepted membership in the organization. The AAU's constitution described the organization as having been "founded for the purpose of considering matters of common interest relating to graduate study." While coordination was integral to the association's activities, the AAU's constitution stressed that "no act of the association shall be held to control the policy or line of action of any institution belonging to it." Recognizing the association's position as a collection of elite institutions and seeking to establish the association as the standard-bearer for advanced degrees, the AAU's members developed a clear procedure for future membership: "Other institutions may be admitted, at the annual conference, on the invitation of the executive committee, endorsed by a 3/4 vote of the association."[48] The association did not, however, clearly define the standards for membership, leaving open the question of who might have the requisite common interest in graduate study. The nation's primary arbiters of standards and practices for advanced knowledge and university-based expertise were self-policing.

After unanimously agreeing to form an association from the invited conference members, delegates to the AAU's first meeting set an agenda for the next year's meeting. Proposed topics included a continued discussion of student migration, an examination of fellowships, an assessment of subordinate requirements for the doctoral degree, and the printing of dissertations.[49] It was decided that to facilitate consideration of these matters, Harper, who was serving as the association's chairman, should appoint for each topic an individual educator to prepare a statement of facts concerning the major issues involved.

Having formally established the association and set an agenda for the next meeting, attendees also took action on a number of matters. They decided not to send association representation to the Paris World Exposition and not to seek legislation from Congress regarding the acceptance of graduate degrees abroad. Despite Hoyt's request of

Angell and others that his national university proposal be considered, there is no record of the matter being addressed.

From the outset, the AAU was concerned with national policy. Though its influence was limited, the Bureau of Education had been invited and did send a representative to attend the meetings. However, rather than work through the federal government and its agencies, the association wished to work with foreign universities and educational ministers directly. In this manner, the AAU began to develop its significant role as an independent agent of the federal state, establishing what would come to be national standards and policies.

Establishing Credentials: Formal Alignment and the Certification of Expertise

Graduate education would grow in the early years of the twentieth century, and so would the significance and reach of the AAU. In the year after its founding, the AAU continued to examine one of the three issues that had been articulated in Wheeler's initial invitation—graduate student migration—as well as several specific issues pertinent to graduate education: fellowships, the publication of dissertations, and the course work required of doctoral students.[50] Again held in Chicago and hosted by Harper and the University of Chicago, the meetings were attended by all of the association's members except for Yale. The previously skeptical Hadley had expected to attend but was called back to New Haven due to his young daughter's having contracted what was feared to be a deadly case of pneumonia.[51]

The association's scope was limited in this initial period, compared to what it would become. However, the 1901 meeting marked the beginning of a formal annual meeting of university leaders who had until this time shared information and expectations mainly through a loosely coupled network based on position and friendships. The AAU was not the first gathering of such men as Eliot, Harper, and Angell; many of the presidents of AAU institutions were also active participants in the NEA. However, the NEA meetings were large, pluralist affairs where the course of graduate education and university-based expertise were only minor concerns. With the formation of the AAU, these leading academics had developed an organization dedicated exclusively to their collective agenda.

At the close of the 1901 meetings in Chicago, it was agreed that the association's 1902 meetings should be held in New York City, with Columbia's Nicholas Murray Butler serving as chairman. The proposed agenda reflected the association's efforts to expand its scope as well as its desire to more fully define its nature and purpose. Even before the 1901 meetings in Chicago, Michigan's Angell had expressed to Harper his wish to see the AAU's membership consider "the scope and character of the dissertation required for the degree of Doctor of Philosophy."[52] This topic became the first item on the agenda for the 1902 meetings, coupled with a continuation of the discussion regarding whether there should be a requirement that the doctoral dissertation be printed.

On the one hand, it seems somewhat remarkable that a little over forty years since Yale awarded the first American PhD (in 1861), no standardized requirements for the content or presentation of the doctoral degree had been established. On the other hand, it should be remembered that the number of PhD's granted by American universities remained relatively small. More important, the informal network of loosely coupled university presidents meant that while no formal standards for the doctorate had been set, the elite universities were familiar with one another's training of graduate students and with the research and expertise they produced. For its first thirty years, the PhD been essentially the exclusive property of these elite institutions, and no need for standardization or formal requirements existed. The end of the twentieth century had witnessed a significant rise in the number of institutions calling themselves universities and granting the PhD. In the most extreme case, the relatively obscure Gale College in Wisconsin awarded fifteen doctorates in 1900; this was equal to the combined number of PhD's granted by California, Cornell, Michigan, Princeton, and Virginia in the same year.[53] The institutional entrepreneurs who ran universities needed to clearly define advanced degrees and protect one of their distinguishing features. These schools did this not only for themselves but also to further establish the authority of these credentials.

Formalizing Peers: The Question of Membership

The creation of the AAU provided academic leaders a unique opportunity to bring definition and clarity not only to advanced degrees but to their universities overall. In order to accomplish this, the members of the AAU needed to give greater definition and clarity to the association itself. The second item on the 1902 agenda would help in this regard. The AAU's executive committee, comprised of Michigan's Angell, Columbia's Butler, Chicago's Harper, and California's Wheeler, was charged with reporting to the association regarding its membership policy.

The committee was to focus primarily on two questions:

1) Should the membership be enlarged? If so, on what principle of selection?
2) Should the association devote its attention wholly to questions concerned with the organization and conduct of graduate work; and if so, should graduate work in law, medicine, theology, and applied science be included?[54]

Though the two questions were not necessarily dependent on one another, they were related. The criteria and procedures for membership would certainly influence the scope of the association. Conversely, the prescribed scope of the association would influence both the who and the how of future membership. The executive committee recognized this relationship but sought to keep the issues distinct.

Reporting to the full membership at the 1902 annual meeting, the committee began its report by stressing that the matters referred for its consideration involved "two separate questions." The committee reversed the order of the questions from how they had been presented to them. They thus began by addressing "the range of topics which should be treated by the association in its discussions, and the desirableness of a change in the constitution to provide for such increased range." On this topic, there was little difference of opinion among committee members. Generally, it was "thought desirable to include within the scope of the discussions of the association all those questions and problems which arise in organizing really advanced instruction in the various departments of university life."[55]

The committee saw little reason to distinguish between advanced knowledge and expertise applied to "academic" questions, on the one hand, and advanced knowledge and expertise applied to professional ones, on the other. Stressing this point, the committee continued:

> It is impossible to draw a distinction between university studies which are non-professional and those which are professional in their character; because in our modern institutions much of the so-called non-professional work of the graduate departments is intended as a preparation for the calling of the teacher, and much of the work of the professional schools is occupied with actual research. The problems of the different departments are so connected and interwoven that they have to be treated together in the universities themselves; and it seems desirable that a body like the Association should treat them in the same way.

For the committee, extending the reach of the association from purely graduate studies to professional ones was a natural step that mirrored the development of universities themselves. To not include the consideration of questions regarding professional education would have been to develop an artificial and unnecessary division. Thinking that the relationship between graduate and professional education was so apparent as not to necessitate a change in the AAU's constitution, the committee stated, "the very fact that the different things are thus necessarily connected is of itself sufficient to justify the treating of these wider problems as germane to the original purposes of the Constitution."[56]

The first step in expanding the reach of the association had been taken. The membership unanimously supported the committee's recommendation. The AAU had stepped forward as an organization that would set national standards not only for graduate education but for professional education as well. Thus, in the years to come, the AAU and its members, not the federal state, would primarily define national standards for advanced knowledge and its related credentials.[57] Strikingly, it was 1909 before the association finally issued a full and comprehensive report on the whole of academic nomenclature. At this time, the AAU's decision to extend itself into matters of professional education marked a significant step in the development of formal alignment among elite universities and their activities as active partners and independent agents of the national state.

The committee presented a clear and definite recommendation in regard to the scope of the association, but it was unclear and conflicted in regard to "the policy to be adopted with regard to increasing the membership of the Association, in order that the numerous applications submitted to this body may be wisely and intelligently handled." In fact, the executive committee reported to be split, with two equally valid, but opposing, lines of argument.

The report summarized proponents of expansion as follows:

> Those who advocate an increase say it is unjust to institutions which are doing excellent work to leave them out of a body of this kind. They think that the effect of omitting these institutions will be to prejudice the influence of the Association, to stimulate jealously, and perhaps to lead to the formation of a rival body which should be more extended in its scope.[58]

Concern regarding competing associations was genuine, especially in terms of public institutions. That previous summer, merger discussions had taken place between the National Association of State Universities and the Association of American Agricultural Colleges and Experiment Stations.[59] Like Hoyt's attempts to establish a national university, these merger efforts recognized the ever-increasing importance of formal national coordination. If the AAU were to be the preeminent coordinating organization, proponents of expansion argued, it would need to ensure that it was broad enough so as to legitimately oversee the advancement of knowledge and the definition of expertise through the development of uniform standards and practices.

Opponents of AAU expansion stressed the value of exclusivity and familiarity that they believed allowed for candor and encouraged relevance. To them, the association's small size was simply a reflection of the small number of "true" universities who could contribute to discussion regarding graduate education. The original members were included in the association because of their value and contribution as peers. Additionally, opponents of an increase feared that expanding membership would place the AAU in the distasteful position of having to make formal and public judgments on petitioning institutions. They did not see any need to publicly declare the requirements for membership. Instead, they believed the association to be detached from the public view. The report summarized:

> Those who oppose such increases of membership say that the value of the discussions which we have hereto had is in large measure the result of the smallness of the membership; and that any attempt to admit all those institutions whose claims we cannot publicly disprove would make the body so large as to interfere with its original purpose.[60]

For opponents of expansion, broadening the scope of the association did not necessarily imply a need to increase the membership. Both sides in the debate expected and welcomed the fundamental role the AAU would play in shaping American higher education. Their differences grew from competing visions of how the association would go about developing this role.

Understanding that the question concerned more than simply an increase in the number of members, the committee recapitulated the issues at the core of the debate.

> The real question seems to be one concerning this fundamental purpose. Is our body an organized association, intended to take in all who reach a certain grade of merit, and charged with the duty of establishing an objective grading of standing among universities? Or is it a club for mutual improvement and enjoyment, without the necessity of telling them the reasons for this exclusion in a form for publication? Accordingly as we regard the association in the one light or the other, our policy with regard to membership will be totally different.[61]

With an understanding of the stakes involved, the executive committee did not recommend a specific course of action. Instead, it unanimously called for further discussion and deliberation, effectively tabling all proposed expansion for at least a year.[62] The new association continued to evolve, from a simple conference called to discuss the acceptance of American degrees abroad in 1900 to a formal association highly aware of its growing importance and stature only a few years later.

Even with unanimous approval of the executive committee's recommendations regarding further deliberations on the subject, the fires of controversy still surrounded the question of membership. Responding to the request of a number of members—notably, Columbia's Butler and Yale's Hadley—regarding the timing of the meetings, the 1903 annual meeting was held on December 29 and 30, 1902. The meetings were again held in New York. For the first time, in conjunction with the meetings, an alumni dinner was held for graduates of AAU institutions. Seemingly an ancillary event, this dinner would ignite arguably the most vociferous and detailed attack on the association in its formative years.

Among those invited to the dinner were a number of alumni who now served on the faculty of New York University (NYU). A little over eighteen months earlier, NYU had asked to be considered for membership in the AAU, but no offer—and essentially no explanation for the absence of an offer—was extended from the association. In response to the invitation for the alumni dinner, the faculty took the opportunity to issue an open letter, addressed to the committee sponsoring the dinner but also published in the *New York Times* and delivered to the presidents of AAU institutions "as one(s) who may be interested in its subject matter."[63]

The faculty began by offering their regrets and rationale.

> The undersigned professors of New York University respectfully acknowledge your invitation for Tuesday December 30th. We regret that we cannot take part in the dinner because of what seems to us to be the policy of the Association. For this apparent policy we recognize that your Committee is in no way responsible, since it has no official connection with that body. Yet as you are seeking to serve the Association, we will frankly describe this seeming policy which forbids professors of New York University accepting your invitation.

Rather than simply decline the invitation, the NYU faculty detailed the history of their efforts to join the association.

> Early in 1901 the New York University Senate presented to the Association the question of admission of other Universities than those represented at the first meeting, and the question of the conditions of membership in the Association. It was not until after a very long delay and the sending by us of an urgent reminder that any report was received from President Harper of

Chicago, the secretary, in regard to the action taken by the Association at their meeting, March, 1901, in response to the communication of the University which we have the honor of serving. The report when received failed to present any complete statement in regards to the conditions of membership in the Association, and why certain Universities are admitted while others are not admitted.

The faculty then took the opportunity to specify their grievances and outline criticisms of the membership policy. For NYU's faculty, the AAU's treatment of their application represented undue exclusivity and bordered on being a monopoly. They stated this position in no uncertain terms.

This University doubts both the academic expediency and the moral right under these circumstances, of a few Universities assuming such an exclusive title as "The Association of American Universities." It is suggestive of the methods of the commercial combines of our day (against which the Government is now proposing to move in order to secure greater publicity), much more than of the open liberal methods of the greater Universities of the world. We feel that we cannot in any way support or wish success to the Association until it frankly announces worthy conditions by the fulfillment of which any American University may become entitled to membership.

While the NYU professors were not directly aware of the debate within the association regarding its membership practices, they were cognizant of the fact that some members wished to expand the organization. The NYU faculty concluded their letter, "we may add that letters received by New York University nearly two years ago, from the presidents of several of the Universities included in the Association, conveyed to us the impression that they were in sympathy with the position which is taken by New York University."[64]

Despite the pleadings of the NYU faculty, it would still be another two years before the AAU expanded its membership. When it did, it was the University of Virginia, not NYU, that was asked to join. The association still considered institutions on a case-by-case basis and refused to establish any criteria for membership, other than the approval of three-quarters of the institutional members. NYU's membership in the association (1950) would be many years in coming.

The NYU faculty members were unsuccessful in their appeal. However, they had been fair in assessing the association's unique position. None of its members would characterize the association as an academic monopoly or cartel. However, there remained some conflict over the organization's exclusivity. Associated with these concerns was an overall recognition of the potential influence of the association. Though not necessarily founded to counter the national university movement or other efforts at standardization and coordination, the AAU became the preferred alternative. Over the next fifteen years, the association, institutionalizing a formal alliance among the leading universities, would come to define national standards not only for graduate and professional schools but for all of higher education.

Extending the Influence and Reach of Elite Institutions

In 1904, the leading universities were among those supporting an enlargement of the federal Bureau of Education and an elevation of its status through the formation of a department of commerce and labor, within which the Bureau of Education could be housed. Writing a confidential letter to his colleague Nicholas Murray Butler, Chicago's William Rainey Harper noted that he had recently discussed this effort with Charles Eliot and other members of the association. In conjunction with general support for the plan, there existed a belief that such an effort could not be effectively undertaken if the aging William T. Harris remained commissioner of education. Harper recounted:

> certain questions were presented which involved the future tenure of office of Mr. Harris. As a matter of fact, it seems impossible to go forward with the enlargement of that bureau and the securing for that bureau its proper recognition by the government so long as Mr. Harris occupies the position. His great worth and value are acknowledged from the educational point of view, but his ability as an administrator is questioned.

Harper proposed what essentially amounted to a buyout plan.

> He is now an old man and the question has been suggested whether a few universities might not unite in inviting him to occupy a lectureship on educational questions which would make provision for him for a few years, and constitute a call to a higher work than that which he is now doing.[65]

Harper's plan called for offering Harris somewhere between twelve to fifteen lectures a year, with the reasonable stipend of six hundred dollars per lecture. Butler replied by saying that he held such an appreciation for what Harris had "done for education in this country and his intellectual gifts" that he would with pleasure urge the trustees of Columbia to offer Harris a lectureship.[66] Butler passed Harper's note and his own reply along to Yale's Arthur Twining Hadley, with the request that Yale participate in the scheme as well.[67]

Despite the efforts of Harper and Butler, the effort to move the Bureau of Education out of the Department of the Interior never gathered any steam. Harris would remain commissioner of education for another two years. The discussion between Harper and Butler represented the dependency federal educational policies and administration had on the established universities. Their failure did not detract from the attempts of the nation's most prominent universities to develop collective influence.

University presidents were often the ones who would direct government's relationship to America's institutions of higher learning. The foundation of the AAU marked the beginning of formal alignment and the institutionalization of coordination. Over the next twenty years, federal policies would be further shaped by the pursuit and application of research and expertise. The AAU did not drive all such efforts, but through their training of scholars, their prominent public positions, and their active efforts to maintain societal relevance, the institutions of the AAU came to define standards for American higher education as a regulatory agency, if not to arguably serve as branches of a "national university." A contemporary observer might think of these in opposition. However, emanating from the founding framework of the University of Michigan[68] and other public institutions of higher learning, many public universities were established to serve as regulators as well as educators. The collection of institutions that comprised the AAU helped define education not only for themselves and their states but for the developing nation as a whole.

7   Working for Service

The Rise of Formal Alignment
and the Furtherance of Agency

Entering the twentieth century, the nation's elite universities continued to grow in both the size of their programs and the breadth of their investigations. Correspondent to this internal growth was an expansion of the university's relationship with the national state. More students, more subjects, and more research meant more opportunities to develop active partnerships and to serve as independent agents.

The formation of the Association of American Universities greatly facilitated this expansion. When institutional entrepreneurs sought to develop new programs and demonstrate new relevancy in conjunction with the federal state, they could quickly bring their colleagues on board. Similarly, when working in place of (rather than in conjunction with) the federal government when extending the reach of the national state, the AAU served to bring elite universities together in a more formal manner than through personal friendships. The formation and emergence of the AAU did not mean that university presidents lost their intimacy and personal connections. Instead such intimacy and personal connections were now supplemented by a formal organizational structure that not only facilitated but also encouraged collective action.

Defining Alignment: Coordination and Competition

To understand the relationship between universities and the American state, we must assess not only the relationship itself but the context of its development. While the turn of the century was recognized as a milestone, the mere turn of the calendar did not drive the creation of new programs and the growth of others. In addition to responding to various forces of governmental and societal complexity, the institutional entrepreneurs who ran American higher education were driven by dynamic forces in their own domain as well. The rise of multiple higher education organizations and disciplinary associations encouraged formal coordination and facilitated service to and on behalf of the state. The growth of elite universities was accompanied by the individual development of their national presence and the correspondent rise in competition among peers. These seemingly opposed, but actually reinforcing, forces of coordination and competition drove universities to work with the developing American state.

The AAU was not the first formal organization of universities and colleges. America's land-grant colleges created the Association of American Agricultural Colleges and Experiment Stations (AAACES) in 1887. Formed as an offshoot of the National Educational Association[1] and headed by University of Mississippi president Robert Fulton, the National Association of State Universities (NASU) was formed in 1895. The NASU included Morrill institutions as well as state universities—such as Fulton's—that were not beneficiaries of the Morrill grants but that had been supported by earlier "seminary of learning" grants.

Though these two organizations predated the AAU, their initial influence and interaction with the national state was generally limited. First, since they represented exclusively public institutions, the AAACES and the NASU were unable to claim that they spoke for higher education as a whole. Second, their public focus meant that these organizations did not count some of the nation's oldest and most influential institutions—that is, Harvard, Yale, and Columbia—among their members. Finally and perhaps most significant, neither association had the flagship institutions of their class as active members. The role of the land-grant institution Cornell University in the AAACES was marginal at best. The nation's foremost "seminary" institutions—the Universities of California, Michigan, and Wisconsin—did not even attend the 1900 NASU meetings.[2]

Managing Competition: The AAU and Rationales for Alignment

A supposedly elitist organization would impact the definition of higher education most significantly and most broadly. The AAU was not the only association attempting to align the institutions of higher education. It would be the only one whose influence would extend far beyond its own membership and that would look to the federal state as an active partner rather than simply as a wealthy patron. The AAU would not only coordinate relations between the nation's leading universities and set standards for all of higher education, but it would take the lead in defining universities' relationship with the national state as well.

Not all university efforts were coordinated. Formal alignment took time to develop, and many university-government efforts remained focused on individual institutions. Additionally, competition continued between the leading universities. Noticeable tensions arose as newer wealthy institutions, such as Rockefeller's University of Chicago and Leland Stanford's Stanford University, arrived on the scene at the same time as established universities sought to take on a greater national presence. These tensions both resulted from and ramped up institutional entrepreneurship. The AAU was not founded as a mediating organization, but its attempts at coordination served as a counterweight to this modern push of institutional competition.

The University of Chicago and Stanford University were recently founded institutions with sizable endowments and generous benefactors. In keeping with the polite demeanor of the period as well as with their personal familiarity with the universities' leadership, presidents of other established institutions often offered advice and guidance to these fledgling schools. Notably, the institutions most often called on to offer such advice and guidance were the two that these new schools most directly challenged, the Universities of Michigan and California.

Michigan and California were quick to share and treated these newer institutions as peers. However, they also privately worried about the threat Chicago and Stanford posed. Berkeley's Benjamin Ide Wheeler, writing to Michigan's James Burill Angell regarding their individual efforts to secure funding from the state, summarized such sentiments: "It will be very unfortunate for the state university idea if the University of Michigan is at this late date outridden by a private institution like that at Chicago. We have the same danger before us in the case of Stanford."[3]

Due to its more established reputation, its national presence, and its geographic distance from Chicago, Michigan was not as overtly threatened by the University of Chicago's presence as Berkeley was by Stanford's. Angell's son, James Rowland Angell, even took his first faculty position at Chicago. Michigan did keep a competitive awareness of its rival to the west. James Burrill Angell sustained a statesmanlike detachment from such concerns, but others, such his Board of Regents, kept a protective watch over Michigan's institutional position. For example, to Angell's general inquiry regarding rumors of a University of

Chicago plan to buy the Michigan Military Academy in 1903 for use as an annex, Regent Levi Barbour responded with a lengthy complaint regarding Chicago's perceived encroachment on Michigan's territory. Barbour explained that he had not heard of such a plan but had heard of a Chicago plan to buy Kalamazoo College. More significantly, Barbour saw a pattern.

> The establishment of a private school in Detroit, practically under the wing of Chicago, the purchase of the Military Academy, the ardent work they are doing to proselyte the West shore of the state and the upper peninsula are attempts which would seem quite properly to excite our jealousy and indicate rather an over buying disposition.

Barbour also reported that the university had established a presence in Michigan through extension courses by its professors and addresses by its administrators. Coupled with Chicago's purchases, Barbour feared that such activity "may lead our citizens to forget that Michigan has a university." Barbour confessed that his disposition was "wicked enough" to rejoice in Chicago's failed attempt to create a private school in Battle Creek and expressed his belief that the Military Academy would not pay as a school.[4]

Angell might not have shared his regent's "wickedness," but he did recognize the potential influence of a wealthy competitor and sought to work actively with, rather than against, it. Angell and Harper would confer on everything from faculty hiring practices to how to rein in what they viewed as the scourge of football. Berkeley's Wheeler and Stanford's David Starr Jordan also shared administrative and academic questions. Of the major associations, the AAU was the only one to include both public and private universities; thus, while it did not initiate coordination and agreement between potential competitors, it did a great deal to further their agreement.

Institutional competition was not solely between older public institutions and newer private ones. Even the oldest and most established of the nation's universities took notice of the activities and appearance of peer institutions. Such notice was not always favorable. For example, in response to a request that his university participate in the upcoming Paris Exposition, Yale's president Arthur Twining Hadley complained to J. Howard Rogers, the director of education and social policy for the U.S. delegation, about the nature of university exhibits at the last major world's exposition: "Most of the things at Chicago which were called educational exhibits from higher institutions of learning were not educational exhibits at all, but simply displays of wealth."[5] He noted that because the university's corporation did not wish to compete in terms of wealth and have the exhibit simply be a show of material resources, the university was unlikely to partake in the event.

Hadley might have scoffed at others' displays of wealth, but he and his institution's alumni recognized the need for active fund-raising. Not long after taking over as Yale's president, he undertook efforts to establish a fund to coincide with Yale's bicentennial anniversary, in 1901. Though not a public capital campaign, it represented Hadley's first active attempt to raise funds to secure and further Yale's position. Reflecting a developing approach of institutional entrepreneurs, Hadley sought funds and secured challenge gifts from a variety of wealthy benefactors. Through the generosity of such alumni as Cornelius Vanderbilt, William Crocker, and others (including a small gift from the University of Chicago's benefactor, John Rockefeller), Hadley was able to raise two million dollars. While impressive and certainly the most money ever raised by his school, Hadley would soon learn that his fund-raising was not enough to keep pace with Yale's primary competitors.

Gifford Pinchot, whose family's generosity and own efforts had only a few years before been instrumental in the creation of Yale's forestry school, wrote of a meeting he had recently had with Bishop Laurence, president of the Harvard Alumni Association. Laurence had mentioned to Pinchot that a Harvard alumni committee was currently raising $2.5 million for additional faculty and salaries. For Pinchot, this triggered memories of a conversation with Hadley during the bicentennial fund drive. Pinchot had suggested pursuing more than twice the target of two million dollars in order for Yale "to keep pace with similar institutions which are making such notable progress all over the country in general equipment for their work." Both men would eventually conclude that such a figure was unrealistic. However, in light of Harvard's effort, Pinchot felt it was "absolutely essential to the welfare of the university that it should meet, by conspicuous progress on its part, the very notable steps in advance which are being made by so many of the other universities of the country and especially by Harvard." Pinchot did not wish to seem intrusive but did want to stress his belief that Yale needed to step up its fund-raising if it were to maintain its position.

> You will not, of course, misunderstand me by thinking that I have lost faith in the slightest degree either in the present or in the future of Yale. I have not. But it seems to me obvious that if Yale is to continue to hold her place in the very front rank of American institutions of learning, and is not to be sup-

planted in her standing and influence, some definite and successful effort must be made to raise the funds without which the equipment of Yale can neither be placed nor be kept on a level with that of the more progressive of her sister institutions.[6]

Having worked closely with Pinchot on developing Yale's forestry school, Hadley did not misunderstand him, and Yale quietly undertook another sizable fund-raising effort.

Yale's rivalry with Harvard was by no means unidirectional. As he had already done a few years earlier, Harvard's Charles Eliot was quick to criticize Yale's academic reforms of the period. Writing to Michigan's James Burrill Angell in anticipation of a visit to Ann Arbor, Eliot offered his critique.

> Yale is simply repeating the precise steps which succeeded each other here in the development of the elective system, but she is repeating them at the interval of from twenty-five to thirty years, during which she has lost a great deal of ground in the university race. The most curious fact about it is that the men concerned with these changes at Yale seem to have an impression that they themselves invented them.

As bemused as he was by Yale's administration, Eliot was equally baffled by the response of Yale alumni, a number of whom objected to such reform: "we have a large number of young Yale graduates in our Law School, and the sentiment among them is distinctly adverse to the recent changes at Yale. They seem to think that Yale had better stand still—a suicidal policy to my thinking."[7]

In addition to Yale's curricular "reforms" and the objections of its alumni, Eliot also was puzzled, or one might say offended, by the fact that the dean of Yale's divinity school had begun actively trying to attract students to New Haven.

> One curious development at Yale is the adoption of the drummer policy at their Divinity School. The present Dean of that school gives most of his time to travelling for the purpose of direct solicitation of recruits for his school. We are all accused of indirect advertising, and there is some truth in these accusations, but the frank adoption of the commercial traveler system seems to me an undesirable novelty.[8]

To contemporary observers, accustomed to large admission offices staffed by a multitude of recruiters, Eliot's comments might seem quaint and anachronistic. However, just as telling as his criticism of Yale's divinity school dean was his admission of indirect advertising. As Eliot notes, most all of the leading universities were taking a more active role in managing their public image. In part, such concern stemmed simply from the universities' sheer size and national presence. However, underlying such efforts was an emerging institutional competition. With regional monopolies weakening, universities were more actively competing for students, dollars, and even, as I will discuss in chapter 8, federal partnerships.

The extent to which universities protected their national presence and compared themselves to one another could be seen in an exchange between James Burrill Angell and Arthur Twining Hadley. As the elder statesman of university presidents, Angell almost always stayed above the fray, often receiving combative words regarding other schools, but rarely (if ever) offering them. However, in response to a Cincinnati speech by Hadley in which the Yale president allegedly referred to the "local constituency and provincialism of Western state universities," Angell offered a lengthy defense in his university's alumni magazine. Granting that Hadley very well might have been misquoted, Angell still set out to show the diverse constituency of the Michigan student body, a constituency "more national than many Eastern colleges." Using the 1905–6 Yale catalog and the 1906–7 University of Michigan catalog, which were the latest he could obtain, Angell did an enrollment comparison (see table 3).[9]

Angell was quick to point out that Michigan had seventy-six students from New England, and he suggested that his institution's size might account for the larger percentage of in-state students. Defending western institutions as well as his own, Angell noted:

It may be maintained that the University of Michigan is exceptional among western institutions. But an exactly similar condition of things stands at the University of Chicago. The truth is that certain colleges in the East, like certain others in the West, have a constituency almost wholly local in character. But there are certain western colleges where the constituency is quite as cosmopolitan as that of any of their eastern colleagues.

TABLE 3.   Angell's Michigan/Yale Comparison

	Michigan	Yale
Students	4,836	3,806
States represented	All 48	All 48
U.S. territories represented	3	2
Foreign countries represented	17	16
Students in state (%)	50	33
Pennsylvania students	181	188
New York students	299	603
Ohio students	408	135
Illinois students	315	147

Angell concluded with a wry comment on the nature of provincialism.

> Moreover, it is well in this connection to recall what a clever writer recently has said of the Hub—"Boston is not a place—it is a state of mind." So provincialism is not determined by topography and geography. It is an affair of the mind, and if, as it is urged, it is chiefly characterized by a hypersensitiveness to one's own virtues, it seems improbable that the West has or soon will have any monopoly of it.[10]

Hadley, appropriately chastened, was contrite in his response, simply apologizing for any misunderstanding and stressing that his comments were certainly not meant to refer to Michigan or any other of the leading universities of the West. Hadley's comments had riled Angell a tad, but they were soon forgotten. A little over two years later, Angell wrote Hadley to praise his annual report as "excellent" and to express his strong agreement with Hadley's emphasis on the importance of professors teaching as well as conducting research.[11]

While rarely overtly contentious, rivalries certainly existed among many of the nation's leading universities. Institutional competition crossed many divides: old/new, east/west, and public/private. Institutional competition also greatly influenced two forces that defined the universities' relationship to the national state, entrepreneurship and coordination. University leaders actively pursued new opportunities, often in regard to government service, with a desire to develop and maintain their institution's national stature. As rivalries grew, so did the push toward formal coordination. Recognizing the danger and difficulties of unbridled competition, universities continued to work together informally and established structures that aligned their interests more formally.

Reflecting the overlap between entrepreneurship, coordination, and public service, the chair of the 1909 reunion of alumni of the Massachusetts Institute of Technology, James Munoz, wrote Angell to ask him to join a variety of leaders in offering a few words to those who would be gathered. Munoz stressed that the alumni association wished to encourage a greater sense of service and that they felt Angell would be just the person to help do that: "We are urging the Institute to emulate those universities in direct service to the upbuilding of the state and nothing could help us more than to have the greatest president, and the chiefest builder, come to the gathering of our alumni."[12] Competition was not necessarily an explicit reason for such emulation, but the leading universities had set a variety of formal and informal standards for institutional activity, and ambitious schools, such as MIT, were quick to learn and follow.

Education and Agency: Universities, National Standards, and the Rise of Formal Alignment

In the later half of the nineteenth century, informal cooperation had been essential to university efforts to define national standards and expectations for both secondary and higher education. The continuation of this systemization of American education at the beginning of the twentieth century was greatly assisted by the formal alignment of elite universities through the AAU. Additionally, the AAU worked closely with the burgeoning private foundations—most notably, the one established by Andrew Carnegie—to ensure that these standards reached more than its own members. Their serving as standard-bearer for all of education meant that the reach of America's elite universities stretched broadly across the nation.

The prestige and position of these institutions and their entrepreneurial leaders enhanced their influence over educational policy, the development of professions, and a variety of other public initiatives. Their prestige was enhanced by cooperation and coordination, which furthered the development of a national system of education. This system still reflected local differences, but it established more rationalized structures and uniform procedures across the country. Not directly supported by the federal state, the universities' efforts at rationalization and standardization were tacitly sanctioned by it. As independent agents of the national state, universities continued the practice, begun with the Morrill Act, of not only working in conjunction with the federal state but broadening policy initiatives independently.

Continuing Agency, Limited Formalization: Universities and Secondary Education

High school accreditation, examination boards, and admission by diploma were the primary mechanisms by which universities helped set national education standards in the later half of the nineteenth century. These systems of admissions both established and elevated expectations for secondary schools. By 1900, a loosely coupled, but highly influential, national system had evolved, with the nation's leading universities acting as independent agents of the American state.

The general expansion and growing complexity of education led to calls for more formalized arrangements. Existing organizations, such as the National Educational Association and the Middle States Examination Board, sought to expand the scope of their activities. Newly founded organizations, such as the AAU, expanded opportunities for meetings and discussion and demonstrated the possibilities of formal alignment. Upon his inauguration, Yale's Arthur Twining Hadley encountered this push toward nationalization when, just weeks into office, he was asked by A. S. Downing, principal of the New York City Training School and chairman of the NEA's Department of Superintendence, to address the NEA's annual meeting that coming February. The invitation had been forwarded by Nicholas Murray Butler of Columbia University, which had incorporated a teachers college within its institution just one year before. Butler noted that between 750 and 1,200 of the nation's leading superintendents, principals, and normal school teachers attended the annual meeting every year, with the midwestern delegation being particularly strong. Butler described the meeting as "one of the most important and influential" gatherings of those concerned with secondary education. He stressed that he knew of "no [other] meeting at which educational opinion is more effectively moulded [sic] because those who attend tend to report back at length to their neighbors and colleagues the ideas and plans which have been presented."[13] Hadley respectfully declined the invitation, as it fell during a particularly busy time of year for Yale.

More striking than Hadley's particular decision to attend or not are the limits of the NEA's influence that are belied by Butler's characterization and praise of the association. The NEA could count many of the leading figures of higher and secondary education among its membership, but its size and diversity made authoritative coordination highly difficult. Charles Eliot's efforts to establish a national secondary school curriculum through the Committee of Ten in the mid-1890s was the closest university leaders came to wielding authoritative influence through the organization. By 1900, the NEA was still large and in fact growing, but it was not an effective vehicle for setting national standards in secondary education.

Rather than working through the association, Hadley found himself working within a "personal presidency." Despite the dawn of the modern university, alumni and others would still write to him asking for guidance. For example, in response to an inquiry from the parent of a prospective student, Hadley noted that Yale did not accept diplomas as basis for admission, as all prospective undergraduates were subject to examination. In response to the same parent's question regarding where his son should "prep," Hadley stated that it was "almost invidious to make suggestions" regarding such schools but that he would recommend Andover, Hotchkiss, St Paul's, Hill, Lawrenceville, or Taft.[14]

Hadley's "personal presidency" did not end with advice regarding choice of preparatory school. When asked, he also offered recommendations to parents regarding college selection. Herbert Beecher of Port Townsend, Washington, had written to Hadley explaining that his son wished to be a lawyer and was considering Yale, California, MIT, or Cornell for college. With striking candor, Hadley discounted MIT and Cornell as options—the former because of emphasis on technology, the latter because of the nature of its students.

> I would send him to a college where he will see a great many kinds of people, and not be narrowed down to the study of one specialty. This shuts out a purely technical school like the M.I.T.; which, however excellent in its instruction, does not give a young man contact with men of letters. While Cornell might naturally suggest itself as a compromise between a technical school and a college, in the broader sense, I should not, on the whole, advise his going to that place. The men whom he meets there would be likely to be very different from those with whom he would be thrown into association in after life, if he makes a really successful career as a lawyer.

Hadley could see value in choosing Berkeley or, obviously, Yale. He concluded by stressing that Yale would be his strongest recommendation.

> If he decides to go to an institution on the Pacific coast, he cannot do better than at Berkeley; if he comes East, I think he will meet more kinds of men at Yale, and get at once a clearer foretaste of what is before him in professional life, and a set of acquaints which will be of more services to him in the hard early stages of his career, than he would be likely to do anywhere else.[15]

More striking than Hadley's recommendation is his rationale; it is largely functional and careerist. Throughout his tenure, Hadley would often speak of the need for educational institutions to develop good, moral citizens; but in this particular case, he seems to be appealing to baser instincts.

Beyond the details of these two anecdotes lies a more fundamental fact of the college presidency at the turn of the century. Notwithstanding the expansion of university presidents' institutional roles and missions and their burgeoning relationships with one another as well as with the national state, there still existed a personal—one might say anachronistic—element to their influence. Hadley was far from the only president to receive such letters requesting advice. Other presidents, such as Michigan's James Burrill Angell, would receive letters asking not just for educational advice but for guidance on matters ranging from grammatical usage to the physics of train travel. One might expect such inquiries at a public institution. However, Hadley was guiding a private university. More important, Angell was of an earlier generation, in which such personal attention to any and all inquiries was expected. Hadley came from a younger generation and a more bureaucratic tradition. Yet he still replied to those seeking academic advice, as it was one way in which he could be assured of influencing educational matters. Such personal advice was by no means a substitute for national efforts at standardization. It was, however, a clear indication that even if academic leaders did not necessarily express their views publicly, they did hold strong opinions as to the proper approach to and course of education.

Moving toward "The Big Test": Coordinating Entrance Examinations

The NEA did not offer the most effective mechanism for coordination, but it did offer a significant forum and springboard for ideas. Nicholas Murray Butler returned from the association's 1899 meeting motivated to establish standard entrance examinations among the leading eastern colleges and universities. Until this period, loosely coupled, parallel systems of admission worked reasonably well. While it was not very formally defined and somewhat fragmented regionally, the nation's leading universities had established a broad national standard for admission that, in turn, had the effect of regulating secondary education. No one trigger event or force led Butler and others to push for more formal alignment and coordination in regard to standards of admission and the corresponding expectations of high schools. However, the increasingly national makeup of the student bodies of the leading universities (with the resulting implicit competition for students), the overall growth of education as a field, and a general push toward formal organization were all contributing factors.

Butler organized a meeting in Trenton, New Jersey, for December 1899. He and his colleagues gave their effort the somewhat unwieldy title "College Entrance Examination Board of the Middle States and Maryland" (hereinafter referred to as the Middle States Board).[16] Meeting again in May 1900, the group adopted a constitution and governing documents. Membership was open to all colleges and universities in the region who had more than fifty freshmen in their incoming class.[17]

Previously, individual institutions had administered examinations and communicated with secondary schools and one another regarding standards and expec ations. The proposal of the Middle States Board did not suggest a new role for universities regulating secondary education. Rather, it was an attempt to bring more formal coordination

among the regulators themselves. Interestingly, unlike almost simultaneous efforts to coordinate regulation of higher education through the
AAU and other organizations (which I will discuss in greater detail
later in this chapter), Butler and his colleagues did not initially attempt
to establish a national system. They recognized the difficulty in immediately replacing the existing parallel systems and instead sought to
graft onto them. They limited their plan to one region, but the ambition
was, from the outset, national. As significant as the nature and ambition of such coordinated efforts was the fact that it was driven by university-based institutional entrepreneurs. National and state government agencies or bureaus were not the primary forces driving
standardization.

Unfortunately for Butler's ambitions, Princeton was quick to declare
its autonomy. President Francis Patton forwarded a faculty statement
to Butler and the Middle States Board. The faculty stressed that they
would not consider "even temporarily" relinquishing the right to
examine students.[18] Recognizing that the plan of the Middle States
Board depended on the quality as well as the quantity of members and
accepting institutions, Butler wrote his friend Arthur Twining Hadley
to describe the effort and to inquire as to Yale's willingness to accept
the results of the board's exams for admission.

Butler stressed to Hadley that though noticeably absent from membership on the Middle States Board, Princeton had agreed to accept the
board's exams for admission. He described the advantages of the Middle States approach, presenting a rough procedural outline of the
exams and maintaining that "for the first time they furnish what has so
long been desired—a uniform test for admission to college upon a prescribed series of subjects." Despite the geographic limits of the initial
membership of the Middle States Board, Butler hoped its exams might
be national in the scope of their acceptance. Recognizing the regional
differences that characterized admissions practices, Butler expressed a
hope that the exams would be used both by schools that admitted on
diploma and by those that admitted on examination.[19]

Saying he always welcomed opportunities for cooperation with his
peers, Hadley expressed cautious interest. He also noted that the Yale
faculty was very unlikely to relinquish the opportunity to examine
prospective students.[20] Butler replied by noting that the Middle States
Board had hoped "it might be possible for the Yale Faculty to attach
such weight to the exams so that they serve as satisfactory alternatives
to the passing of Yale's exams." Butler stressed that the plan was not to
relieve individual institutions of their autonomy through exams that

would lead to the admission of "any student to any college." Rather, he emphasized, plans called for the results to be expressed in percentages, with individual colleges and universities using them as they saw fit. While the Middle States Board would seek to set minimum standards for secondary schools, it would not attempt to standardize universities' expectations. Butler concluded by noting that in reading Yale's catalog, he learned that students who passed Columbia, Harvard, and Princeton's exams were granted unique standing. With this in mind, he hoped the Middle States exams might be granted similar status.[21]

Harboring the doubts he expressed to Butler, Hadley nonetheless remained intrigued by the idea of a coordinated examination board. In fact, soon after the public announcement regarding creation of the Middle States Board, he supported a meeting to consider the formation of an examination board for the New England states; but no formal agreement came of it. Despite his colleague's lobbying, Hadley settled into a position of "wait and see." Summarizing his view, Hadley responded to a Brooklyn reporter's question regarding cooperation between institutions of higher learning by noting that the success or failure of the Middle States effort would greatly influence nascent efforts in New England but that, regardless, "there is sure to be progress toward harmony in requirements." He explained, "This does not mean that every college will require the same amount of study for entrance, but that the requirements of each college, as far as they go, will be framed as nearly as possible on the same lines with its neighbors." Continuing on, Hadley referenced the loosely coupled relationships between institutions, speaking of a "good deal of quiet work" that had been done regarding admissions among the New England schools: "It has not advertised its existence nor passed formal resolutions, but this has made its work more effective rather than less so." As for his colleagues at western schools who worked under a parallel system of admission by diploma, Hadley could only state, "the State Universities of the West are doing such different things that it is impossible to generalize concerning them."[22]

The "quiet work" would continue, but Hadley and others—most notably, Harvard's Charles Eliot—would be frustrated in their efforts to develop more formal coordination among the New England colleges. After a conference of New England colleges in November 1901, Hadley and Eliot both expressed disappointment at their inability to achieve consensus and raise standards. Butler somehow heard of their dissatisfaction and was quick to again offer both institutions a place on the Middle States Board, "in view of the fact that the smaller New England colleges seem to fear so strongly the competition of Yale and Harvard, and since this fear on their part apparently operates to hold them back from any cooperative movement." Butler argued that acceptance of his offer would not require an adjustment in Yale's or Harvard's standards of admission or represent abandonment of the New England effort. In fact, Butler believed that joining Yale and Harvard to the Middle States Board would serve as a catalyst for other institutions of the region. He concluded,

> I cannot help feeling that you would begin to accomplish in New England what we feel that we have already begun to accomplish here, namely, an elevation in standard and change of point of view on the part of institutions that now admit on very easy examinations or no examinations at all."[23]

Hadley and Eliot preferred to remain autonomous in making admissions decisions. However, they also embraced their responsibility to act as an independent agent, helping facilitate the development of national standards for secondary education. It was the mechanism, rather than the mission, that limited Butler's ambitious plan for formal alignment.

Simultaneous to efforts among eastern institutions to coordinate and establish a series of standard examinations, western universities that primarily admitted students on the basis of graduation from a properly accredited high school were also looking to create a more formally organized structure through which they could coordinate their efforts. The North Central Association had been founded in 1895, with a somewhat broad and overly ambitious mission.[24] Through its formative years, the NCA exuded little formal influence. In 1901, attempting to actively pursue its avowed goals of excellence and coordination, the NCA formed the Commission on Accredited Schools. The commission consisted of university leaders and high school principals from across the West.[25] Similar to efforts in the East, these meetings represented a formalization of loosely coupled cooperation regarding accreditation.

By its second meeting, the commission broached the possibility of having the association, rather than individual institutions, make accreditation visits. Michigan was quick to raise objections to the idea. Returning from the NCA meetings, University of Illinois president A. S. Draper wrote James Burrill Angell expressing concern over the NCA's plan. He noted the committee's assurances that it wished not to replace or "take control" of individual institutional inspectors but, rather, simply to ensure greater coordination of visits and so forth. Despite such assurances, Draper was worried that the NCA would seek to take control of the inspections, and he asked Michigan to share in issuing a statement stressing that if that were the case, the leading universities of the West would "not enter into any agreement to act in concert."[26] Angell was quick to state his support for a shared expression of autonomy.[27]

Not unlike Hadley and Yale in their response to shared grading, Angell and Michigan did not object to greater coordination and standardization of expectations but did object to losing the ability to define standards and apply expectations as they saw fit. Western institutions continued to informally consult with one another regarding standards for admission and accreditation of high schools during this push toward more formalized regulation of secondary education. However, as evidenced by the responses of Hadley and Angell, the leading universities' efforts at greater and more universal coordination generated an increased emphasis on—or at least awareness of—institutional autonomy.

In addition to witnessing attempts to create more formalized standards of admission among the eastern and western universities, this era also saw occasional efforts to bring greater uniformity to the two parallel systems of admission. Again, the debate was not over standards; the leading universities of the East did not question the expectations and regulation of secondary schools in the West. Instead, the debate revolved around the mechanism by which these standards would be established, gauged, and enforced.

The 1905 meeting of the NEA's department of education was devoted almost exclusively to considering the relative merits of the "western system of admitting students through certificates from duly inspected secondary schools" and the "eastern method of admitting only by exam." The meeting did little to settle the question. However, it did provide the opportunity for Missouri's R. H. Jesse to recognize Angell as the "father of the Western system." Angell politely demurred, reminding Jesse that this title actually belonged to Angell's predecessor, interim president Henry Simmons Frieze. Underscoring Angell's influence and respect among his peers, Jesse wrote to the Michigan president after the NEA meeting:

> May I politely contradict you—Prof. Frieze may have planted the seed of the idea, but the plant as an effective plant was developed during your administration at Ann Arbor and has spread from Ann Arbor all over the country from the crest of the Allegheny mountains to the shore of the Pacific Ocean. The system is blooming splendidly in Missouri and we copied it consciously from you and from Michigan.[28]

More than simply reflecting the respect and admiration with which western university presidents viewed Angell, Jesse's comments also reflected the challenges facing any efforts at formal coordination among the "admission by diploma" schools. How valuable would meetings regarding the practice be without the active input of its "father"?

Though no formal merger of the two parallel systems took place, competition for students and a desire to maintain a national presence encouraged greater overlap in the practice of admissions that characterized the regions. The leading western schools had always offered the opportunity for students to be admitted by examination and now began to offer exams more frequently and in more locations in the East. Such institutions as Michigan and Wisconsin did not, however, seek to join the examination boards, preferring to continue their autonomy. Conversely, even the most retrograde of institutions, Yale, would become a more active member of the examination boards in 1917, in response to the demands of its Sheffield Scientific School. Additionally, Yale's western alumni complained that the university's unwillingness to modify its examination system greatly hindered efforts to attract qualified students in that region. In 1911, the dean of admissions declared that Yale was "not going to have any certificate system, even if the Western Association of Yale Clubs tells us to."[29] In 1917, however, the school did establish an alternative admissions process by which a student's high school record was considered and the number of exams minimized.

Overlap would have little to do with the formalizing organizations. The North Central Association as well as the Middle States Board and the proponents of a New England examination board had sought to formalize relations between universities and secondary schools. They also had sought to institutionalize the mechanisms by which widely acknowledged but loosely structured national standards could be defined. However, the desire for institutional autonomy meant that university efforts as independent regulating agents were haphazardly piecemeal. Disagreement over mechanisms and a desire for exclusivity meant that formal alignment in regard to secondary schools was limited.

Defining Agency and Self-Regulation: Higher Education, the AAU, and Alignment

Efforts to standardize admission requirements failed primarily because of institutional exclusivity and concerns regarding the nature and depth of coordination. Interestingly, these same forces drove the formation of the AAU and accounted for its success. The AAU emerged from a broader atmosphere of coordination that developed at the very turn of the century. Columbia president Nicholas Murray Butler expressed his sentiments about this atmosphere when writing to James Burrill Angell to thank him for granting leave to one of Michigan's faculty, James Hyslop, so that he might teach at Columbia.

> We are, I am glad to think, entering upon a new era of university life in this country, when the various institutions of the higher learning will come to look upon themselves not as rivals in a struggle for students or for individual influence, but rather as sympathetic and helpful members of one group of cooperating forces in the development of higher civilization. It will be an important stimulus to this development, as well as evidence that it is near at hand, if such representative institutions as Columbia and the University of Michigan can lead the way in bringing about such an interchange of instructors as is suggested.[30]

Butler perhaps overstated the end of competition. However, he did appropriately highlight the need for greater cooperation as well as the role of "representative institutions," such as Michigan and Columbia, in serving as standard-bearers and models for the whole of higher education. Additionally, Butler's suggestion also underscored the demands made by the rise of specialized knowledge and expertise among the faculty and the need for a mechanism to facilitate sharing skilled teachers and researchers. Columbia had no one to teach Hyslop's specialty of politics and ethics and was grateful for his services. Butler stressed, "the time has come when the universities of the country are sufficiently well organized and developed to permit them to undertake the occasional interchange of members of their teaching force." He also expressed his belief that such an exchange was of "great advantage" to the institutions and to professors, who gained a wider outlook and a broader experience.[31]

Demand for cooperation alone would not drive alignment and facilitate agency. The leading universities wished to coordinate with only select institutions and hoped their collective efforts would in turn influence others. Daniel Coit Gilman, upon learning of his nomination to lead the Carnegie Institution, neatly summarized these notions of exclusivity and leadership. Having been informed that Michigan's James Burrill Angell, Harvard's Charles Eliot, and Cornell's Andrew Dickson White were among those who had secured his nomination, he wrote to Angell, "we have lived to see wonderful progress in our highest institutions and Harvard, Cornell, and Michigan stand together in the front line of the marching column."[32]

Unlike examination boards or accreditation agencies, the AAU was not conceived as—nor did it ever attempt to be—an umbrella organization, inclusive of all who wished to participate and who felt the organization was an appropriate vehicle within which to voice their concern. Instead, the AAU was essentially an organization that formalized the loosely coupled institutional cooperation (based on personal relationships) that characterized the leading universities in the post–Civil War era. Formal alignment did not arise out of the demands of independent agency or active partnership, but it greatly facilitated these efforts. This was especially true in regard to regulating the development of higher education. Rather than a federal agency, it would be the AAU, with significant support from the Carnegie Foundation, that would formally articulate and publicly present standards and expectations for academic degrees and departments, professors and facilities.

In an interesting institutional twist on America's culture of aspiration and notions regarding equality of opportunity, the AAU's exclusivity reinforced its ability to regulate the domain and to serve as standard-bearer. For example, while criticizing the AAU as a "Ph.D. trust," University of Illinois president Edmund James also actively worked to secure his school's membership, which it gained in 1908.[33] Thus, while some academic leaders might have complained of the AAU's "monopoly," almost all of them accepted (though sometimes grudgingly) its leadership role. Additionally and perhaps most important, the federal government did as well, calling upon the AAU to facilitate partnerships, consistently attending its annual meetings, and allowing the AAU to define, standardize, and speak for all of higher education as an independent agent.

Aligning Resources: The AAU, the Carnegie Foundation, and the Rise of Association Authority

Having primarily been founded as a simple extension of the loosely coupled relationships that defined elite universities' early coordination, the AAU did not immediately exert a strong organizational influence. The association did serve a significant agenda-setting function, but even this was not without its hiccups. For example, in the association's formative years, Henry Walcott, a professor at Harvard, wrote to ask Yale's Arthur Twining Hadley if he would sign a letter of support and assist in bringing to the AAU a resolution requesting that Congress pass legislation to provide tariff relief for the importation of specific research materials. Possessing his own separate agenda, Hadley was curt, to say the least.

> After making such inquiries as I can, I hardly regard this as a wise thing to sign. Our leading universities have an important change in legislation in view which is vitally necessary, namely, the repeal of the US inheritance tax. This involves many hundred times as much as is connected with any matter about wax models. Under the circumstances, I think that the Presidents of our large institutions should concentrate all their attention and influence on this vital point. For that reason I am making no minor demands on the Finance committee either of the Senate or the House which distract attention from this, or can possibly weaken our influence in insisting upon it.[34]

Hadley concluded by saying that he hoped Walcott, upon consideration, would agree with his thoughts on the matter. History does not record whether Walcott ever chose to advocate Hadley's agenda. However, properly chastened, Walcott did not call upon the AAU for support. As for the inheritance tax, despite coordinated lobbying of Congress supported by the AAU, efforts to repeal it failed. Nonetheless, the episode reflected the beginning capabilities of the association as a coordinating and agenda-setting institution.

Beyond institutional coordination and collective lobbying, the creation of the AAU allowed member schools to cooperatively pursue support from the growing number of wealthy individuals and the newly developing private foundations. Higher education had already witnessed the influence of such patronage with the founding of Rockefeller's University of Chicago.[35] With the foundation of the Carnegie Institution in 1902 (a research facility in Washington, D.C., initially headed by former Johns Hopkins president Daniel Coit Gilman) and the Carnegie Foundation for the Advancement of Teaching in 1905, the nation's leading universities and the institutional entrepreneurs who guided them would work actively to cultivate the philanthropist's generosity.

Reflecting the multidirectional relationship between universities and their benefactors, Andrew Carnegie did not unilaterally develop an agenda for supporting higher education. Instead, the Carnegie Institution and the Carnegie Foundation relied on the often-coordinated entrepreneurship of university leaders. Specific foundation support was often crucial for the development of agency. The Bureau of Education's limited reach correlated with its limited resources. Universities could not rely on the government to subsidize its efforts to define national standards for higher and professional education. Instead, leading academics worked with the Carnegie Foundation to develop standards. With the power of the purse, these national standards quickly grew to be authoritative—the criteria by which universities were assessed and to which they aspired.

One of the first efforts to cultivate specific support was spearheaded by Henry Eddy of the University of Nebraska. Writing to Cyrus Northrop of Minnesota, Charles Van Hise of Wisconsin, and James Burrill Angell of Michigan, Eddy recounted the "difficulty of providing adequate support for carrying on and enlarging graduate work." Emphasizing that "such work has an increasingly important role in the development of higher education in this country," Eddy expressed concern that a shortage of resources inhibited state institutions who were attempting to actively pursue graduate work.[36]

To illuminate his point, Eddy provided a comparative analysis of graduate work (see table 4). Using data from the commissioner of education's latest annual report (1903), Eddy concluded that private institutions were conducting graduate work of much greater value and with much greater efficiency. He also argued that the support private universities received from the Carnegie Institution contributed to this imbalance. The disparity presented troubled Eddy. Accurately foreseeing graduate education as crucial to the development of universities overall, he was alarmed by its relative absence in public institutions.

> Without it [substantial graduate programs] we [state universities] are likely to suffer a steady deterioration in the morale of undergraduate faculty and students; nor need I speak of the devitalizing and asphyxiating effect of the

TABLE 4. Graduate Education at Public and Private Institutions, 1903

	Private Institutions	Public Institutions
Number of undergraduates	1,997	1,924
Number of nonprofessional graduate students	455	126
Number of instruction staff	213	150
Number of volumes in library	356,500	148,000
Value of apparatus, etc. (in million dollars)	1.098	0.243
Annual income (in million dollars)	1.021	0.557
Number of fellowships	38	2
Number of doctorates in last five years (1898–1903)	138	15

Source: U.S. Commissioner of Education, 1903 statistics.

Note: The private schools included in this analysis are: Columbia, Cornell, Harvard, Pennsylvania, and Yale. The public schools included are: California, Michigan, Nebraska, Ohio State, and Wisconsin.

constant withdrawal of advanced students to other institutions and the vir-
tual discrediting of the state universities thereby.[37]

For Eddy, the discrepancy was best addressed by active entrepreneurship—specifically, pursuing support for graduate fellowships and
instruction from the Carnegie Institution. He continued: "in what way
is it possible to make such a change? It seems to me that the duty and
privilege of making an effective and authoritative presentation of the
pressing needs of this graduate work to a well disposed and liberal capitalist rest with the leading state universities themselves." Pursuing this
end, Eddy asked Northrup, Angell, and Van Hise to enlist the cooperation of other state university presidents with the hopes of "bringing
such a powerful combined influence to bear in its favor as to insure its
success." Demonstrating the tiering existent among schools, Eddy concluded by acknowledging that while the leading state universities—
such as Minnesota, Wisconsin, and Michigan—might not feel the need
for such a push, it was hoped that they would be willing to support the
"general cause."[38]

Northrup, Angell, and Van Hise all generally supported Eddy's proposal. Northrup underscored his belief that if graduate education were
to flourish at public institutions, it would need significant support from
private benefactors, such as Carnegie.

> I have always felt that we, who are connected with State universities, must
> keep in mind the fact, that the duty of the State is, first to provide education
> for the masses and that only as the lower education can be fully provided for
> has the State the right to spend its money for the higher education. As a
> result I have never felt the freedom in using the money of the State for grad-
> uate study that I feel in using it for undergraduate work.[39]

Angell and Northrup continued to communicate and plan their
approach to the Carnegie Institution. They decided that Angell, by
virtue of his position as elder statesman and his relationship with
Carnegie's leadership through the AAU, should make the initial
inquiry.

In reply to Angell's inquiry asking about the possibility of Carnegie
supporting graduate education at public institutions, R. S. Woodward
of the Carnegie Institution noted that Angell had offered a difficult
proposition. On the one hand, Woodward stressed, even Carnegie's
generosity was not enough to ensure the success of research and graduate education. On the other hand, Woodward recognized, foundation
support could be useful. Woodward expressed general support for the
idea but was noncommittal.[40] As Angell and his other public institution

colleagues would soon learn, there were other pressing issues that would come to top the foundation's agenda.

At the same time that Angell and his colleagues were attempting to garner Carnegie's support for graduate research and fellowship, MIT's president, Henry Pritchett, left Cambridge to assume leadership of the Carnegie Foundation. The foundation was founded to expand on the particularized research work of the Carnegie Institution and provide for the general improvement of American education. In pursuit of this end, the foundation's first priority was the establishment of pensions for college faculty. Pritchett had first proposed such a system while at MIT. As head of Carnegie's newest effort, Pritchett had the opportunity to make his entrepreneurial ambition a reality.[41]

Upon taking the foundation position and learning of Angell's efforts, Pritchett politely suggested to Angell that the latter's energies might be better spent elsewhere. Specifically, Pritchett advised that Angell focus on having public universities included among the institutions for which Carnegie might endow professors' pensions. As Carnegie was currently considering which institutions were to receive such funds, Pritchett's "judgment" was "that it is not well now to raise any further question with him concerning the state universities until this has been decided." Pritchett candidly stressed that his advice to Carnegie was that he refrain from including state universities "until the experiment had been tried elsewhere." He also expressed his belief that since state universities had succeeded in establishing clearly the principle that the state should support higher education, he doubted the wisdom of wholesale endowment for all the states and believed they would not suffer if they waited a year or two.[42]

In addition to providing guidance regarding an appropriate agenda for public universities' cultivation of private philanthropy, Pritchett also worked to further interactions between Carnegie and the AAU. The Carnegie Institution had hosted the AAU's annual meeting the year before, and upon taking the leadership of the Carnegie Foundation, Pritchett built on this relationship. The CFAT itself would soon become an invitee. Thereafter, the AAU's executive committee, of which Pritchett was a member, would often meet in the CFAT's offices. Once Carnegie committed to endowing pensions for professors, AAU institutions would have a significant influence over the process. Pritchett actively communicated with Michigan's Angell, Wisconsin's Van Hise, California's Benjamin Ide Wheeler, Harvard's Charles Eliot, Columbia's Nicholas Murray Butler, and many others. The AAU thus worked with the Carnegie Foundation in a fashion similar to how it had partnered with the federal government. The association often found itself speaking not only for its members but also for all of higher education as a domain.

The relationship between alignment and agency could most readily be seen in the controversy over pensions for professors at publicly supported institutions. When the CFAT formally announced the establishment of the pension fund, it listed forty-six colleges and universities whose faculty were entitled to support.[43] Noticeably omitted from the list were Rockefeller's University of Chicago as well as "all institutions having formal denominational ties" and "all institutions controlled and supported by a state, province or municipality." Additionally, as in most every "national" initiative in American higher education, schools from the South were sorely underrepresented. The announcement stressed that "a number of these institutions, in time, might make clear their right to a place in the list." It also stated that public universities would have their status considered as a class at the next meeting of the Carnegie trustees, scheduled for the coming November.[44] Such assurances did little to mitigate the inevitable controversy that followed. The foundation justified its initial decision with the argument that it hoped state legislatures would provide for such support. The presidents of state-supported institutions derided such an assumption as "highly unrealistic."[45]

The November 1906 meeting of the Carnegie trustees did nothing to settle the question of public universities, and over the next year, negotiations between the representatives of public institutions and Pritchett would continue. Ostensibly, the National Association of State Universities was to discuss appropriate standards and expectations with the Carnegie Foundation. However, as negotiations continued, Pritchett and Harvard's Eliot, who was chairman of the foundation's trustees, worked almost exclusively with their colleagues from the AAU, Wisconsin's Van Hise (whose institution was a member of the NASU), and Michigan's Angell (whose institution was not), in an effort to reach a compromise. Beyond the issue of state legislatures' responsibility for the pensions was the question of exact qualifying criteria that should be applied to petitioning institutions.

After meeting with Pritchett and Eliot in Chicago in January 1908, Van Hise expressed to Angell his disappointment with the fact that Pritchett seemed permanently wedded "to [the] view that ultimately state universities should provide for their own retirement allowances." Van Hise still was hopeful, as further conversations with Eliot suggested that there might be room for compromise. With this in mind, he attached a statement for publication, which he requested Angell join his fellow public university presidents in signing. The brief statement simply urged the Carnegie Foundation to broaden its scope and stressed the belief that "the great and admirable purpose of CFAT to elevate the profession of teaching in American cannot be accomplished until tax-supported institutions are embraced by it."[46]

Angell signed Van Hise's statement and, more important, continued to work with all of those concerned (Van Hise, Pritchett, and Eliot) to develop an acceptable set of standards. Additionally, all four men worked closely with their colleagues at the AAU to ensure consensus among the leading universities. In March 1908, Carnegie wrote Pritchett of his intentions to add to the fund in order to extend opportunities to public institutions as well: "from the numerous letters I have received from pensioners and their wives and the warm approval of the press and the public, I am satisfied that this Fund is, and must be for all time, productive of lasting good, not only to the recipients but to the cause of higher education."[47] Though subtly, Carnegie's announcement underscored the significance he placed on the development of standards.

With this motivation, Van Hise, Angell, and Pritchett intensified their efforts. Among the largest hurdles was a debate between Van Hise and Angell over whether the foundation should have separate standards for public institutions in regard to income and endowment. Angell believed such distinctions were necessary, as state legislatures were rarely as generous in their appropriations as private benefactors were in their endowments. Van Hise disagreed with Angell. In a letter to Pritchett that he forwarded to Angell, Van Hise argued that there should be general rules governing all institutions. Saying that the "gracious thing" would be to have a strictly general rule, Van Hise asked, "why should a good college named a university and supported by the state be treated differently than private schools" with the same name.[48]

After another series of meetings and further letter writing, Pritchett, Eliot, Angell, and Van Hise finally came to a workable compromise. In May, the CFAT issued a public statement establishing criteria for public universities that could petition it. Admission to the "list of approved institutions" was open to "all universities whose educational standard, plan of government, and endowment" met CFAT standards, which were specified at length. Fearing that bad publicity and a backlash might come from the perception that it was forcing these pensions on the states, the foundation stressed that public institutions would need the support of the governor and the state legislature to apply. However, the foundation also "reserve[d] the right to decline application of a school if it is subject to political control or interference which, in the opinion of the Trustees of the Foundation, impairs its educational efficiency." The foundation also reserved the right to discontinue the program for any school not meeting requirements but stressed that such an action should not affect those already granted pensions.[49]

Despite these restrictions, a number of public universities applied for consideration. Initially, only four were accepted, three in the United States (Michigan, Minnesota, and Wisconsin) and one in Canada (the University of Toronto). Writing Angell to inform him of the foundation's decision, Pritchett implied that others who were possibly worthy of acceptance but did not meet all of the foundation's stated requirements, such as California and Virginia, had their applications "postponed" in the belief that such a decision would lead these state universities to "take action" in order to make "academic progress."[50]

By including public universities as well as private, Pritchett and the Carnegie Institution, with the significant assistance of Angell and Van Hise, had now brought greater force to efforts at standardization and regulation of higher education. Notably, the federal government was all the while a bystander. The pension fund had become a mechanism for enforcing standards and expectations and furthering pursuit of a "national university." Carnegie's money had become the carrot that those seeking to improve the quality of higher education attached to the stick of minimum expectations. A minimum definition of a college or university had been established. The foundation's authority was by no means absolute, nor was it necessarily arbitrary.

Strikingly, the standards had been primarily defined through a consensus between members of the AAU and representatives of the Carnegie Foundation. Pritchett, Eliot, Angell, and Van Hise all represented a plurality of interests. Pritchett might have been president of the CFAT, but he was also chairman of the AAU's committee on purpose and scope. Thus, the Carnegie Foundation provided the required money and power to support efforts at standardization, while the AAU provided the necessary credibility and institutional authority.

Defining by Degrees: The AAU and the Standardization of Credentials

Correspondent to their efforts in conjunction with Carnegie, members of the AAU worked actively to define the specifics of higher education. Their work with the Carnegie Foundation had focused primarily on internal factors: income, admissions, and governance. The AAU, on its own, sought to more thoroughly define and standardize universities' relationships with one another as well as with the national state and society as a whole. Thus, while the Carnegie Foundation established expectations to which universities could aspire, the AAU set about developing a common language and universal expectations by which all the nation's universities could interact.

As had occurred with the joint Carnegie-AAU efforts to establish minimum requirements, the common language and shared expectations were developed not by the government itself but, rather, by coordinated universities working as its agent. The uniqueness of this arrangement was even more apparent when one recognized that the AAU and its member institutions would frequently stand as representatives of American interests in dealings with foreign governments. The leading universities often served as academic ambassadors, doing so not just as active partners of the national state—such as when sending delegates to international conferences—but also as independent agents making their own entrepreneurial arrangements on behalf of American higher education.

One remarkable example of this was the creation of the Theodore Roosevelt Professorship in 1905 between Columbia University and the University of Berlin. Less than fifteen years before their two nations would be at war, Columbia's president Nicholas Murray Butler had arranged for a leading American scholar to be appointed to the University of Berlin faculty for a year to lecture in areas that "reasonably well represent the field of American History and Institutions." In Berlin, the appointments were to be formally made by the Prussian ministry of education, with the emperor's sanction. Contrastingly, in the United States, nominations to these professorships were to be made by Columbia, in consultation with the nation's "other leading universities."[51]

In the previous year, the Prussian ministry of education not only decided to accept bachelor's degrees from AAU institutions as the equivalent of certificates from gymnasiums but also agreed to grant credit for graduate work done at AAU institutions. With this Prussian acceptance in mind, as well as a general desire to facilitate "graduate migration" (students attending graduate school at institutions different than those at which they went to college), the AAU set about trying to define what various academic credentials and curriculum meant. In doing so, the AAU had quickly moved beyond its initial concern with solely graduate education. The AAU's leaders did stress that their primary concern was "advanced study," but this term was purposely vague and taken to include even sophisticated undergraduate work.[52]

Since the leading universities were becoming ever more concerned with "advanced study," the association's scope naturally expanded in relevance, if not in breadth. The association's two broadest efforts to define standards involved university nomenclature and academic credentials. Both efforts were critical not only for seeking standards and expectations but also for attempting to create a template by which American universities could interact with one another and with other organizations and institutions, even those of other countries.

The association's Committee on Nomenclature presented its first report at the meeting of January 1909. The committee expressed frustration at the fact that "no consensus" existed even among the nation's leading institutions on the definition for such common terms as *course, school, college, department,* and *division.*

> It appears from the foregoing that universities, the institutions which are supposed to systematize and advance knowledge, which ought to illustrate the principles of education in their organizations as far as practicable, have permitted without protest a hopeless confusion of nomenclature which would not be tolerated in any of the sciences.

In sorting through the confusion of academic phraseology, the committee stressed the importance of the term *college.*

> It is clear that the history of the college in America, worthy of its English source, demands that the term should be the largest and most dignified in the university. The very fact that this term has been applied at Columbia, Harvard, Yale, and Princeton, from one to three centuries, for their colleges of liberal arts, or what was until recently almost their entire institutions, requires this.

The committee continued on to define the terms *school, course, department,* and *division.* The committee stressed that such specificity was necessary for the appropriate systemization and specialization of higher education concerns.

> The definitions suggested appear to your committee to assign to the various terms the meanings which are the fairest compromises they have been able to work out under the principles of giving each term its best and widest uses, and at the same time, restricting each term to a single meaning, and this last must be done if the theorists of education are ever to gain the respect of the scientists.[53]

To the modern observer, it might seem a bit elementary and pedantic to define such terms as *college, school,* or *course.* However, as newly redefined organizations, the leading universities sought to establish parameters through which their activities, their missions, and their relations to state and society would be universally understood.

Having defined the structures that housed specialized knowledge and expertise, the AAU next sought to define the degrees and credentials that publicly represented such knowledge and expertise. Once again, as good organizational men of the early twentieth century, these academic leaders did not undertake this effort through a large, inclusive and democratic initiative. Instead, they assigned a committee to study the matter. After surveying their membership as well as others, the AAU's Committee on Academic and Professional Degrees reported to the association in November 1916.

The committee began by stressing it had worked under two assumptions. Its first assumption was that it was the "function of the committee to formulate an acceptable statement of principles regarding academic degrees and the conditions under which they should be conferred." The committee maintained, "Advice rather than precept is intended." In presenting this report, the committee and, by extension, the overall association did not wish to appear autocratic. However, as I will discuss further, they also had reason to believe that their recommendations would be heeded. The committee's second assumption was that "the existing status is comparatively satisfactory as regards the degrees more commonly conferred."[54]

The committee then summarized their assumptions regarding the shared standards for academic degrees: a four-year curriculum for a bachelor's and at least one year of advanced work beyond the bachelor's for a master's. It was believed that the PhD should be only "conferred for advanced work in which independent investigation occupies an essential place." The committee stipulated: "The results of this investigation should be set forth in a thesis worthy of publication. The amount and character of the work should be such that the degree rarely could be attained in less than 3 years following the attainment of a bachelor's degree or its equivalent."[55]

Having developed standards for the primary university credentials, the committee then undertook efforts to coordinate these fundamental degrees with professional degrees, helped by the American Medical Association, the Society for the Promotion of Engineering Education, and the Association of American Law Schools. After conferring with these professional associations, the committee reported back with eleven specific recommendations. Some recommendations—for example, that "multiplication of degrees is to be avoided" and that bachelor's students who complete a second bachelor's curriculum should get a second bachelor's degree—were fairly obvious. Other recommendations were more substantial and reflected significant efforts to bring order to the chaotic academic marketplace. Among these was the acceptance of the growing practice, driven by ever increasing special-ization, of supplementing degrees with the fields of study, as with a "BA (Commerce)." The committee also felt that while the sciences and the professions offered opportunities for research, such efforts were not "higher training in research as opposed to practice"; they thus believed that, rather than the PhD, efforts at advanced work in a professional field should be recognized with the degree Doctor of Science. Though ambitious in its recommendations, the committee also recognized that there would be limits to its influence. It stated in its report: "certain exceptions to the principles above outlined have become so firmly established in practice that they must be regarded as permanent. Chief among these is the degree of MD."[56] The committee recognized the great flux and transition of higher education in the early twentieth cen-tury. Not wishing the association to be stagnant or caught unaware of credentialing challenges that would naturally occur with the increase in specialized knowledge and expertise, the committee concluded,

> "for dealing with outstanding cases and others that will probably arise, the committee recommends creation of a standing committee to observe the development of academic and professional degrees, to aid so far as feasible in directing such development along lines acceptable to the Association, and to report to the Association."[57]

The association unanimously accepted the committee's recommen-dations and gladly established a standing committee. The accomplish-ment in establishing basic standards was substantial. Incidents from a prospective graduate student inquiring as to the possibility of receiving a PhD in absentia for practical life experience and individual research to university presidents suggesting the creation of new degrees (e.g., Western Reserve University's Phillip Twilling proposed a Doctor of Arts)[58] showed that a shared understanding of the specific scope and meaning of university credentials was lacking. The AAU, acting as an independent regulatory agency, provided that necessary commonality for the American state.

The Authority of Aspiration: Formal Alignment
and the Expansion of Membership

Considering the AAU's authority and ability to influence the shape of higher education and, thereby, all the fields, disciplines, and profes-sions that relied on universities for the production and codification of specialized knowledge and expertise, one is still left wondering from whence its authority came. The power underwriting the influence of such an organization as the Carnegie Foundation was clear. Colleges and universities needed to meet specific standards enforced, if not fully established, by the CFAT for their professors to be eligible for pensions. The authority of the AAU was much subtler and thus, I would argue, much more significant.

The association's authority was built on two independent but very highly related factors, exclusivity and aspiration. As an organization consisting of the leading universities in the country, the AAU would provide a benchmark for all of higher education. Correspondingly, many universities and their presidents who were not members of the association would eagerly seek membership even, as I have discussed earlier, while criticizing the association as monopolistic. The AAU's authority was enhanced by the sanction it received from the federal state. By turning to the AAU for representation at international meetings or for guidance in partnerships with universities, the federal government acknowledged the AAU's role as arbiter and overseer and, more important, its position as a collective "national university." The association's relations with and parallels to foreign governments' ministries of education served to enhance this position as well.

The association was keenly aware of the stir its perceived exclusivity and membership practices caused. Recognizing its standardizing and sanctioning role, especially in regard to American schools and their students' relationships with foreign universities, the association expressed a desire to ensure that all "reasonably qualified" institutions were admitted. In 1904, the University of Virginia was admitted. Over the next few years, a large group of institutions would ask to be considered for membership. Among them were a number of midwestern state universities (Illinois, Indiana, Iowa, Kansas, Minnesota, Missouri, Nebraska, and Ohio State) that would eventually be admitted to the AAU. The inclusion of these schools would expand the representation of western institutions, but the South, aside from Virginia, remained an essentially nonexistent presence on the national academic scene. The association accepted the midwestern state universities gradually. After announcing its interest in expanding in 1906, the AAU, upon receiving the applications of all those interested, chose to postpone action. Van Hise reported to Angell:

> There were such a large number of institutions considered and no one or two of these could be picked out as distinctly superior to the others, that the Association took no action in favor of admitting any institution, and no nominations were made for admission for next year, so that question seems to be postponed for at least two years.[59]

The University of Illinois and the University of Minnesota were admitted soon thereafter. The process of expansion had begun.

Typical of the pursuit of membership were the efforts of Northwestern University. In 1908, Northwestern asked to be considered for membership. Before formally contacting the association, the university's president, A. W. Harris, asked for the advice of his colleague James Burrill Angell, former AAU secretary. Harris claimed (one would assume mistakenly rather than falsely) that when the associated was founded, Northwestern had been asked to join but, owing to the absence of the university's President from the country, was not able to attend the initial meeting.[60] Harris expressed understanding that the AAU was "adverse" to expansion of its members, but he said that he felt compelled by this historical anecdote—no matter its accuracy—to ask for consideration. Additionally, he stressed:

> We have been embarrassed, as I suppose other institutions have been, by the fact that membership in this association has been made the basis for public recognition of graduate work in this country, and I am now troubled by finding that it is likely to interfere with the foreign recognition of some of our professional degrees.

Harris was hesitant to push the issue but maintained that "the embarrassments noted above and the admission of several universities at the last meeting of the Association make me feel that I ought to do so."[61] Angell was less than encouraging, underscoring the association's desire to remain limited in size.[62] Harris was grateful for Angell's advice. However, again he felt compelled to press the question despite his personal misgivings: "it seems a little like presenting myself at a social function uninvited. But I feel I am forced to do so because of the embarrassment to which you refer arising out of the action of the foreign universities."[63] Angell understood Harris's concerns and forwarded his request to the AAU's secretary for consideration. No formal application procedure existed, but Harris's request was acknowledged and forwarded on to the AAU's committee on aim and scope.

At its next meeting, in October 1908, the committee considered Northwestern's request as well as that of the University of Louisville. Both were "passed over without prejudice." Disappointed and concerned about the consequences for its professional and graduate students seeking experience in Europe, Harris still expressed understanding. The AAU's charter was to focus on "advanced study," and the lack of a formally organized graduate school did not help Northwestern's chances. Not coincidentally, soon after the university formally organized a graduate school in 1917, it was asked to join.

The AAU clearly was in many ways a club. However, exclusivity was not its only asset; tangible benefits in terms of recognition of degrees and opportunities to define the national educational and public agenda through partnerships and agency accompanied membership. Reflecting generally on his efforts as president and specifically on pursuit of AAU membership as well as Carnegie funding, Edwin Alderman of Virginia dramatically explained his ambition. In a fairly personal expression, Alderman underscored to his friend Henry Higginson that AAU membership and placement on the list of Carnegie institutions were fundamental to his efforts. He then spoke of his overall aspirations.

> I came to the University of Virginia because I believed it to be a creative Institution. The University of Virginia was in sore need of more means and better organization and of a more democratic attitude towards society. In architectural setting, in material equipment, in number and strength of faculty, and a certain dignity of achievement, it was, and is, unquestionably the most considerable educational achievement of the States between the Gulf and the Potomac river. I sought to enrich it, and to organize and to democratize it, as its Founder intended, by so relating it to all the other phases of education as to achieve unity of purpose in our whole educational order, and to introduce into it a concept of service to the state and Nation as the ruling idea.
>
> My desire was to do all this, and yet not vulgarize or cheapen its conceptions of culture, nor to put out of sight its fellowship with high feeling and poetic understanding. In other words, I wished it to be what Jefferson intended it to be, the leader of a great region entering into an industrial democracy, and somewhat tardily getting ready to reap the benefits and face the perils of such a social order. I think I have done a number of these things under conditions of fair difficulty. There is a new spirit, compounded of reasonableness and hope and adaptation to environment and passion for service to the State and country.[64]

Needless to say, membership in the AAU and inclusion in the Carnegie fund were not solely responsible for Alderman's sense of accomplishment. However, his words reflect a desire to establish and maintain a national presence.

Before the foundation of the AAU, a university's national presence and ability to shape the American educational and policy agenda was largely dictated by personal connections. The AAU did not eliminate such considerations, but it did institutionalize relations that had been previously informal. More important, it greatly expanded the capabilities for coordination. As witnessed by the AAU's relations with prospective members, such coordination accentuated the ability of leading institutions to act as independent agents of the national state. It was not only the prestige of the AAU but also the opportunity it represented that provided leverage and led to its essential position as a practical substitute for a federally chartered university and/or regulatory agency.

The Great War and Redefinition: The AAU as Network

The escalation of tensions in Europe and the United States' eventual entry into World War I did not alter the AAU's fundamental role as primary coordinator and representative of America's higher education interests. The war would place new demands and expectations on America's universities. Starting with the height of the war and especially intensifying at its conclusion, public debate began over the role and function of education generally and higher education specifically.

Some academics, such as Columbia Teachers College dean James Russell, complained that not enough time was being spent "teaching democracy" and stressed a desire to free American education from "German standards of scholarship and efficiency which have controlled the policy of our universities."[65] Others, such as an editorialist identified in the *New York Times* only as "a university professor now in the service of the United States," praised universities' work on behalf of the war effort and suggested that, after the war, they would become simply "schools for national efficiency." He continued: "if ever an institution has justified itself, in the eyes of the public at a time of national crisis, it is the American university of today. It rendered an invaluable service in helping to mobilize and direct the nation's resources."[66] This sentiment had been expressed earlier in a report by Secretary of the Interior Arthur Lane. Lane, in conjunction with a number of leading academics, issued a report "upholding higher education."

> In the progress of its work the committee has sought to show how essential it is, if the Government's far-reaching military plans are to be carried out successfully, that the processes of higher education be maintained at the highest possible efficiency, especially those which have to do with the future supply of men and women trained in scientific and technical subjects, including teachers in these fields. The people of the United States should recognize that the maintenance of the war strength of the nation in its full power demands the utmost efforts of all existing well organized and adequately equipped colleges, universities, and technical schools. This means ever increasing and more devoted bodies of students as well as faculties.
>
> Young people . . . should develop especially those scientific and practicable branches of study which are essential to the winning of the war, to the development of our industries and commerce, and to accomplishment of the

tasks of the civic and political life of the nation. Educational institutions should use every effort to make the opportunities and privileges of training for public service accessible to all suitably prepared men and women of college age.[67]

As the war came to its conclusion, the debate still raged, with many of the leading universities taking a centrist position. On the one hand, academics wished to continue emphasizing research and expertise. On the other, the war experience had cautioned them against pursuing expertise for its own sake. Speaking soon after the war, Columbia's Nicholas Murray Butler warned:

> We have forgotten what we study for. There has been too much study of the machinery and details of government, and not enough comprehension of the principles on which good government is based.
>
> The war has taught the lesson that the proper place of efficiency is the servant of a moral ideal. We shall make a criminal blunder if the war teaches us to imitate Germany in any particular.[68]

At the same time that academics pursued such moral ideals, there also remained a fear of excessive patriotism and emotion in governance, at the price of rationality. Speaking at Yale's 1919 convocation, Hadley stressed that the expansion of the national state had heightened the need for the university to pursue expertise and supply calm.

> Democracy is a very different thing now from what it was twenty years ago. The public demands government action on a great many matters which previous generations left individuals to settle for themselves. The motives for demanding government action are generally good; but the results are often bad.
>
> It is just this emotional attitude of passion that creates the chief danger to American politics today. Men have a zeal for God, but not according to knowledge. They mistake prejudice for fact, and think that good intentions can take the place of careful examination of evidence. No government which manages its affairs on the basis of prejudice rather than evidence can long endure. We must help the community to examine evidence and exercise self-control; and the best way that we can do this for many years to come is by ourselves setting the example of self-control.[69]

At war's end, the university, like much of American society, found itself undergoing redefinition, especially in regard to pursuing research and defining expertise.

Crucially, the leading universities had mechanisms in place to facilitate this process. The recently expanded AAU would be essential in maintaining and refining universities' relationships as active partners and independent agents of the national state. The association's agenda for its annual meetings of 1919 and 1920 dealt almost exclusively with the role of research and specialized knowledge in universities' relations with government, private industry, and one another. Correspondingly, as the primary organization responsible for defining such relationships, the meetings of this supposedly exclusive organization were attended not only by member institutions but by representatives of forty-three other colleges and universities, as well as representatives of a variety of related organizations.[70] Despite the upheaval accompanying the war, the formal alignment and institutional prestige of the institutions of the AAU had helped collectively establish the association and its members as a defining force for the American state's enterprise of expertise.

8 Facilitating Shared Service

Formal Alignment and Active Partnerships

The beginning of the twentieth century witnessed not only the expansion of this nation's global reach and international presence but also, in some ways correspondingly, the continued extension of the national state. Universities facilitated this growth by providing expertise in the form of manpower and knowledge. From relationships with long-established agencies, such as the Department of Agriculture, to relationships with newly developing bureaus, such as the Forestry Service, university-driven partnerships actively extended the reach of the federal state.

These partnerships between the university and the national state were stimulated by the formal alignment most clearly reflected in the AAU. The AAU worked with the federal government from its first meeting. However, it did not monopolize university relations with the national state. Some collaborations were initiated by individual universities acting autonomously, while others were developed as group ventures. As a whole, they reflected the influence that more formal alignment had on the university's support of the new American state.

Evolving Alignment, Defining Partnerships, and Establishing Expertise

The rise of the AAU as well as other academic organizations meant that the nature and scope of active partnership would come to be defined collectively. For the nation's leading universities, the formation of the AAU and the nature of institutional competition would lead to a more collective agenda, a greater uniformity of structure, and an increasing standardization of expectations. These forces would not only define universities' relationships to one another; they would shape their relationship to the national state as well. Responding to the demands of institutional entrepreneurs, the federal government began to devote greater resources to research and the pursuit of expertise. Yale president Arthur Twining Hadley's *Facilities for Study and Research in the Offices at the United States Government in Washington,* issued in 1909 as a bulletin by the Bureau of Education, cataloged this development.

Of course, not every partnership would be of such a nature as to demand a collective solution; but whereas the later half of the nineteenth century had seen even the most ambitious partnerships developed on an individual or loosely coupled basis, the beginning of the twentieth century would see the national state undertake partnerships with academic associations as well as individual institutions. In tracing the variety of partnerships between the national state and universities in the first part of the twentieth century, we witness not only the development of specialized knowledge and expertise but the rise of formally structured, cooperative organizations that greatly assisted this development.

Individual Entrepreneurship and Institutional Competition: *Forestry and the Evolution of Partnership*

Founded in 1900, Yale's forestry school represented one of the clearest examples of partnership between universities and the national state. As the recently established federal Bureau of Forestry needed trained and expert foresters, Yale created a school to provide for such training and the development of expertise. In addition to shedding light on the provision of manpower and the creation of credentials, the school's founding highlighted the importance of entrepreneurship, the institutionalization of skills and knowledge, and the extent to which even such modern efforts were dependent on simple familiarity and social connections.

An active and generous alum, as well as head of the federal Bureau of Forestry, Gifford Pinchot first broached the subject of a forestry school with Yale president Arthur Twining Hadley in December 1899: "It has occurred to me that certain of the course already being given at Yale, possibly with some modification, might be put together and described in the Catalogue as a group of studies or courses preparatory to professional training in forestry." According to Pinchot, there were between twenty and twenty-five students at Yale who had decided to or were seriously considering adopting forestry as a profession. He had little doubt that this number would increase if existing courses were arranged systematically so as not to conflict and if new courses were possibly added. Stressing the value of such a program to Yale, Pinchot offered to suggest the names of courses and instructors, in the hopes of assisting those already at the college as well as attracting others who were considering either "a technical forestry school or one abroad."[1]

Hadley was very receptive to the suggestion. Pinchot, assisted by his deputy and fellow Yale alum Henry Graves, quickly sent along proposals for two sets of courses to prepare students—one based in Yale College, the other based in Yale's technical branch, the Sheffield Scientific School. Having convinced Hadley of the value to Yale, Pinchot then expressed the expectations of the Bureau of Forestry: "It would I think, be of great value to us here if men who have taken these studies, or any part of them, whether post-graduates or undergraduates, could receive certificates specifying the studies pursued and the marks received." Pinchot's preferred approach was to develop a school of national reach through partnership with his alma mater rather than advocate a federal forestry academy. Moving beyond the general scope and objectives of his plan, Pinchot suggested offering, at the beginning of every academic year, a talk to Yale students about the nature of the forestry profession. Pinchot outlined a few areas for improvement, stressing that such efforts would allow Yale to effectively serve the state and naturally gain a reputation as the preeminent institution for forestry study.[2] For Pinchot, if Yale were to found a forestry school, it would not simply be a provider of manpower and issuer of credentials, it would also have to be the national standard-bearer for the profession.

Pinchot could make such demands because Hadley shared his aspirations and his notions of service. Hadley was grateful to Pinchot for his and Graves's efforts, expressing his sense of "great obligation." Hadley hoped that the list "might amount to more formal organization." Hadley allocated two hundred thousand dollars for an upgrade that Pinchot felt was necessary for the botanical garden, and Hadley asked if any additional funds would be needed to get the garden up to standard. He acknowledged that such a scheme as the one Pinchot had devised would require significant fund-raising as well as organization. However, he believed that with the help of Pinchot and others, Yale could be at the forefront of defining and providing expertise: "We should have every advantage in bringing our work into line with the actions of the Govt. and of private individuals who are practically promoting intelligent applications of the subject."[3]

After a series of letters and informal discussions, Pinchot and Hadley had laid out the parameters for the establishment of such a school. Pinchot, who came from a wealthy family, would donate $150,000, as well as a tract of land in Pennsylvania (purchased by his family from the federal government), for research and instruction. As part of its responsibilities under the deed of gift, Yale would provide income for courses and "other necessary uses and purposes" incidental to the gift, as well as a suitable headquarters for the school. In accepting Pinchot's gift and its terms, Hadley expressed, on behalf of the corporation, Yale's gratitude for "the opportunity thus placed at their disposal of advancing the knowledge and practice of sound forestry in the United States."[4]

The school's founding was integral to the development of the federal Bureau of Forestry. Just as important, however, was its impact on Yale and its sense of public mission. Pinchot certainly was a driving force behind the establishment of the school, and his generosity was essential. For example, in making plans for the opening of the school, Pinchot wished to hire William Ludworth of the Bureau of Forestry as an instructor. Discussing Ludworth's salary with Hadley, Pinchot noted the amount required and mentioned that, "if necessary," he would "be very glad to be of assistance" in meeting that salary. However, just as important to the school's establishment was Hadley's receptiveness and desire to serve the national state. In the same letter regarding faculty hiring, Pinchot discussed with Hadley the general development of the school. Pinchot outlined plans for the course bulletin and concluded that he was "very deeply glad to bring the school about." He also praised Hadley: "you will remember that it was your suggestion that started me to consider the matter so that you have to thank yourself for it first of all."[5]

Yale's partnership with the national state was indicative of the personal exchange between Hadley and Pinchot. With Hadley as Yale's president and Pinchot as the school's dean, their entrepreneurship meant they pursued every opportunity to further the reputation and reach of the forestry school and its expertise. Typical of such efforts was a letter by Hadley to Herbert Myrick, editor of the *New England Homestead*. Myrick had written Hadley and attached an article regarding efforts by the White Mountain Forestry Association to coordinate the use of materials and lands. Hadley expressed interest in the association's work but was "surprised to see no reference to cooperation w/the Dept of Forestry at Washington." He wrote, "The work done by this Dept in the direction in question is so intelligent that I have some doubt as to the wisdom of an independent organization—at any rate, until after careful consultation to avoid cross purposes."[6] Hadley actively promoted the Bureau of Forestry, and Pinchot continually championed Yale's program.

While Yale's newly founded school had been a success, the nation's first school of forestry, established at Cornell a few years earlier, had not found consistent support. The Cornell trustees had decided to close its New York State College of Forestry after Governor Benjamin Odell had vetoed their request for funding. Interestingly, rather than actively lobby to sustain the school as head of the Forestry Service, Pinchot, as dean, hoped to have Yale take advantage of Cornell's closure. Stressing that Cornell's decline was "purely the result of bad administration," not the result of poor students, Pinchot suggested that Yale might "relax a little the severity of [its] entrance requirements," in order to accept transfers from Cornell.[7] Hadley was happy to make amendments. Pinchot responded by noting that there would also be a need for additional funds to take on transfers but that he expected "little difficulty" in obtaining the required amount by August.[8]

The developing competition between schools of forestry could also be seen in Ann Arbor. Unaware of the decision by Cornell's trustees, the head of Michigan's program, Filbert Roth, sought funds to retain a second instructor by comparing the university's commitment to forestry with that of schools in the East. Arguing that removing funding for a second instructor "could not help doing mischief to school and scholars, by giving the matter a bad appearance and insufficient attention," Roth even offered to contribute a portion of his own salary. Roth argued that since Yale had three instructors and Cornell had three also, "it would be too bad to let Ann Arbor be the 'one horse' forestry school of our country."[9] In keeping with the newly developing nature of the discipline and its partnerships, Roth, rather than look to the federal government for assistance, secured funds from the state forestry commission.

As the Bureau of Forestry and various schools of forestry were quickly developing, it would not be long before Michigan and other programs were competing for federal funds. At the end of 1908, Pinchot announced plans to place a forestry laboratory in the upper Midwest. Similar to agricultural experiment stations, such a laboratory would provide significant reputational and financial benefits to the university chosen. Michigan was one of three universities—Minnesota and Wisconsin were the other two—strongly pursuing this opportunity for active partnership. In its pursuit of the laboratory, the university was assisted by both its congressional delegation and its timber industry. James McLaughlin of the House Agriculture Committee and Sam Smith personally met with the Bureau of Forestry to present the university's case and also arranged for the university's regents to make a presentation.[10] Additionally, the state's major lumber companies, responding to Filbert Roth's intelligence that the laboratory choice would probably be between Wisconsin and Michigan and would depend largely on how much money each institution would be able to offer the Bureau of Forestry for installation, guaranteed four thousand dollars to supplement the university's bid.[11]

Despite such efforts, Michigan's bid had its shortcomings. The Michigan state legislature offered general "support" but did not offer any financial assistance. Angell attempted to call on Pinchot during a visit to Washington, D.C., but the forester was traveling and thus unable to meet with him.[12] A little over a month later, Pinchot wrote to Angell with the unfortunate news that Wisconsin had been selected. Saying that the decision was a "most difficult" one, Pinchot apologized to Angell that he could not have selected all three proposals. Assuring Angell there was nothing more that could have been done by the university, its regents, or the Michigan delegation in Congress, Pinchot said, "no one factor led to this decision."[13] Upon receiving Pinchot's decision, Angell noted disappointment but also expressed understanding and a desire to continue working toward active partnership with the national state.[14]

Pinchot did more than encourage competition between the leading universities and schools of forestry; he also sought to facilitate coordination. The AAU and the AAACES had discussed the value of advanced study in various fields and domains including forestry, but Pinchot wished to gather the foresters himself and thus issued a call for a conference of all universities and colleges where forestry was taught, to be held in December 1909 at Washington, D.C. Pinchot believed that such a conference would be "of great value to the progress of forestry as well as to the universities and to the forest service which employs so many of their graduates and which is vitally interested in the best training of foresters."[15] Beyond the mere agenda and practice of the conference, Pinchot's effort reflected the evolution of active partnerships between the state and the university. Having begun as individual relations between universities and the bureau that were mediated by Pinchot's personal connections, these partnerships evolved into competitive and coordinated efforts to serve the national state.

Extending Entrepreneurship: Efforts in the Philippines

Developing partnerships generally worked well for both the American state and the university. Universities could be assured that their students were receiving relevant training, and the state could recruit interested talent. Additionally, government specialists could take advantage of university knowledge, advances, and equipment, while the university could offer more and varied courses. Such partnerships were also integral to universities' broader effort to serve the "public," an effort that grew more and more to mean linking with the federal state. At the same time, the federal state itself grew as America extended its reach to "colonial" possessions, such as the Phillippines.

Various universities would actively support federal efforts in the Philippine territory. One of the first efforts in this regard was advocated to Hadley by Pinchot and involved bringing Filipino students to study at Yale. Newly appointed colonial governor William Howard Taft had been a classmate of Hadley's at Yale. Pinchot's friend Harris Proctor, civil service commissioner, called for Taft and the Philippine Commission to select a small number of students to pursue advanced studies at Yale and then return in order to assist the commission in its governance. Pinchot had already begun discussions with administrators in the Philippines about sending students to Yale's forestry school. Proctor and he wished to see Yale provide scholarships for these students as well as those in other areas of professional expertise, such as law, medicine, and engineering.

By training Filipinos and providing them with various practical skills and social knowledge, Pinchot and Proctor not only hoped to educate young men but also sought to facilitate the United States' rule over the territory. In this way, they reflected a belief that university partnerships with the national state could help extend the reach of the federal government beyond its own borders. Expertise and specialized knowledge could be applied to all areas of government concern. As Pinchot summarized in concluding the plan, "I lay it before you with the most confidence because it seems to me to be in line with the policy of cooperation with the Government which I have heard you express."[16] Hadley agreed with the sentiments of Proctor and Pinchot and secured funding for the program.

These scholarships were not the only example of universities assisting the national state's governance of its territories. Individual appointments often substituted for institutional programs. In one telling instance, in response to Taft's request for a "good man" to oversee the Philippine judicial system, Hadley recommended Charles Vander Graff, from Yale's graduating class of 1881. Hadley wrote that Vander Graff was a "first rate" lawyer and a "leading man in every way," who possessed the expertise Taft felt necessary for the position—a good knowledge of Spanish and an extensive familiarity with Roman law, which he had developed through his practice in New Orleans. Alleviating any concerns Taft might have had about a previous lack of public service, Hadley stressed that Vander Graff's lack of "political advancement" could be attributed to the fact that he was "uncompromising in his position as a good Democrat."[17]

Vander Graff was soon offered and accepted a position in the colonial administration. Clearly, Vander Graff's familiarity with Hadley and Hadley's connections to Taft were of great help in securing him the position. However, this familiarity was coupled with the formal training and specialized knowledge that Hadley and Taft believed the position required. Additionally, partisan political connections were certainly not necessary, since Vander Graff's standing as a "good Democrat" did not keep Hadley from recommending him or Taft from appointing him. This is not a minor point, for in the new American state, institutional loyalties could outweigh partisan ones.

Keeping with the developing relationship between higher education and the federal state, the partnership between the nation's colleges and universities and its Philippine territory included more than occasional requests to fill individual positions. More systematic and formal relationships were also developing. In addition to supporting colonial governance and administration, institutions of higher learning were also called on to provide teachers for the colony. In June 1901, Lt. Col. C. R. Edwards, the chief of the War Department's Division of Insular Affairs, asked Hadley to recommend ten men "of strong scholarship" for teaching positions in the Philippines. Hadley soon thereafter sent along the names of recent graduates.[18] Yale's peers, such as Columbia and Harvard, also recommended individuals for such teaching posts. At the end of the summer, Edwards found his need to be greater than anticipated and asked Hadley if he might be able to recommend any additional individuals. Hadley replied that he desired to assist Governor Taft and the Philippine Commission in any way possible but could not be of immediate assistance: "I regret very much that the prosperous times have caused so large a number of our graduates to find good places elsewhere that we have exhausted the list of those whom we are at present able to recommended."[19]

A lack of sufficient personnel was not the only challenge universities encountered when seeking to develop partnerships with the foreign extensions of the national state. University experts were sometimes torn between their desire to be of service and their own personal interests and satisfaction. Hadley's Yale was at the forefront of university partnerships with the Philippines, but it was not the only institution to undertake such efforts. Angell's Michigan also worked with Taft's government, and from this partnership came a strong example of the conflict between personal desire and national service.

Michigan professor Paul Freer had been serving the Department of the Interior in the Philippines as head of government laboratories since early in Taft's administration. His initial appointment was scheduled to last through May 1903. Soon after Freer's arrival, Taft requested and Angell granted an extension of Freer's service through September 1903. In May 1903, Angell formally recalled Freer to ensure his return by September. This recall triggered Secretary of War George Edmunds to write Angell at the request of Taft. Acknowledging Angell's previous "kindness" in extending Freer's leave, Edmunds mentioned that Taft wondered if Freer might be released to the federal government for another two years and asked that Angell "recognize the urgent necessity" of his request and grant Freer further leave.[20]

It required the shuffling of some teaching responsibilities for the coming year, but Angell was quick to pass the request of Taft and Edmunds along to the regents, with his full endorsement and understanding of Freer's significance to the Philippine efforts. They soon granted approval, so that Freer might continue his "very special and important work."[21] Not everyone was pleased with this arrangement, most particularly Freer himself. Writing to Angell, he expressed his displeasure, tempered by a sense of obligation: "the Government seems to be impressed with the importance of my remaining for that length of time and owing to the great pressure brought to bear on me I did not see how I could refuse if the Board of Regents were willing." While understanding the demand for his services, Freer was eager to return to Ann Arbor, as he felt he had gained all that he could from his experience: "It has been a very interesting experience out here and very valuable to me, but I think I am coming to the point where I have all the experience I need and all of value that is possible." Freer went on to say he was ready for his return and was hoping he might combine his work in Ann Arbor with service to a government laboratory.[22]

Unfortunately for Freer, Taft insisted he remain. The government had bought a large number of sick animals, and the task of immunizing them had fallen to Freer's labs. Reiterating the fact that he was very disappointed with having to stay, Freer continued:

> The Governor [Taft] seems to be afraid that everything would go wrong if I were to leave. I never realized that I was quite so important an individual

before, and personally I do not suppose I ought to give my thanks to Congress for passing the $3 million [in emergency funding], because it is this matter that has held up my proposed trip home.

Freer recognized the obligation his expertise carried and tried to be accepting of the fact that he was remaining in the Philippines. He ended his letter to Angell, however, on a very melancholy note, stating, "the lack of change in temperature grows monotonous in time, and the beauties of the tropics fade very much when you are face to face with a disappointment such as I had today."[23]

In addition to representing the human element of such efforts, Freer's tale also underscored the limited formalization that defined many of these partnerships. Freer's appointment was not part of a prescribed program that had a specific length of time or included a readily available replacement. While not fully established, such efforts did represent the extended reach of expertise as it was sought by American interests across the Pacific as well as closer to home.

Despite occasional difficulties, these formalized, but still not fully systematic, partnerships remained an important link between the national state's colonial and diplomatic interests and universities' available expertise. The partnerships were not unidirectional. Freer might have complained about the service, but initially he coveted his appointment in the Philippines, believing it would be of great benefit to his research and career. Additionally, universities often greatly benefited from such assignments, using the federal government to gather research materials for its museums and laboratories and experience for its faculty and students. Freer, for example, might have remained in the Philippines at the request of colonial governor Taft, but his work benefited the University of Michigan as well the colonial government. Previously, when Michigan and other institutions wished to obtain specimens for their collections, they would either have to fund a research expedition themselves or buy collections from dealers. With the expanded reach of the American state, the federal government could obtain materials from around the world on a university's behalf, saving the university from expending a great deal of time, money, or manpower.[24]

Worldly Expertise: Institutionalizing Government Service

University efforts to support the American state abroad would not be limited to individual postings. Institutional entrepreneurs would seek to extend their schools' service and societal relevance through a variety of means. One of the most ambitious undertakings in this regard involved Hadley's attempt to build a curriculum to train staff for the nation's "colonial efforts." Hadley's attempts were rooted in the most basic forms of partnership and simple personal relations, but they extended to a systematic program.

Writing Taft to congratulate him on his appointment as governor of the Philippines, Hadley also took the opportunity to propose a new course of study. After praising Taft and wishing him the best in his new position, Hadley began by stating Yale's priority of service and synopsizing the partnership already undertaken with Pinchot.

> In this connection I have an ax of my own—or rather of Yale's—to grind. Ever since Pinchot has been in the forestry dept he has been keeping his eyes open with regard to possible teaching in forestry which should meet American administrative needs and the upshot of it is that we shall next month be able to publish the prospectus of a school of forestry, with excellent equipment, ample endowment and, best of all, living connection with the needs of the government and the country.[25]

Hadley was pleased with the forestry effort and wished to extend Yale's partnership with the federal state further. He continued, "now I have at heart, and have had at heart for the last two years, the development of an institute or department of instruction which should have the same sort of living connection with our administrative work, and particularly with the problems of colonial administration."[26] Noting that Yale had one professor who had done much study in the area and had others who could add "a great deal if we just knew what was most wanted," Hadley maintained, "This last information can only be obtained by keeping our eyes open and seeing what there is to be seen." Hadley greatly valued Taft's appointment, as he concluded, "I believe that you will be in a position to tell better than any other man what kind of preparation is wanted for the men who are going to go out into our new possessions and what steps Yale can take toward meeting this need."[27]

Taft and Hadley corresponded regularly about the administrative and personnel needs of the territory. Both saw the value of the school Hadley proposed, but the money necessary to make the program a reality was not immediately forthcoming. In a letter to Taft outlining a variety of fund-raising priorities associated with Yale's bicentennial of 1901, Hadley estimated the amount necessary for starting an Institute of Colonial Administration and Public Law to be two hundred thousand dollars.[28] However, neither Taft nor Hadley had as much fund-raising success as Pinchot (who was able to call on his colleagues and especially his family for resources), and the school remained only an aspiration.

In November 1905, still frustrated in his fund-raising for the endeavor and worried about potential competition, Hadley proposed to Nicholas Murray Butler that Yale and Columbia undertake a jointly established program (the two had discussed the possibility earlier, in passing). Writing to Butler, Hadley recounted discussions he had recently had with a wealthy benefactor, Frederick Boas, regarding patronage for a school of colonial service: "I understand that there is a chance of funds being provided to help in the enterprise if we are pre-pared to formulate the scheme in the near future."[29] Butler had also spoken to Boas and was very receptive to the idea.[30] Butler agreed that Yale and Columbia should offer such instruction without duplication.

For Butler, such an effort would not only be of great service to the national state; it would also underscore to other universities the value of alignment and the excesses of competition, especially in regard to specialized knowledge and expertise.

> In addition to the possibility that such a grouping of courses might serve the present need, the act itself would serve to illustrate and carry out one of my favorite notions, which is that in the higher and special reaches of university work it is unwise and uneconomical for institutions to duplicate each other's instruction, and that the end that we all have in view might be better served in many of these respects by cooperation. Perhaps we might be able in this way to set an example that would be followed in years to come.[31]

Butler and Hadley communicated throughout the holiday season, and by the middle of January 1906, they developed a scaled-back plan, which they detailed in an "outline of proposal to establish a course of study preparatory to diplomatic, consular, or commercial service in the East, through the cooperation of Yale and Columbia." Both Yale's cor-poration and Columbia's trustees "gave hearty approval to the plan for cooperation between Yale and Columbia in preparation for a program in Oriental Life and Service."[32] While receiving the support of both governing boards, the program failed to attract more than a handful of students at a time and thus failed to become institutionalized as part of either school's regular curriculum. Despite its limited success, the part-nership revealed an entrepreneurial desire to anticipate and meet the expected needs of the federal state and its agencies.

Hadley pursued partnerships with the national state wherever and whenever possible. Demonstrating an entrepreneurship that was driven by both competition and coordination, he extended both the breadth and the depth of Yale's relationship to the federal government. As striking as Hadley's achievement was his ambition. In his annual report of 1906, Hadley summarized a variety of programs, including the work of the forestry school, the placement of teachers in the Philippines, and the collaboration undertaken with Columbia.

Additionally, Hadley used discussion of a proposed forestry museum as an opportunity to the stress the competitive importance of service to the national state. Summarizing the progress and importance of the forestry school as well as the plans for the forestry museum, Hadley stated:

> I have purposely confined attention in this summary to the public activities which we already are in position to exercise without mentioning those which are projected. A word should, however, be said of the plan for a Forest Museum which is in the mind of Mr. Gifford Pinchot. The Yale Forestry School was organized just at a time when the American public was beginning to see the importance of the subject. We have had the good fortune to take the lead in this line of education, so that students come to us from every quarter of the world.
>
> It is Mr. Pinchot's belief that the museum would allow Yale "to take the same position before the public as a whole that our courses of instruction have given us in the minds of students and specialists, and to make Yale the center to which the whole world will turn for its record of progress in forestry in the past and its suggestions of possible lines of progress for the future."

For Hadley, the success of the forestry school and the effort to build new partnerships were natural extensions of Yale's evolving public role—a role that would not only rely on coordination with other institutions but also be the product of institutional entrepreneurship and initiative. Hadley concluded his discussion of the forestry school and museum by stressing their greater significance: "I mention it at this moment as indicating the kind of public work which makes the modern university something more than a mere group of schools and elevates it to its highest possible rank—that of public servant."[33]

Hadley and Pinchot did not limit their concept of service to within Yale's walls. Among their more ambitious (albeit unrealized) efforts was an attempt to host "a series of talks . . . given by Government officials in New Haven, broadly upon the topic of university training for Government work and upon the opportunities for valuable service under the Government." Pinchot had intended to invite various cabinet officials and others to address administrators and faculty of the leading universities, with the hope that this "would help very powerfully in setting the trend of student thought . . . toward Government work."[34]

Though this effort failed (in no small part due to the fact that Pinchot was unable to coordinate such a conference from the wilds of West Virginia, where he was stationed for most of the year), it still underscores the extent to which active partnership with the national state was gradually becoming an increasingly collaborative effort for America's leading universities.

Partnerships and Alignment: The AAU as National Coordinator

Collaboration between leading universities involved more than informal advice, joint programs, and occasional conferences. The creation of the AAU established a formal alignment that greatly enhanced universities' impact. The benefits of alignment were not unidirectional. On the one hand, the elite universities could petition the federal government as a unified body and, by virtue of their prestige, appear to speak for all of higher education. On the other hand, when the federal government wished to call on the specialized knowledge and expertise of the nation's leading institutions, it no longer had to call on each institution individually. As I have discussed, individual acquaintance and connection still occasionally cemented active partnerships. However, universities increasingly began to see themselves as a collective body, not only in relation to one another, but in their coordination with the national state as well.

Alignment and Ambassadorship: The AAU
as National Representative

The AAU was founded to facilitate acceptance of American degrees by foreign universities as well as simply to engender further and more formal communication between the institutional entrepreneurs who ran American universities. It quickly grew into an organization concerned with standards and practices in all of higher education. Having been involved with the organization from the outset, the federal government was well aware of the group's concerns and interests. When the Bureau of Education needed American universities either as hosts for visiting dignitaries or as representatives at foreign meetings, it would call on the AAU. Both collectively and through its individual members, the AAU came to stand for American higher education internationally.

An early example of this partnership was the Bureau of Education's request that the AAU send a delegation to Chile for the First Pan American Congress on Higher Education. The conference had been called in order to secure closer ties between Latin American universities and the universities of the United States. The conference had been organized by the Chilean ministry, and the Latin American nations were represented by their ministers of education.[35] The United States' invitation had been sent to the federal Bureau of Education. The bureau in turn asked the AAU and other agencies and organizations to appoint delegates. Though not formally officials of the federal government, these delegates would be granted the "proper credentials to constitute them its lawful representative to serve under such instructions" as would be determined by the commissioner of education.[36] The delegates of the AAU were thus ambassadors for American higher education. They served as both expert representatives, speaking authoritatively on the condition of higher education in the United States, and representatives of expertise, promoting the broad application and utility of specialized knowledge.

Spurred largely by the lobbying of Angell, Hadley, Butler, and other AAU presidents of influence, the Congress appropriated funds for ten delegates.[37] The AAU would send four of them, the most from any one organization. Other delegates funded by Congress included representatives of the Department of Agriculture, the Smithsonian Institute, and the Isthmian Canal Commission.[38] Additionally, the AAU contingent was supplemented by five professors from member institutions who were in South America for research and service, including Charles Curtis of Michigan and Bernard Moses of California. All told, over half of the delegates from the United States were from AAU institutions.[39] The attendance of so many representatives from the nation's leading universities was well appreciated by the conference's hosts as well as by the other attending nations. At its outset, Curtis reported back to Angell that the conference was "arousing much interest in South America." He continued, "The prompt action of the Government of the U.S. and the AAU in providing for a liberal representation at this Congress has made an exceedingly favorable impression in educational and official circles down here."[40]

The federal government was eager to have the service of America's leading universities, and attendance at the conference was not a burden to the AAU schools. In addition to further solidifying the AAU's position as the primary defining body for American education, AAU members could also pursue relations with the developing nations of Latin America. No formal exchanges between the United States and the countries of Latin American were adopted at the Congress, but informal agreements between South American governments, such as Chile and Argentina, and members of the AAU were. For example, the universities of Michigan and California agreed to accept eligible and interested Chilean engineering students. The Chilean government had been sending such students to France but were displeased with that arrangement, as they felt that the students returned "strong in theory, but not in ability and practice."[41]

With the advent of World War I, the AAU would coordinate active partnerships of much greater breadth and of far larger significance to the national state. Additionally, because of its members' extensive relations to international institutions, the AAU would often facilitate relationships with foreign ministers of education implicitly on behalf of, rather than actively in conjunction with, the national state. The seemingly minor coordination and partnership involved in supplying representatives to such gatherings as the First Pan American Congress on Higher Education highlighted two factors that would be crucial to the AAU's broader coordinated efforts as active partner and independent agent of the state. The first was the association's ability to position itself as a representative of and spokesman for all of higher education. The association did not necessarily include every institution of higher learning in the United States, but to the federal government and foreign officials, it essentially included all those that mattered. The second factor was the ability of the association to maintain publicly uniform and cohesive positions even in the face of competition and disagreement.

A neatly emblematic example of this ability can be seen in the initial debate over the role of AAU delegates at the Chilean conference. James Warren of Harvard, the secretary of the AAU, upon initially receiving the invitation from the Bureau of Education, wrote Angell, who was serving as president of the AAU, to suggest that the association's members possibly bypass the meetings. He felt the AAU had been slighted, since it had not been extended a formal invitation by conference organizers.[42] Angell replied that he felt such a suggestion was rash as the oversight could easily be explained by "the lack of a comparable organization in Latin American countries."[43] The conflict never spread beyond the confines of the organization, because at the same time, various member presidents and the association itself were making appeals to Congress for delegate funding. The AAU's members certainly had their differences of opinion on a variety of issues, but when working as active partners, they spoke with a collective voice.

Alignment and Armaments: Universities and Military Preparedness

Since the passage of the Morrill Act, military training had been a characteristic of American university life. The act stipulated that land-grant institutions offer military training; it did not require that such training be compulsory. A few prominent institutions, such as Cornell, initially mandated that students partake in such training, but they quickly abandoned that idea in the face of student protests and a shortage of equipment and instructors. While not a required part of the curriculum, military instruction remained an aspect of campus life, though other demands on the military often made provision for such a partnership difficult.

Not until World War I would universities' formal coordination and alignment influence its partnerships with the military. Before the advent of the conflict in Europe, such partnerships were almost haphazard in nature. From plans for naval architecture to professorships in military science, universities worked as active partners of the federal government on a school-by-school, case-by-case basis. Institutional tradition and personal relationships, rather than standards and systemization, defined collaboration, with no appreciable defects or notable complaints. However, the rise of formal alignment among universities, coupled with the advent of the Great War, would change these partnerships and solidify the importance of coordination among universities as active partners.

The Great War and Formal Alignment: Seeking to Maximize the Resources of Expertise

Both debate over U.S. involvement in the Great War and the eventual entry of the United States into it would have a profound impact on partnerships between universities and the federal state. In addition to developing a more formal and extensive relationship with the American military, universities also publicly debated, for the first time, the proper nature and extent of their service to the state. Providing manpower as well as expertise, universities and the institutional entrepreneurs who oversaw them stressed their utility, relevance, and necessity. Most significantly, while the war did not start the process of formal alignment and coordinated service, it did greatly accelerate and clarify it.

As war began among the major European powers in August 1914, students from many of the leading American universities were concluding their time at military camps sponsored by the War Department. The camps had been started the summer before by General Leonard Wood, in conjunction with a collection of university presidents. Wood initiated the idea and was greatly assisted by the support of Arthur Twining Hadley of Yale, Lawrence Lowell of Harvard, and

John Grier Hibben of Princeton, who, along with Henry Sturgis Drinker of Lehigh, formed the Advisory Committee of University Presidents. This committee mobilized the support of their colleagues to build a national reserve among college students by training students at summer camps. The camps were well attended and deemed a success by all.

With the sinking of the Luisitania in May 1915, the European war became a pronounced American concern. As tensions grew and debate over America's potential entry intensified, Hadley began to stress the need for military preparedness and the role of universities in such efforts. In his annual report of 1915, excerpts of which were reported in the *New York Times*, Hadley praised General Wood and the existing system of camps, stating, "I have no hesitation in saying that, wholly aside from their military value in preparing a reserve of trained officers for possible service in event of war, the events have an educational value that much more than justifies their organization and its maintenance."[44] In addition to promoting the camp system, Hadley also recommended giving college credit to those who attended the camps and extending the summer camp program to the school year by offering lectures on military duties on campus. He stressed, however, that he did not believe such classes or service should be compulsory.

Hadley was not alone in such sentiments. In November, Wood called a meeting of the Advisory Committee of University Presidents, in New York. Joining the committee and Wood were a number of other university leaders, including Michigan's Harry B. Hutchins and Cornell's James Schurman. Wood had not formally coordinated the War Department camps with the AAU, but its members were well represented. Three of the four advisory committee members came from AAU institutions, and 50 percent of the overall university attendees came from AAU schools.

In 1916, former Princeton University president Woodrow Wilson campaigned for and won reelection to the U.S. presidency, with the promise of keeping the United States out of the war in Europe. Despite such assurances, Wilson's former colleagues in the AAU did not wish to be caught unprepared and continued with plans to discuss the place of military service in their institutions. At its January meeting, the association had planned the agenda for its next meeting, to be held that coming November. During those meetings, held less than a week after the election, one of the primary topics of discussion was military training in universities and colleges. The association did not wish to make any formal recommendations or proposals. The topic was addressed largely to specify alternatives for members and to further their relations with Wood and the War Department.

With the passage of the National Defense Act in the summer of 1916 came provisions for the establishment of the Reserve Officers Training Corps on college campuses. By the time of the November meeting, only a few AAU schools had organized ROTC units. However, the session offered the association's members an opportunity to discuss how best to incorporate the program into their existing partnerships as well as a chance to collectively discuss their role in the preparedness effort with a member of the War Department. Three main presentations were made on the topic. The first presentation was made by Colonel Wood, who provided a general overview of the War Department's needs and expectations. The other two were made by representatives of member institutions, who discussed their schools' particular approaches to partnership with the military. Two alternatives were offered. Yale's Hadley presented an overview of the summer camp system, and University of Illinois dean David Kinley spoke (in place of the university's president, Edmund James) as a representative of an institution where military training had been in existence for some time.[45] Hadley not only stressed the need for coordination between universities but also emphasized the importance of cooperation with military planners and authorities. Kinley did not disagree with the need for coordination and cooperation but cautioned against simply turning over universities to the military brass.[46] Demonstrating universities' concern with preparedness, the meeting underscored the importance of formal alignment in the universities' partnership with the federal state. Unlike the Civil War, where individual schools established their own battalions with little concern as to what other schools were doing, America's leading universities were working closely with one another to facilitate public service.

University service included more than training of students. The founding of the National Research Council (NRC) in 1916 was also a significant part of the preparedness campaign and later war efforts. Established by congressional charter and placed under the auspices of the National Academy of Science and the National Science and Technology Society, the NRC was chaired by George Ellery Hale, an MIT-trained astronomer who had overseen observatories for both the University of Chicago and the Carnegie Institute. The NRC was established with the purpose of linking academic, governmental, and industrial research efforts. The NRC and its leadership worked closely with AAU members upon its founding, though its influence would be more profoundly felt in the decade to follow. The NRC would largely define the development of academic science, helping define parameters and procedures in a particular area of expertise. The NRC would help facilitate partnerships between universities and the national state, but it also would rely heavily on the efforts of institutional leaders and coordinating institutions.

The AAU continued to extend its role as the primary representative and coordinator of higher education institutions. Congress declared war in April 1917. By early May, the AAU's members had been called to Washington for a meeting organized by Hollis Godfrey of the Council of National Defense, a quasi-governmental organization whose mission was to gauge and facilitate national preparedness. To meet this goal, Godfrey called a meeting between representatives of major universities and of the various agencies of the federal government, "to consider the vital problems for our institutions of higher education arising out of the war and the immediate creation of a great army."[47]

Though not the only universities invited, AAU institutions were a prominent force, owing to their prestige and the public presence of their leaders. According to the association's president, G. Stanley Hall of Clark University, the AAU viewed the purpose of the meetings as twofold:

1) to impress upon the National Government, through concerted action, the fundamental importance of conserving and properly utilizing our institutions of higher education.
2) to mobilize all our educational forces, not only for the service of the country through the war, but also for the difficult period after the war.[48]

Academic leaders throughout the country pretty much shared the AAU's position. Out of patriotic obligation as well as entrepreneurial opportunism, university leaders sought to extend their partnerships with and service to the federal state.

Among the AAU's primary functions was to speak collectively on behalf of the leading research institutions, both to facilitate partnerships and to protect their interests. At its 1917 meeting, the AAU passed a resolution that acknowledged the need to suspend trade "with the enemy" (Germany), but it also called on the Congress to grant such importation "so far as such action assists important work of research and is consistent with the safety of the US or the successful prosecution of the war."[49] Often coordinated by the AAU, the nation's leading universities were active partners with the federal state. However, it would be mistaken to assume that the universities' agendas simply became whatever the state demanded.

The passage of the Selective Service Act in May 1917 had had a significant impact on student enrollment and campus life. With the start of the fall term, universities witnessed dramatic changes in their student and faculty populations. In an effort to mitigate the impact of the draft, the association discussed the necessity of placing certain students and highly trained men in one of the later draft classes. Following these meetings, a special committee organized by the association to address the issue proposed new regulations regarding opportunities for enlistment. At the time, medical students and interns could maintain their schooling and enlist with the surgeon general. The AAU committee requested that this privilege be extended to a variety of other specialties. The committee believed their plan was a reasonable modification of existing policy that would benefit both the national state and the university, stating, "these requests are prompted by the firm conviction that if granted the most efficient service of scientifically trained men will be secured for the conduct of the War, and that some of the unforeseen, unfortunate complications which have resulted from the first draft will be obviated."[50]

The committee stressed that its proposal was motivated and justified by a number of observations. Their first observation was that "the maintenance of the National interest, other than purely military concerns does not seem to have been given sufficient weight by the District Boards." Second, the committee believed that many highly trained professional scientific men (engineers, chemists, physicists, etc.) could be more effectively used if they were assigned properly. Finally, the AAU committee argued:

> by voluntary enlistment of university men in service for which they are not best fitted the ranks of the educational institutions have already been alarmingly depleted as regards students, teachers, and research men. The university men have shown the highest type of patriotism irrespective of their own interests and have probably responded to the country more enthusiastically than any other class of men. There is an immediate danger that without specific provision to the contrary the universities will lack the teachers and students necessary to provide the Army and Navy with the highly trained men who will be required for the successful conclusion of the War.

The committee emphasized that they were not seeking special privileges for all men that fit the categories described. The students, faculty, and researchers who received such privileges would only do so "on recommendations of the presidents of the institutions concerned." "For others," the committee maintained, "the decision [would] rest with the authorities designated by Secretary of War."[51]

The AAU special committee had succeeded in fully mobilizing its members and other organizations, such as the NRC and the Bureau of Education, in support of the proposal, but it was not able to convince the War Department of the proposal's merits. Speaking for the War Department, Newton Baker wrote to the AAU committee to inform them of his decision. Baker noted that the War Department's judgment was shared by the officers of the Naval War College and by the army's chief of engineers.[52]

Baker assured AAU president Ray Wilbur that the department appreciated the difficulties the war situation presented to the nation's universities and technical schools, but he did not think the AAU had offered a viable or workable alternative.[53] Baker's response underscored a limit of institutional entrepreneurship and active partnership: in times of crisis, such as war, universities and academic leaders, no matter their institutional prestige or personal connections, found their initiatives constrained.

Perhaps no single incident reflected the constraint placed on individual initiatives as much as the experience of Gifford Pinchot while trying to work on behalf of the Agriculture Reconstruction Committee of the National Board of Farm Organizations (NBFO). Reflecting the growing pains associated with the new American state and its application of expertise, Pinchot's career had taken an interesting turn. He was relieved of his duties as head of forestry by William Taft in 1910 after a conflict with the secretary of the interior, Richard Ballinger. The Ballinger-Pinchot Affair, as it was known, is credited with being one of the driving forces in Theodore Roosevelt's Progressive Party candidacy of 1912. Pinchot himself ran a losing campaign for senator of Pennsylvania as a progressive Republican in 1914. He would find electoral success later, being elected governor in 1922 and 1930.[54]

In September 1918, with the war still raging, Pinchot wrote to tell Arthur Twining Hadley of plans to visit European nations[55] in order to examine the status of European farmers, to determine what changes should be made in farming practices during reconstruction after the war and how these changes could best be brought about. He asked Hadley for letters of introduction and suggestions as to whom he should see. He apologized for imposing on Hadley with such a request but noted that he was less hesitant because his work was of academic and public value.[56] Hadley questioned the timing of Pinchot's research trip but said he would be happy to assist in any way he could.[57]

Hadley was not the only one who wondered about the timing of such an excursion. In November, with the armistice declared but wartime restraints still in place, Pinchot wrote Hadley stating that when he asked for letters of introduction, he thought there would be no difficulty in securing his passport. He was sorry to say this was not the case.[58] Pinchot attached a letter to the NBFO from Alvey Adee, a second assistant to the secretary of agriculture, saying that it did not appear that Pinchot's proposed trip was "of such urgent necessity as to warrant the issuance of passports at this time."[59] Pinchot also attached a letter he addressed directly to Robert Lansing, asking the decision be reversed.

> The organized farmers of the US have the unquestionable right to seek, in their own way and through their own agents, first hand information on any agricultural subject provided only that their doing so does not interfere with the military operations of the govt. The denial of this right would be in line not with American democratic ideals but rather with the policy and practice of autocratic governments. No free people could afford to accept it.
> To refuse any but official information to the people of a democracy amounts to destroying their power to check up and control their official servants. In numerous instances passports have been issued to enable commercial and other organizations to secure unofficial info of value to them. It does not appear why an org of farmers should be treated differently.[60]

Despite his impassioned plea, Pinchot's appeal was denied.

Pinchot's appeal raised an interesting question regarding the democratic right of private citizens and their organizations to pursue their own research agenda. Though not working on behalf of a university, Pinchot was still affiliated with Yale's forestry school, and his effort reflected the desire to apply specialized knowledge to particular problems. He was denied the opportunity to do so, because his application was not in keeping with the national state's priorities. This does not mean that partnerships between universities and the national state were exclusively defined by the federal government, but it does show that the crisis of World War I tipped the balance of partnership primarily toward state interests.[61]

This wartime shift in the balance of partnership did not preclude all university initiatives. The leading universities continued to seek ways to both support the war effort and avoid wholesale disruption of their campuses due to enlisting volunteers and the draft. As head of a War Department advisory board on educational interests, University of Chicago dean James Rowland Angell offered a plan in May 1918 "to provide military instruction for the college students of the country during the present emergency." Working closely with a number of AAU presidents, especially Yale's Arthur Twining Hadley, the son of the legendary Michigan president James Burrill Angell[62] proposed the establishment of a Student Army Training Corps. The purpose of the SATC was to "1) develop as a military asset the large body of young men in the colleges, and 2) prevent unnecessary and wasteful depletion of colleges through indiscriminate volunteering, by offering students a definite and immediate military status."[63]

AAU presidents quickly signaled their support, and the program was soon in place. The SATC allowed students to be both scholars and soldiers, as they took classes and participated in training. Introduced to minimize disruption, the program largely led to chaos. The effort to merge military and academic demands did little to help the military and much to disturb the university. Students were called out of class to participate in drill, professors were required to show passes to enter buildings, and the campus began to resemble encampments. The armistice of November 1918 thankfully cut the program short. Despite its limited existence, the program demonstrated that universities could effectively bring their experience and knowledge to bear on a variety of problems, but assisting the military in organizing students was difficult and demonstrated the strains the war placed on efforts at active partnership.

The Evolving Partnership and an Accelerated Return to Normalcy

As the war ended and the nation attempted to return to normalcy, the nation's leading universities also sought to return to prewar conditions, not only in their own activities, but in their relations with the American state. Writing in *Harper's Monthly*, Yale's Arthur Twining Hadley summarized the reflection that the end of the war had brought to American campuses.

> For two years past the American public has been interested in knowing what our schools and colleges have done for the war. Today it is beginning to ask what the war has done for our schools and colleges. What merits has it emphasized and what defects has it brought to light? What improvements in the course of study has it suggested? What direction is it likely to give to the development of our educational system?

The crisis of war had produced greater state control and definition of its active partnerships with the nation's leading universities. Hadley, however, did not view this imbalance as permanent: "the American college of 1919 looks singularly like the American college of 1916. The military excitements of 1917 and the military organizations of 1918 have left few visible traces behind them." Hadley contended that while universities were returning to broader, less militaristic missions, the primacy of partnerships with and service to the national state should and would remain: "underneath this quiet there is a sense of impending change. Professors, students, and graduates realize that their responsibilities to the nation have not ended with the armistice, and that we must use the lessons taught by the war to enable us to meet the country's problems in time of peace."[64]

For Hadley, the key to further partnerships and service did not lay only in the improvement of the intellectual rigor and quality of individual institutions. It also lay in even greater coordination among these institutions.

> The problem of the higher education of the community can never be solved unless we realize that it is a national and not an individual one, an economic and not a psychological one.
>
> We must find some means of regulating an indiscriminate competition which results in multiplying specialists in subjects for which there is no considerable or elastic demand. In other countries division of labor between universities is recognized as a legitimate and natural thing. This will mean real nationalization of our educational system; not the sort of nationalization which is involved in imposing one scheme or method of instruction upon everybody, but that which comes from appropriating the work to those who are likely to do it best, and leaving each group of men free to do it in their own way.
>
> If we can grasp these great economic principles affecting education, the high cost of living may prove to be a blessing in disguise to the teaching profession, by compelling the public to face the problem of national education in its entirety, as part of the great problem of national efficiency.[65]

The disruptions of the war were therefore offset by the opportunities of partnership and service they exposed.

Hadley's colleagues shared his views. The war had confirmed—at times painfully—the importance of active partnerships between universities and the national state. It also had underscored the value of formal alignment among universities and the need for coordination. However, while the war effort had demonstrated that the institutional entrepreneurs who ran America's universities were adroit in their attempts to link with the state and to offer it specialized knowledge and manpower, it had also demonstrated that there were limits to the institutional capacity of even the elite universities to meet the demands for service and coordination. The Great War did not begin a new process of partnership, but it did heighten, intensify, and accelerate the already existing one.

9   The Modern University
and the Question of
Contemporary Public Service

At the end of this discussion, one might wonder why early university support of the state found academic leaders occasionally falling short of their ambitions and what implications this has for contemporary considerations. I would argue that the failure of some specific efforts was to be expected, given the haphazard evolution of the state itself. American state building is indicative of American exceptionalism. The fragmentation that allowed universities a defining role in creating the new American state also limited the reach of their success. Beyond specific programs, however, the emerging universities' impact has been so absolute as to almost be unrecognized in retrospect.

Today, doctors who provide care, teachers who educate, and lawyers who define justice are all in some ways regulated by the state, but only after they have been first credentialed by the system of higher education that has its roots in this era. The domains of health care, education, and justice are arguably the most visible, but by no means the only, areas where the university continues to frame the relationship between the state, practitioners, and the citizenry. Just as important, beyond specific domains, administration of the state as a whole is subject to such framing.

The Modern University and Public Administration

Though historical in its approach, my work seeks to continue the scholarly tradition of studying American political development to illuminate contemporary questions of politics and policy. I am advantaged in this effort not only by the work of Skowronek and Eisenach, who offer a useful overview of the institutional and intellectual legacy of the era under consideration, but also by Cook's suggestions for a modern approach to public administration.

Having traced the development of America's administrative state from the colonial era to the present, Cook recognizes that America's "fundamental commitment to limited government, the Jacksonian notion of democratic administration, and concerns about the distorting effects of professionalism" have driven historical skepticism and contemporary criticism of government bureaucracy and public expertise.[1] Despite such political and cultural forces, Cook advocates revitalizing public administration in America. Before outlining his plan for revitalization, Cook offers his rationale. Building from the extensive influence of the Progressive Era's pursuit of efficiency, Cook emphasizes that administration is not a neutral instrument but, rather, an influential enterprise. Offering the thoughts of Progressive journalist Herbert Croly, Cook summarizes this role: " 'Indeed [American government] is organized for efficiency chiefly because in the absence of efficiency no genuinely formative popular political experience can be expected to accrue.' Even from a late-twentieth-century perspective, Croly's initial juxtaposition of two values—efficiency and education—does not seem all that odd."[2] While cautioning readers to be wary of Croly's unquestioning embrace of efficiency and expertise, Cook still finds value in his sentiment and its consequences.

The influential nature of the administrative state thus calls attention not only to the state's activities but to its development as well. Cook acknowledges that the political and cultural forces that have driven the rise in America's skepticism of the administrative state might hinder attention to such development. Despite such a context, Cook argues that an understanding of administration's full influence will not only rekindle emphasis and attention but also redefine how public officials are educated and how the university serves the state. For Cook, the effects of such redefinition are far-reaching: "Recognizing administration's constitutiveness will bring about a reorientation in the education and training of public administrators. It will, more significantly, stimulate changes in the concepts, incentives, and practices of public policy design."[3]

Notably, in keeping with his desire to build from the Progressive Era, Cook almost reflexively looks to universities as the driving force behind such reorientation. In response to questions of what advanced knowledge and skills can offer this process, Cook suggests:

The answer lies in how public administration is constitutive of the regime, particularly in its embodiment and promotion of practical reason in the public sphere. The education of public administrators, and any claims they may make to expertise beyond narrow technical specialties, must center on a commitment to the development and exercise of practical reason in public affairs.[4]

Cook acknowledges he is "not adequately equipped" to offer a treatise on practical reason. He does, however, suggest a role for universities in helping reorient the American administrative state. Such reorientation depends on redefining the education of bureaucrats and government officials. Cook stresses that "first, public administration education must be grounded in political science, but a political science in what might be called its classical sense; theory joined to practice, specifically to the practice of liberal democratic politics."[5] Cook reminds readers that such an approach was standard in the first forty years of the discipline. However, since the rise of "an aggressive positivist approach to political studies" in the 1950s, Cook explains, "political science and public administration had for all intents and purposes parted company."[6]

Some scholars of public administration, such as Nicholas Henry, suggest that the split was inevitable and that revitalization of the field is best served independent of political science.[7] Cook argues for the opposite approach.

Every political science program should be tied closely to, if not housed within a political science department. Program curricula should be grounded in normative political theory with empirical research of several different designs tied closely to it. Likewise, any graduate program in political science that does not have public administration scholars on its faculty and does not interweave public administration throughout its curriculum is deficient. The study of the moral, ethical, and constitutional dilemmas faced by administrative officials, in the context of particular agencies and their histories and operations, is particularly important.[8]

Cook's call is for a modern reorientation. Its roots, as he acknowledges and emphasizes, lie in the Progressive Era's pursuit of public management grounded in specialized knowledge and expertise. Thus, just as universities were crucial to the process of building a new American state at the turn of the century, they are fundamental for modern reorientation of public administration.

The Modern University and Its Societal Position

I am highly sympathetic to Cook's proposal but would suggest that there are contextual hurdles to implementation that also need to be addressed.[9] I will allow others to debate precisely the best way to educate public administrators. Instead, I wish to focus here on the implicit assumptions that Cook and others make regarding universities' willingness and capacity to pursue the approaches suggested. Cook looks to the Progressive Era's notion of a prescriptive political science as a model for reinvigorating the practice of public policy. The influence of university-based expertise on the development of the American state goes without question. However, understanding the historical process of university support highlights a number of factors that will greatly influence the viability of public administration's revitalization, within political science or elsewhere. The unique societal position held by universities, the modern universities conception of service, and the nature of contemporary political science all continue to shape relations between institutions of higher learning and the administrative state.

As I have discussed throughout this work, the emergence of the American university was predicated on more than its support of the administrative state. Underlying such efforts at service was the development of the university as a national institution dedicated to the promotion of America's democratic community, industrial competitiveness, and intellectual vanguard. The development of leading universities' national identities and their promotion of democratic community, industrial competitiveness, and an intellectual vanguard were not coincidental or supplementary to their pursuit of expertise. Rather, they were fundamental to such pursuit, as they provided a rationale to justify their efforts to those who might criticize as undemocratic or impractical their focus on research and specialized knowledge. Building on their entrepreneurship and coordination, university leaders effectively portrayed their institutions as serving the greater good of the nation, rather than bound to a particular technocratic or administrative agenda. At the turn of the twentieth century, the American university was in the unique position of being an autonomous and largely self-sufficient organization while, at the same time, being a very public institution.

Universities remain very public, very national institutions. However, some critics, such as James Twitchell, have suggested that American institutions of higher learning are no longer driven to pursue and disseminate knowledge as much as they are dedicated to crafting and providing an experience. In a *Wilson Quarterly* essay provocatively titled "Higher Ed., Inc.," Twitchell does not say universities have abandoned the work of ideas; rather, he suggests that such work is no longer central to their identity.

> What used to be the knowledge business has become the business of selling an experience, an affiliation, a commodity that can be manufactured, packaged, bought, and sold. Don't misunderstand. The intellectual work of universities is still going on and has never been stronger. Great creative acts still occur, and discoveries are made. But the *experience* of higher education, all the accessories, the amenities, the aura, has been commercialized, outsourced, franchised, *branded*.[10]

Though Twitchell is slightly inflammatory in his tone, his "branded" university does not inherently abdicate its unique societal position. It is still national in its orientation. The promotion of America's democratic community, industrial competitiveness, and intellectual vanguard can still be incorporated within Twitchell's experience-centered institution.

Additionally, I would suggest that a focus on students' experience rather than simply their learning is by no means a modern phenomenon. Recall that in a letter (cited in chap. 7) to a prospective student's father, Yale president Arthur Twining Hadley suggested that the student attend Yale or Berkeley rather than MIT or Cornell, not because of the instruction he would receive, but because of the quality of men he would encounter.[11] Historical perspective, however, does not fully dismiss Twitchell's concerns about the intensification of university "branding." The corporatization of intercollegiate athletics stands as just one example of how university efforts to develop their identities and define their communities have threatened to become an end in themselves rather than the means to the greater end of education and service.

Twitchell sees the focus on experience as a danger but not as an inevitability. Others are more pessimistic, fearing that universities have abandoned their greater mission. Support for American industrial competitiveness has long been seen as part of a larger effort of university service. However, Eyal Press and Jennifer Washburn, in their sensationalistically titled piece "The Kept University," argue that any assumptions about the public benefit of such work is naive, if not dangerous. Press and Washburn detail the dramatic rise in university research partnerships with major national and international corporations at institutions across the country.[12] While the specifics of such collaboration might not seem to be of immediate interest to those concerned with the university's relationship to the administrative state, its rationale and justification are of vital importance to any assessment of how universities develop and transmit specialized knowledge.

In their piece, Press and Washburn summarize the arguments of Gordon Rausser, dean of the College of Natural Resources at the University of California at Berkeley and a leading proponent of partnerships with large corporations. According to Rausser, such initiatives, "far from violating Berkeley's public mission, would help to perpetuate the university's status as a top flight institution."[13] Press and Washburn note that Rausser's view is more and more the norm, as academic administrators throughout the country turn to the private sector for an increasing percentage of their research dollars.

This trend greatly concerns Press and Washburn, and they conclude their discussion by offering Rausser's most compelling argument but then immediately questioning its consequences.

> University-industry collaborations, Rausser argues, have brought important new products—anti-AIDS treatments, cancer drugs, etc. to market, and have spurred America's booming biotech and computing industries.
>
> This is a powerful argument, but a troubling one. In an age when ideas are central to the economy, universities will inevitably play a role in fostering growth. But should we allow commercial forces to determine the university's mission and academic ideals? In higher education today corporations not only sponsor a growing amount of research—they frequently dictate the terms under which it is conducted.[14]

For Press and Washburn, corporate control, rather than mere corporate patronage, drives such apprehension.[15]

Though darker in their outlook than Twitchell, Press and Washburn do not suggest that universities have abdicated their unique societal position. Rather, they believe that universities are exploiting their position for institutional gain without necessarily serving the public good. Again, historical context suggests more measured concern than alarm. Since its correspondent development with the Industrial Revolution, the modern university has long had corporate patrons, and historians of intellectual freedom would rightfully argue that there has almost always been some tension between the expectations of patrons and the activities of scholars. The University of Chicago's acknowledgment of Rockefeller as founder on its early letterhead comes to mind (see chap. 7, n. 35). The current context threatens greater upheaval, but it also offers greater opportunity, as institutional entrepreneurs from a broader range of institutions can look further afield for support.

Business and industry are not the only enterprises where some fear that university support has veered from a sense of broader public purpose. While the enterprise of government has long relied on a variety of academic disciplines, political science has historically been fundamental to state initiatives. Interestingly, contemporary concern does not center around a fear that government patrons are somehow inhibiting scholars from systematically considering contemporary politics and policy; rather, critics question whether political scholars themselves have any interest in shaping the issues of the day. Cook acknowledges that the rise of positivist approaches in the 1950s might have led the discipline away from issues of administration. Yet he assumes that the need for quality public governance is growing so apparent and necessary as to compel political science to return to such efforts.

Jonathan Cohn is less sanguine about the discipline's role. In a journalistic critique titled "Irrational Exuberance: When Did Political Science Forget about Politics?" he argues that the tendency away from a prescriptive political science has only intensified in recent years. After recounting how, even as recently as the 1980s, such scholars as James Q. Wilson and Richard Neustadt were highly active in shaping public policy, Cohn describes the discipline currently.

> The future of political science . . . lies in the hands of a different breed, which is epitomized by a man named Kenneth Shepsle.
>
> Shepsle, too, is considered among the generation's leading scholars of American government. Yet if you look for Shepsle in the Lexis-Nexis database of newspapers and magazines, you will find not one quotation from him on a contemporary debate about congressional reform, let alone an op-ed or longer essay under his byline. . . . He has never served on a government commission, testified before one of the committees he's made a career of studying or otherwise put his expertise to use in a public forum. . . . If that seems at all strange, then you haven't been keeping up with developments in political science over the past two decades.[16]

I would quibble with the blanket nature of Cohn's argument and suggest that there are some political scientists whose efforts influence policy debates and development—Robert Putnam most readily comes to mind.

Cohn's fundamental assertion that much of political science has lost interest in the basic activities of public life may ring true. He is not the first to raise such issues in recent years. However, similar to the views of Twitchell as well as Press and Washburn, Cohn's critique underscores, rather than undermines, the unique societal position of universities. Concerns about the university's ability to usefully address questions of public concern date back to the very origins of political science: one need only recall that the *New York Times* of the 1880s praised Columbia's and Michigan's programs in political science while at the same time wondering whether offerings would include courses in machine-style manipulations and chicanery.[17]

The debate itself shows the vibrancy of the universities' overall concern with issues of policy and administration. As mentioned earlier, some proponents of revitalizing public administration, such as Nicholas Henry, propose actively separating the study of public policy and education of administrators from the study of political science. Cook believes political science is integral to revitalizing the study of administration. Most important, because of the inherently public mission and spiritedness of the university, its unique position, and its entrepreneurial desire, no one is suggesting that such revitalization efforts, wherever located, are not the responsibility of the university.

The Modern University and the
Responsibility of Institutional Entrepreneurship

While arguably the most relevant for specific consideration of universities' societal position and support of America's national community, industrial competitiveness, and intellectual vanguard, the previously mentioned critiques are far from the only ones regarding America's universities. In "The University and Its Critics," an essay stemming from a larger symposium coinciding with Princeton's 250th anniversary (in 1996),[18] Cornell president Frank H. T. Rhodes noted, "in an era when the people are being asked to 'sacrifice' for the sake of the nation's long term strength, universities are perceived as self-indulgent, arrogant and resistant to change." Rhodes recognized that "these critics are, by and large, insiders who have had a greater degree of involvement with universities than most Americans,[19] and that makes their criticisms all the more troubling."[20]

While not necessarily addressing all of its critics, Rhodes broadly responded to criticism of the university by harkening back to Woodrow Wilson's address "Princeton in the Nation's Service," presented at the institution's sesquicentennial celebration. Rhodes continued: "universities have become, both by demand and by choice, far more actively involved in the large issues of public life. They are now citizens, partners in a social compact that places great responsibility and high expectations upon them."[21] Rhodes's characterization is not unique. In fact, the critics Rhodes seeks to address would likely dismiss his rhetoric as hackneyed banalities. I would suggest, however, that his insight that universities' public role is driven as much by institutional choice as by public demand offers a seed for a common fertile ground. The vibrancy and potential of the university is in fact reflected by both the harshness of its critics and the faith of its leaders.

On the broadest level, universities remain fundamentally public institutions. Thus, debate about their future often reflects a larger and healthier debate about issues of concern to the polity and society. More specifically, to both the practitioner and the researcher of public policy, contemporary questions about the appropriate reach of the national state lead to similar questions regarding the current relationship of universities to government and of expertise to policymaking. Nonetheless, contemporary questions and controversies should not lead us to easily dismiss the university's significance. Rather, in response to such concerns, I would suggest that there is a correspondence between questions regarding the size and scope of the national state and examinations of the leading universities' public role.

As Skowronek emphasizes and many others have noted, the United States has always had "the problem of the state." On the one hand, there is "America's remarkable capacity to regenerate its government peacefully." On the other hand, "there were no unqualified triumphs in building a new American state."[22] Summarizing the complexity this entails, Skowronek stresses:

> The path taken in modern American institutional development has now fully eclipsed the sense of statelessness that so clearly marked our early politics, but that past was not without consequences for present difficulties. Its impact is uncovered in the political and institutional struggles that attended the formation of the state in which we now live.[23]

Correspondingly, while the university was the most significant contributor to the development of the new American state and was arguably the most influential institution to emerge from the era, its success was also not unqualified.

Needless to say, the American state and the nation's leading universities were and are distinct institutions. However, owing to their related growth, they are, to some extent, committed to shared fates. As I discussed earlier in this work, one of the major qualifications of the universities' triumph was the fact that no matter the nature and extent of their public service, universities have been criticized at various times for being elitist. At its worst, this criticism has found universities characterized as unresponsive to popular opinion and unaware of genuine public concerns. The American system's federalism and pluralism make it difficult for any public institution to be universally praised. Therefore, despite their regional appeal and sporadic efforts at inclusiveness, American universities have found themselves under attack from the public they have sought to serve.[24]

With this in mind, one could argue that contemporary condemnations of higher education are simply reflections of the inherent, historic limits of the reach of both higher education and the national state. The questions raised by such condemnations do not simply concern how universities are called on to support the national state and how they offer to do so. Instead, the questions involve the more fundamental matter of what issues are deemed to be of public concern. While supplying the manpower for the national state, universities have also defined its capabilities. Since their emergence in the later half of the nineteenth century, universities have defined which social and political issues are appropriate state concerns and how the state should go about addressing those concerns.

Obviously, university efforts at agenda setting are driven somewhat by government incentive and public sentiment. However, universities have frequently brought to issues the initial awareness that fostered government incentives and nurtured public sentiment. Beyond illuminating the process by which university-based expertise came to be crucial for the development of the new American state and its associated reforms, appreciation of universities' role in agenda setting further highlights the contemporary significance of institutions of higher education in shaping the parameters of policy and the scope of reform.

To those of us witnessing the current climate of university relations with the national state and understanding universities' fundamental role in supporting and defining state capacities, it seems appropriate to begin asking the broader question: as the development and application of public policy evolve, how, too, will the university-based system of expertise? This is not to say that the system of university-based expertise created in concert with the development of the national state is irrelevant to contemporary concerns. However, as the national state has been and will be questioned with regard to its efficiency and equity, the system of university-based expertise has been and will be similarly scrutinized.

University support for the American state was fundamental to the Progressives' efforts at reform and to later expansions of the federal government in the New Deal and Great Society eras. Though without pithy definition, the current era has been marked by the enactment of welfare reform, calls for redefinition of education and health care, and renewed attention to America's role in the world (stemming from the terrorist attacks of September 11, 2001), all of which have significantly altered the expectations and practice of administration as well the overall relations between the state and its citizenry. Responding to both demand and desire, universities have, to varying degrees, shaped this redefinition. In the American state, the university's authority—its ability to support such redefinition—derives from its credibility and its relevance. The biggest threat posed by the critics that Frank Rhodes and others address is not their critique; it is their potential indifference. If the university comes to be broadly perceived as simply a vested interest inhibiting the consideration of reform, rather than as an agenda-setting institution, its unique societal position—its relevance—is lost. This is not to say that the university does not possess and pursue a public agenda; even the state itself occasionally acts as a competing political interest. But acknowledging the agenda-setting role of the university emphasizes that the privileged position the university has held—the unique role it has played—stemmed from its place as a forum for transparent competition between public ideas as well as its position as a mechanism for national coordination of them.

A Note on Sources

In conducting my research, I relied primarily on the archives of the University of Michigan, the University of California, Yale University, Harvard University, Columbia University, and Johns Hopkins University. My work in these archives was supplemented by published collections of these schools' and other educational institutions' annual reports as well as by various federal bulletins, contemporary newspapers, and secondary histories of the period generally and of higher education specifically.

I have drawn heavily on the personal papers of University of Michigan president James Burrill Angell. The Angell Papers, housed at the university's Bentley Historical Library, are enormously helpful for any scholar of higher education's development and its role in greater society at the turn of the twentieth century. The papers are valuable for a variety of reasons. First is the length and breadth of Angell's career: Angell served as president of the university for a remarkable period of thirty-eight years. Beyond this impressive biography, however, lies Angell's open mind and quiet nature. These traits not only guided his governance and service but also defined his relations with his peers. Thus, the Angell Papers comprise an exceptional repository not only of his ideas and opinions but of those of his colleagues from across academia and public life. Owing to both his tenure and his position as a linchpin between the established private universities of the East and the developing public institutions of the West and the South, Angell invariably found himself involved—not necessarily as an arbiter, but as a sympathetic ear—in the various debates that shaped higher education's contribution to the national state. Angell was not always the most vociferous participant in these debates. However, he was often the most central one—a conduit and a sounding board.

While certainly fundamental to this project, the Angell Papers and other documents at Bentley Library were by no means the only resources I employed. I also visited a number of other campuses, focusing primarily on the papers of their various leaders. While an individual assessment of each collection does not seem necessary, a few observations are in order.

First, while seemingly mundane, a discussion of variations in the organization of the archives themselves is worthwhile. The Angell Papers were the best-cataloged and best-organized collection, in no small part owing to the exceptional staff and relatively abundant resources of Bentley Library and the University of Michigan's School of Information. Interestingly, unlike the papers of every other university president I visited, Angell's papers were organized strictly in chronological order. Delving into his papers, one encounters the gamut of administrative activities, from discussion of how to structure the archives of the federal government to an explanation to the parents of one sophomore that their son had been suspended for debauchery, including consorting with women that the parents would not entertain in their own home.

At other institutions, presidential papers were generally organized by correspondent or subject, a system that can cause the researcher some trepidation. For example, while it is certainly helpful to have all of California president Benjamin Ide Wheeler's correspondence with Gifford Pinchot in one file, a researcher cannot help but fear missing out on auxiliary discussions and issues when approaching collections organized according to this method. Inevitably, there are institutional idiosyncrasies. For example, at Yale, Arthur Twining Hadley's incoming correspondence is organized by author, whereas copies of his responses are organized chronologically. Obviously, there is no best method, but for the researcher, there are admittedly varying comfort levels and comparative advantages for each.

Generally, most of the archives at the schools I visited, while not necessarily including the extensive cataloging of Michigan's Bentley Library, were well organized and maintained. One notable exception was at Columbia. Housed in the regal Low Library, the Columbia archives were certainly useful. Unfortunately, at the time of my visit, they were pitifully understaffed and a tad disorganized. Uncertainty abounded as to where collections were actually housed and if they were available. The staff was very professional and courteous but seemingly shackled by a lack of institutional support. I mention Columbia's limits here not as a criticism but as a reflection of the diversity that exists between seemingly comparable resources.

Second, beyond simply adding new resources, these additional archives were essential for confirming the patterns and processes that I discovered. *Triangulation* is a somewhat loaded word stemming from the Bill Clinton–Dick Morris era of politics. However, it is the most apt description of how I used multiple sources to confirm observations. The necessity of this method is perhaps readily understood, but its value should not be underestimated.

Reconstructing history always presents difficulties. Detailing the historical development of a political process perhaps presents more, because decisions not made or actions not taken can have as significant an impact as those that are. The failure to establish a federally sponsored national university is arguably the most striking example of this. However, even small "nondecisions" present challenges, as our understanding of these events often depends on the reminiscences of the participants themselves. These recollections, in keeping with the limits of human nature and memory, sometimes might not be fully accurate. In the course of this work, I encountered the most striking example of this phenomenon in the letters from Northwestern president A. W. Harris to James Burrill Angell requesting advice on how to apply for membership in the Association of American Universities. Harris claimed that when the association was founded, Northwestern had been asked to join but, owing to the absence of the university's president from the country, was not able to attend the initial meeting and so was not included in the association. This seems to be a perfectly legitimate explanation. However, as I mention in my discussion of this request in chapter 7, the letter sent to the original invitees and Benjamin Ide Wheeler's draft letter of invitation make no mention of Northwestern. One might assume that Harris's misrepresentation stemmed from faulty institutional memory rather than purposeful deception: Harris had not been at Northwestern when the AAU was founded. Nonetheless, whatever the reason, Harris's mischaracterization underscores the value of and need for multiple sources when pursuing an accurate historical narrative.

Of course, despite these efforts at "triangulation," there remains the question of source selection. Why did I focus on archives from the leading universities to examine universities' efforts on behalf of the national state? In addressing such concerns, it is important to make two points. First, as I have discussed, my goal was not simply to prove that universities played a significant role in the development of the federal state. Numerous scholars of American political development have recognized universities' influence. Rather, I sought to detail the process by which universities came to play such a significant role. Thus, in pursuit of specificity, I made the nation's leading universities the primary focus of my research. Second, the influence of the nation's leading universities on the whole of higher education, especially in the period considered, cannot be overstated. This influence is significant to the researcher for a number of reasons. First and most obviously, the leading universities produced scholars who would fill professorships and leadership positions not only at research institutions but also at various smaller state schools and liberal arts colleges. Additionally and in some ways correspondingly, this influence also enhances the value of the leading universities' archives. Their peers, including those at smaller institutions, continually called on the heads of these institutions for advice and guidance. Thus, while not necessarily providing an absolutely complete picture, the archives of leading universities certainly provide an exceptionally full one.

Notes

Chapter 1

1. Theda Skocpol, "Bringing the State Back In: Strategies of Analysis in Current Research," in *Bringing the State Back In*, ed. Peter Evans, Dietrich Rueschemeyer, and Theda Skocpol (New York: Cambridge University Press, 1985), 14.

2. Lawrence Veysey, *The Emergence of the American University* (Chicago: University of Chicago Press, 1965).

3. Ibid.

4. Stephen Skowronek, *Building a New American State: The Expansion of National Administrative Capacities, 1877–1920* (New York: Cambridge University Press, 1987), 42.

5. Eldon Eisenach, *The Lost Promise of Progressivism* (Lawrence: University Press of Kansas, 1994), 12.

6. Ibid., 7.

7. Ibid., 3, 103.

8. Ibid., 107.

9. George Marsden, *The Soul of the American University* (New York: Oxford University Press, 1994).

10. Julie Reuben, *The Making of the Modern University* (Chicago: University of Chicago Press, 1996).

11. Jon H. Roberts and James Turner, *The Sacred and the Secular University* (Princeton: Princeton University Press, 2000).

12. Roger Geiger, *To Advance Knowledge: The Growth of American Research Universities, 1900–1940* (New York: Oxford University Press, 1986).

13. Roger Williams, *The Origins of Federal Support for Higher Education* (University Park: Pennsylvania State University Press, 1991).

14. John Aubrey Douglass, *The California Idea and American Higher Education: 1850 to the 1960 Master Plan* (Palo Alto: Stanford University Press, 2000).

15. Michael Dennis, *Lessons in Progress: State Universities and Progressivism in the New South, 1880–1920* (Urbana: University of Illinois Press, 2000).

16. Veysey, *Emergence of the American University*, 455.

17. Hugh Hawkins, *Banding Together: The Rise of National Associations in Higher Education, 1887–1950* (Baltimore: Johns Hopkins University Press, 1992), 13.

18. Peter Evans, Dietrich Rueschemeyer, and Theda Skocpol, "Toward a More Adequate Understanding of the State," in *Bringing the State Back In*, ed. Peter Evans,

Dietrich Rueschemeyer, and Theda Skocpol (New York: Cambridge University Press, 1985), 360.

19. Clyde Barrow, *Universities and the Capitalist State* (Madison: University of Wisconsin Press, 1990).

20. Michael Cohen, James March, and Johan Olsen, "A Garbage Can Model of Organizational Choice." *Administrative Science Quarterly* 17 (1972): 1–25.

21. John W. Kingdon, *Agendas, Alternatives, and Public Policies*, 2nd ed. (New York: Harper Collins, 1995).

22. Along with Skowronek and Eisenach, Brian Cook details the importance of this era, in *Bureaucracy and Self-Government* (Baltimore: Johns Hopkins University Press, 1996).

23. Richard Bensel, *Yankee Leviathan: The Origins of Central State Authority in America, 1859–1877* (New York: Cambridge University Press, 1990).

24. Robert Wiebe, *The Search for Order* (New York: Hill and Wang, 1968).

25. Robert Wiebe, *Self-Rule: A Cultural History of American Democracy* (Chicago: University of Chicago Press, 1995), 143.

26. Richard Hofstadter, *The Age of Reform: From Bryan to FDR* (New York: Random House, 1960).

27. Skowronek, *Building a New American State.*

28. Ibid., 31.

29. Cook, *Bureaucracy and Self-Government,* 1.

30. Skowronek, *Building a New American State.*

31. Ibid., 13.

32. Ibid., 15.

33. Ibid., 31.

34. Ibid., 43.

35. Eisenach, *Lost Promise of Progressivism.*

36. Ibid., 1–2.

37. Ibid.

38. Cook, *Bureaucracy and Self-Government,* 69.

39. Thomas L. Haskell, *The Emergence of the Professional Social Science* (Urbana: University of Illinois Press, 1977), 33.

40. James March and Johan Olsen, *Rediscovering Institutions* (New York: Free Press, 1989),105.

41. Paul DiMaggio and Walter Powell, "The Iron Cage Revisited: Institutional Isomorphism and Collective Rationality," in *The New Institutionalism in Organizational Analysis,* ed. Walter Powell and Paul DiMaggio (Chicago: University of Chicago Press, 1991).

42. March and Olsen, *Rediscovering Institutions,* 30.

43. Max Weber, *Economy and Society,* vols. 1–2 (1922; reprint, Berkeley: University of California Press, 1978); Gianfranco Poggi, *The Development of the Modern State: A Sociological Introduction* (Stanford: Stanford University Press, 1978); Skocpol, "Bringing the State Back In."

44. Skocpol, "Bringing the State Back In."

45. John W. Kingdon, "Politicians, Self-Interest, and Ideas," in *Reconsidering the Democratic Public,* ed. George Marcus and Russell Hanson (University Park: Pennsylvania State University Press, 1993), 76–77.

46. Mary Douglas, *How Institutions Think* (Syracuse: Syracuse University Press, 1986).

47. Skocpol, "Bringing the State Back In"; Douglass North, *Institutions, Institu-*

tional Change, and Economic Performance (New York: Cambridge University Press, 1990); Robert Jackman, *Power without Force: The Political Capacity of Nation-States* (Ann Arbor: University of Michigan Press, 1993).

48. Douglas, *How Institutions Think,* 45.

49. Evans, Rueschemeyer, and Skocpol, "More Adequate Understanding of the State."

50. Skowronek, *Building a New American State,* 15.

51. Eisenach, *Lost Promise of Progressivism,* 31.

52. Veysey, *Emergence of the American University,* ix.

53. Those familiar with the AAU will note that these categories do not include all of its founding members; they exclude Clark University and the Catholic University of America. Though not included in the typology for the sake of design elegance, these institutions are discussed at various points in this work.

54. Caroline Hazard to Charles Eliot, June 11, 1907, Records of President Charles W. Eliot, UAI.5.150, Harvard Archives, Harvard University Library.

55. V. O. Key, *Southern Politics* (New York: A. A. Knopf, 1949); Jack L Walker, "The Diffusion of Innovation among the American States," *American Political Science Review* 68 (1968): 880–99; Richard Bensel, *Sectionalism and American Political Development, 1880–1980* (Madison: University of Wisconsin Press, 1984).

56. Jackman, *Power without Force;* Arthur Stinchcombe, *Information and Organizations* (Berkeley: University of California Press, 1990).

57. Evans, Rueschemeyer, and Skocpol, "On the Road toward a More Adequate Understanding of the State"; Skowronek, *Building a New American State.*

58. The influence of these leaders has been addressed at length in histories of higher education, such as Veysey's *Emergence of the American University* and Rudolph's *The American College and University: A History* (Athens: University of Georgia Press, 1990), as well as in contemporary considerations of universities' societal role—most notably in essays by Harold Shapiro and Hanna Gray in *Universities and Their Leadership,* ed. William G. Bowen and Harold T. Shapiro (Princeton: Princeton University Press, 1998).

59. Justin Winsor to James Burrill Angell, November 24, 1887, James Burrill Angell Papers, box 3, folder 97, Bentley Historical Library, University of Michigan.

60. *Portland Oregonian,* February 28, 1909; *Wheeling (WV) News,* February 28, 1909.

61. Harry Pratt Judson to James Burrill Angell, December 5, 1906, Angell Papers, box 6, folder 225.

62. Hadley's appointment in 1899 itself reflected the evolution of the university, as he was the first layperson to head Yale.

63. Quoted in Thomas Dyer, *The University of Georgia: A Bicentennial History, 1785–1985* (Athens: University of Georgia Press, 1985).

64. Virginius Dabney, *Mr. Jefferson's University* (Charlottesville, VA: University Press of Virginia, 1981).

65. "Virginia University Gets Rockefeller Gift," *New York Times,* April 14, 1905, 6.

66. Veysey, *Emergence of the American University.*

Chapter 2

1. Earl D. Babst and Lewis G. Vander Velde, eds., *Michigan and the Cleveland Era* (Ann Arbor: University of Michigan Press, 1948), 4; Woodrow Wilson, "Princeton in

the Nation's Service," address delivered at Princeton's sesquicentennial celebration, October 1896.

2. Marsden, *Soul of the American University*, 181.

3. Skowronek, *Building a New American State*, 14.

4. Ibid., 31.

5. Eisenach, *Lost Promise of Progressivism*, 7.

6. Cook, *Bureaucracy and Self-Government*.

7. Evans, Rueschemeyer, and Skocpol, "On the Road toward a More Adequate Understanding of the State."

8. Skowronek, *Building a New American State*; Eisenach, *Lost Promise of Progressivism*; Wiebe, *Search for Order*.

9. DiMaggio and Powell, "Iron Cage Revisited."

10. Robert Axelrod and Michael Cohen, *Harnessing Complexity* (New York: Free Press, 2000).

11. Benjamin Wheeler to Seth Low, October 6, 1899, Benjamin Ide Wheeler Papers, BANC MSS C-B 1044, Bancroft Library, University of California, Berkeley.

12. Daniel Kevles, "A Time for Audacity: What the Past Has to Teach the Present about Science and the Federal Government," in *Universities and Their Leadership*, ed. William G. Bowen and Harold T. Shapiro (Princeton: Princeton University Press, 1998).

13. Benjamin Wheeler to Gifford Pinchot, April 3, 1901, Wheeler Papers.

14. "Urge Students to Camps," *New York Times*, November 18, 1915, 3.

15. "Drafting Our Universities," *New York Times*, October 20, 1918, 72.

16. Rudolph, *American College and University*; William Reese, *The Origins of the American High School* (New Haven: Yale University Press, 1995).

17. A. F. Nightingale to James Burill Angell, April 22, 1899, Angell Papers, box 5, folder 173.

18. Skowronek, *Building a New American State*.

19. Paul Starr, *The Social Transformation of American Medicine* (New York: Basic Books, 1982).

20. Rudolph, *American College and University*.

21. "Virginia University Gets Rockefeller Gift," *New York Times*, April 14, 1905, 6.

22. *Biennial Report of the President of the University on Behalf of the Regents to the Governor, 1910–1912* (Berkeley, 1912).

23. Michael Oriard, *Reading Football: How the Popular Press Created an American Spectacle* (Chapel Hill: University of North Carolina Press, 1993); J. Douglas Toma, *Football U.*, (Ann Arbor: University of Michigan Press, 2003).

24. C. M. Woodward, comp., *Opinions of Educators on the Value & Total Influence of Inter-collegiate & Inter-scholastic American Football as Played in 1903–1909* (St. Louis, 1910).

25. Robin Lester, *Stagg's University* (Urbana: University of Illinois Press, 1999).

26. "Columbia Begins a New Era," *New York Times*, October 2, 1894, 9.

27. "Ending College Labors," *New York Times*, July 2, 1880, 2.

28. "The Graduating Season," *New York Times*, June 26, 1880, 4.

29. Arthur Twining Hadley, *Baccalaureate Addresses and Talks on Kindred Themes* (New York: Scribner's and Sons, 1907), 180–81.

30. Ibid., 188–89.

31. "Our Future University," *New York Times*, April 8, 1883, 8.

32. "Liberty in Learning," *New York Times*, June 21, 1885, 6.

33. "President Low's Problem," *New York Times*, February 9, 1890, 4.

34. "Talking about Colleges," *New York Times*, December 30, 1891, 5.

35. Skowronek, *Building the New American State*, 42.

36. "Columbia's Green Old Age," *New York Times*, April 14, 1887, 9.

37. "Advance in Education," *New York Times*, February 28, 1892, 11.

38. "Gov. Roosevelt at Cornell," *New York Times*, June 21, 1899, 5.

Chapter 3

1. Bensel, *Yankee Leviathan*.

2. Richard Hofstadter and Wilson Smith, eds., *American Higher Education: A Documentary History*, 2 vols. (Chicago: University of Chicago Press, 1961), 2:568–69.

3. Roger Williams, *Federal Support for Higher Education*.

4. Hofstadter and Smith, *American Higher Education*, 568.

5. Andrew Dickson White, *The Autobiography of Andrew Dickson White* (New York: Century Company, 1905), 1:281.

6. Morris Bishop, *A History of Cornell* (Ithaca: Cornell University Press, 1962).

7. Bishop, *History of Cornell*.

8. Andrew Dickson White to Daniel Coit Gilman, March 16, 1864, Daniel Coit Gilman Papers, MS 1, box 1.49, Special Collections, Milton Eisenhower Library, Johns Hopkins University.

9. Andrew Dickson White to Daniel Coit Gilman, September 14, 1864, Gilman Papers, box 1.49.

10. Ibid.

11. Andrew Dickson White to Daniel Coit Gilman, November 14, 1864, Gilman Papers, box 1.49.

12. Bishop, *History of Cornell*.

13. Ibid.

14. Andrew Dickson White to Daniel Coit Gilman, May 5, 1865, Gilman Papers, box 1.49.

15. *New York Tribune*, March 20, 1868.

16. Brooks Mather Kelley, *Yale: A History* (New Haven: Yale University Press, 1974).

17. Ibid., 189.

18. "Yale's Unproductive Branch," *New York Times*, March 10, 1893, 6.

19. Verne Stadtman, *The University of California, 1868–1968* (New York: McGraw-Hill, 1970), 24.

20. *Report of the Regents of the University of California Relative to the Operations and Progress of the Institution* (Sacramento, 1872). Prior to this time, California did have institutions of higher learning. In 1851, the Jesuits had founded Santa Clara College, and the Methodists had founded California Wesleyan College (which became the University of the Pacific) in San Jose. In 1853, the New Light Presbyterians founded the Contra Costa Academy in Oakland, which was to become the College of California.

21. Stadtman, *University of California*.

22. Fabian Franklin, *The Life of Daniel Coit Gilman* (New York: Mead and Company, 1910), 118–19.

23. Inaugural address of Daniel Coit Gilman, November 1872, Gilman Papers, box 5.3.

24. Ibid.

25. Ibid.

26. Andrew Dickson White to Daniel Coit Gilman, October 7, 1874, Gilman Papers, box 1.49.

27. Andrew Dickson White to Daniel Coit Gilman, September 20, 1874, Gilman Papers, box 1.49. Ironically, the selection of Noah Porter, rather than himself, as president of Yale was one of the factors that drove Gilman to head to California.

28. Andrew Dickson White to Daniel Coit Gilman, December 8, 1864, Gilman Papers, box 1.49.

29. Daniel Carpenter, "The Corporate Metaphor and Executive Department Centralization in the United States, 1888–1928," *Studies in American Political Development* 12, no. 1 (1998): 162–203.

30. *Biennial Report of the University on Behalf of the Regents to the Governor, 1880–1882* (Sacramento, 1882), 26.

31. *Biennial Report of the President of the University on Behalf of the Regents to the Governor, 1894* (Berkeley, 1894), 10–11. In 1892, no report was issued; the report issued in 1893 covers three years; the 1894 report covers one year.

32. Roger Williams, *Federal Support for Higher Education.*

33. Andrew Dickson White to Daniel Coit Gilman, September 22, 1873, Gilman Papers, box 1.49.

34. Bishop, *History of Cornell*, 254.

35. Charles Kendall Adams to James Burrill Angell, July 19, 1885, Angell Papers, box 3, folder 86.

36. Moses Coit Tyler to James Burrill Angell, August 1, 1885, Angell Papers, box 3, folder 86.

37. Diary entry of Andrew Dickson White, December 1, 1885, quoted in Bishop, *History of Cornell*, 257–58.

38. Bishop, *History of Cornell*, 258.

39. *Biennial Report of the President of the University on Behalf of the Regents to the Governor, 1884–1886* (Sacramento, 1886) 8.

40. *Biennial Report of the President of the University on Behalf of the Regents to the Governor, 1880–1882* (Sacramento, 1882), 9.

41. Ibid.

42. Daniel Coit Gilman to James Burrill Angell, July 12, 1887, Angell Papers, box 3, folder 95.

43. John Swift to James Burrill Angell, May 24, 1887, Angell Papers, box 3, folder 94.

44. Ibid.

45. John Swift to James Burrill Angell, June 14, 1887, Angell Papers, box 3, folder 94.

46. E. W. Hilgard to James Burrill Angell, July 15, 1887, Angell Papers, box 3, folder 95.

47. John Swift to James Burrill Angell, August 7, 1887, Angell Papers, box 3, folder 95.

48. Ibid.

49. William T. Reid to James Burrill Angell, August 30, 1890, Angell Papers, box 3, folder 113. To contemporary observers, Reid's move from university president to school headmaster might seem a step down, but given the political intrigue and uncertainty surrounding the University of California, such a move is not altogether surprising.

Chapter 4

1. Woodrow Wilson to James Burrill Angell, November 7, 1887, Angell Papers, box 3, folder 97.

2. Ibid.

3. Ibid.

4. Ibid.

5. Woodrow Wilson to James Burrill Angell, November 15, 1887, Angell Papers, box 3, folder 97.

6. Woodrow Wilson, "The Study of Administration," *Political Science Quarterly* 2 (1887): 197–222.

7. Ibid.

8. Ibid.

9. Frances Lieber, "An Inaugural Address Delivered on the 17th of February, 1858, on Assuming the Chair of History and Political Science in Columbia College, New York," in *Discipline and History: Political Science and History,* ed. James Farr and Raymond Seidelman (Ann Arbor: University of Michigan Press, 1993), 21–32.

10. "Rearing a Race of Statesman," *New York Times,* February 23, 1879, 1.

11. Daniel Coit Gilman to Thomas Mortimer Cooley, November 16, 1880, Aa 2, box 7, Bentley Historical Library, University of Michigan.

12. Ibid.

13. George Brown to Thomas Mortimer Cooley, December 16, 1880, Aa 2, box 7, Bentley Historical Library, University of Michigan. In this era, the term *postgraduate* referred to all work done beyond the bachelor's—what we today commonly refer to as "graduate work."

14. Brown did not write simply to offer Cooley an opportunity to spearhead the Johns Hopkins program in historical and political science. He also wrote to express his support for Cooley's potential appointment to the Supreme Court and to stress that such long-term prospects should not keep Cooley from accepting the Hopkins post in the short term.

15. Thomas Mortimer Cooley to Daniel Coit Gilman, February 15, 1881, Aa 2, box 7, Bentley Historical Library, University of Michigan.

16. Herbert Baxter Adams to Thomas Mortimer Cooley, October 20, 1880, Aa 2, box 7, Bentley Historical Library, University of Michigan.

17. Herbert Baxter Adams to James Burrill Angell, November 15, 1887, Angell Papers, box 3, folder 97.

18. *John Hopkins University, Annual Report of the President, 1890–91* (Baltimore, 1891).

19. Michigan's plan called for a three year-course of study that would begin after a year of work in the university's College of Literature, Science, and the Arts or after the completion of the sophomore year somewhere else. Over the three years, a student would take courses in the political history of Europe, including studies of Europe's various peoples and nations; the constitutional history of the United States and Britain, including theories and methods of government; political economy and finance; application of social science; civil service in the United States and Britain; city government; management of prisoners and of the poor; taxation and revenue; public health; administrative law; modern diplomacy; and political ethics. Upon completion of these courses and a thesis, a student would earn a PhD.

20. "Scientific Political Training," *New York Times,* July 23, 1881, 4.

21. Ibid.

22. Keeping the careers of all of the Adams's straight can be confusing. Herbert Baxter Adams (1850–1901) helped found the American Historical Association and worked with Gilman to bring the seminar method and the "scientific" study of politics to Johns Hopkins. Henry Carter Adams (1851–1921) studied under Henry Baxter at Johns Hopkins, receiving one of the first PhDs granted in the United States. In

addition to his academic work, Henry Carter Adams served as chief economist for the Interstate Commerce Commission. Charles Kendall Adams (1835–1902) served as president of Cornell and the University of Wisconsin. These men were not related to one another, nor were they related to Henry Brooks Adams (1838–1918), the Harvard historian who, among these men, is the most well known in the popular imagination, for his work *The Education of Henry Adams.*

23. Herbert Carter Adams to James Burrill Angell, July 15, 1885, Angell Papers, box 3, folder 86.

24. Ibid.

25. Ibid.

26. *University of Michigan President's Report, 1889* (Ann Arbor, 1889), 5.

27. In 1914, Michigan again established a formalized program, the Institute of Public Administration, the progenitor of the university's current school of public policy.

28. In 1894, for example, two PhD's were granted in political economy—one with the subfields of sociology and statistics, the other with the subfields of administrative and constitutional law.

29. The American Social Science Association had been founded in 1865. However, more formal disciplinary associations, such as the American Historical Association, would not be founded until 1884; the American Economic Association followed in 1888, the American Political Science Association in 1903.

30. Andrew Dickson White to Daniel Coit Gilman, April 7, 1876, Gilman Papers, box 1.49.

31. Ibid.

32. Attachment, Henry Carter Adams to James Burrill Angell, March 25, 1886, Angell Papers, box 3, folder 88.

33. Henry Carter Adams to James Burrill Angell, March 7, 1887, Angell Papers, box 3, folder 92.

34. Henry Carter Adams to James Burrill Angell, March 25, 1886, Angell Papers, box 3, folder 88.

35. Ibid.

36. Henry Carter Adams to James Burrill Angell, March 7, 1887, Angell Papers, box 3, folder 92.

37. Ibid.

38. Ibid.

39. Henry Carter Adams to James Burrill Angell, July 1, 1887, Angell Papers, box 3, folder 95.

40. Ibid.

41. Skowronek, *Building a New American State.*

42. Ibid., 69.

43. Andrew Dickson White to James Burrill Angell, January 7, 1891, Angell Papers, box 3, folder 117. In addition to Angell, White hoped to include in his appeal Timothy Dwight of Yale, Franklin Carter of Williams, and Merrill Edwards Gates of Amherst.

44. James Burrill Angell to Andrew Dickson White, January 8, 1891, Angell Papers, box 3, folder 117.

45. White, *Autobiography,* 2:118.

46. Erwin Mecates to James Burrill Angell, March 17, 1891, Angell Papers, box 3, folder 120.

47. Andrew Dickson White, "Scientific and Industrial Education," *Popular Science Monthly,* April 1874.

48. Charles Kendall Adams to James Burrill Angell, June 23, 1888, Angell Papers, box 3, folder 100.

49. J. G. Wallace to James Burrill Angell, February 12, 1889, Angell Papers, box 3, folder 103.

50. George Miller to James Burrill Angell, February 14, 1889, Angell Papers, box 3, folder 103.

51. Ibid.

52. Ibid.

53. William Melville to James Burrill Angell, September 23, 1890, Angell Papers, box 3, folder 114.

54. J. H. McGowan to James Burrill Angell, March 8, 1880, Angell Papers, box 2, folder 48.

55. Levi Barbour to James Burrill Angell, March 20, 1880, Angell Papers, box 2, folder 48.

56. James Burrill Angell to Daniel Evarts, March 11, 1880, Angell Papers, box 2, folder 48.

57. Eli Blake to James Burrill Angell, March 21, 1880, Angell Papers, box 2, folder 48.

58. Lerned Moss to James Burrill Angell, March 23, 1880, Angell Papers, box 2, folder 48.

59. Charles Stille to James Burrill Angell, March 23, 1880, Angell Papers, box 2, folder 48.

60. Andrew Dickson White to James Burrill Angell, March 27, 1880, Angell Papers, box 2, folder 48.

61. James Burrill Angell to Andrew Dickson White, April 15, 1880, Angell Papers, box 2, folder 49.

62. Henry Simmons Frieze to James Burrill Angell, October 8, 1880, Angell Papers, box 2, folder 54.

63. James Burrill Angell to Henry Carter Adams, November 2, 1880, Angell Papers, box 2, folder 55.

64. *Manitoba Record,* October 15, 1885.

65. Quoted in William Putnam to James Burrill Angell, February 8, 1887, Angell Papers, box 3, folder 91.

66. Ibid.

67. White served diplomatic missions to both Germany and Russia.

68. Wilfred Shaw, with assistance from James R. Angell, "James B. Angell," in *Michigan and the Cleveland Era,* ed. Earl Babst and Lewis Vander Velde (Ann Arbor: University of Michigan Press, 1948).

69. James Burrill Angell to Andrew Dickson White, October 5, 1885, Angell Papers, box 3, folder 87.

Chapter 5

1. William T. Harris, "The Necessity of Free Public High Schools," *New England Journal of Education* 11 (1880): 53.

2. Between serving as superintendent of St. Louis schools and commissioner of education, Harris assisted Bronson Alcott (Louisa May's father) and Franklin Sanborn in managing the Concord (MA) School of Philosophy from 1880 to 1889.

3. Freize not only created the system of admission by diploma but also intro-

duced coeducation to the University of Michigan. He served as interim president during Angell's diplomatic mission to China.

4. *University of Michigan President's Report of the Board of Regents, 1889–90* (Ann Arbor, 1890). Interestingly, a modified version of such a system of admission returned in the late 1990s as a response to concerns about affirmative action and alleged bias on the Scholastic Aptitude Test (SAT). The most notable example occurred at the University of Texas, where finishing in the top 15 percent of one's high school class granted one admission regardless of test scores.

5. Minutes of the Chicago Board of Education, February 18, 1891, Angell Papers, box 3, folder 120.

6. James Burrill Angell to Shatock Hartwell, June 2, 1891, Angell Papers, box 3, folder 123.

7. *University of Michigan President's Report to the Board of Regents, 1890–91* (Ann Arbor, 1891).

8. Ibid.

9. Dilbert Haff to James Burill Angell, May 14, 1889, Angell Papers, box 3, folder 105. Typical of other instances, Angell received letters in March 1891 from Ira Allen of the Allen Academy in Chicago asking for advice on replacing Latin with German and from Allan Marendorf of the high school in Helena, Montana, asking whether the next building constructed should be a gymnasium or a science laboratory.

10. A. F. Nightingale to James Burrill Angell, May 17, 1894, Angell Papers, box 4, folder 140.

11. A. F. Nightingale to James Burrill Angell, April 22, 1899, Angell Papers, box 5, folder 173.

12. *Biennial Report of the President of the University on Behalf of the Regents to the Governor, 1882–1884* (Sacramento, 1884).

13. Ibid.

14. Ibid.

15. Ibid.

16. Ibid.

17. Ibid.

18. *University of Michigan President's Report to the Board of Regents, 1889–1890* (Ann Arbor, 1890).

19. S. S. Lows to James Burrill Angell, October 10, 1887, Angell Papers, box 3, folder 96.

20. William T. Reid to James Burrill Angell, August 30, 1890, Angell Papers, box 3, folder 113.

21. Charles Eliot to James Burrill Angell, August 2, 1892, Angell Papers, box 4, folder 128.

22. In addition to William T. Harris (the commissioner of education) and headmasters and principals from Massachusetts, New Jersey, New York, and Illinois, the committee included Eliot of Harvard, Angell of Michigan, and the presidents of the University of Colorado, the University of Missouri, Vassar, and Oberlin.

23. Charles Eliot to James Burrill Angell, April 11, 1893, Angell Papers, box 4, folder 132.

24. James Baker to the Committee of Ten, January 1893, Angell Papers, box 4, folder 130.

25. Ibid.

26. Charles Eliot to James Burrill Angell, December 8, 1893, Angell Papers, box 4, folder 138.

27. Nicholas Murray Butler to Charles Eliot, February 26, 1894, Presidents' Papers, University Archives, Low Library, Columbia University.

28. Ibid.

29. Charles Eliot to Nicholas Murray Butler, March 1, 1894, Columbia University Presidents' Papers.

30. Another early effort at formal coordination was spearheaded by Vassar College and its committee on certificate privileges for women in education. The committee's chairman, William Dwight, wrote to Angell asking for his assistance. He explained that Vassar was often asked to accept certificates for the passage of other schools' entrance exams and wondered if Michigan had a similar experience. In view of the frequency of such requests and "of the difficulty in making satisfactory decisions in such cases," Dwight thought it "proper to suggest the possibility of finding some common ground on which the leading collegiate institutions which admit women to their courses, might base a uniform usage with reference to the mutual acceptance of certificates of entrance exams passed by them or accepted by them." Dwight inquired if Angell was willing to join a committee with this purpose, along with presidents of other leading colleges (William Dwight to James Burrill Angell October 14, 1895, Angell Papers, box 4, folder 147). Dwight did not succeed in organizing a formal committee, but like the work of the Committee of Ten, his efforts did spark later discussion of coeducation and examinations for admission, among the Middle States Association and the College Entrance Examination Board in the early years of the twentieth century. Included in these organizations were members of the Association of Collegiate Alumnae (Boston University, Bryn Mawr, California, Cornell, MIT, Michigan, Northwestern, Oberlin, Smith, Syracuse, Wellesley, Wesleyan, and Wisconsin) and representatives of Brown, Adelbert, Radcliffe, and Barnard.

31. A. F. Nightingale to James Burrill Angell, June 23, 1896, Angell Papers, box 4, folder 158.

32. James Burrill Angell to James Rowland Angell, April 6, 1896, Angell Papers, box 4, folder 154.

33. For Columbia and Yale, the renaming was straightforward. Harvard had actually been chartered by the state of Massachusetts as a "university" in 1780. It was not until the creation of the Faculty of Arts and Science—through the combination, under Eliot, of the faculty of the College and the faculty of the Lawrence Scientific School—that the name "Harvard University" came into common usage. Princeton was officially chartered as the College of New Jersey and changed its name to Princeton University in 1896.

34. Kelley, *Yale*, 283.

35. "Her Twelfth President: Yale Installs Her New Head, Dr. Timothy Dwight," *New York Times*, July 2, 1886, 2.

36. "Our Future University," *New York Times*, April 8, 1883, 8.

37. *Memorial of the Johns Hopkins University to the Legislature of Maryland*, February 22, 1898, 5, Gilman Papers, box 1.62.

38. Arthur Twining Hadley to Charles W. Eliot, May 9, 1905, Eliot Records.

39. Eliot's intelligence proved correct. Adams would soon leave to serve as president of the University of Wisconsin, where he served until his death in 1902. Adams's Cornell successor, James Schurman, found the position far more tolerable, serving eighteen years, until 1920.

40. Charles W. Eliot to Daniel Coit Gilman, June 2, 1890, Eliot Records.

41. Cited in Herbert Baxter Adams, *Thomas Jefferson and the University of Virginia*, U.S. Bureau of Education Circular 1 (Washington, DC: Government Printing Office, 1888), 150.

42. Charles Smith, "Southern Colleges and Schools," *Atlantic Monthly*, October 1884, 548.

43. At the time of his honor, Bryce was a distinguished scholar. He would go on to achieve even greater renown as British ambassador to the United States from 1907 to 1913.

44. Martin Scott to James Burrill Angell, December 2, 1890, Angell Papers, box 3, folder 113.

45. James Schurman to James Burrill Angell, February 6, 1893, Angell Papers, box 4, folder 130.

46. Leland J. Stanford to Edward Holden, December 26, 1885, University of California (System), Office of the President, Records: Alphabetical Files, 1885–1913, CU-5, series 1, Bancroft Library, University of California, Berkeley.

47. Edward Holden to Leland J. Stanford, December 29, 1885, University of California Presidents' Records.

48. The academics mentioned are Benjamin Ide Wheeler, Charles Henry Hull, and Andrew Dickson White. Wheeler would leave Cornell to become president of the University of California and would be the driving force behind the AAU. Hull was a professor of history who would remain at Cornell and serve as dean. Though receiving many offers, White never returned to academic administration, instead serving a variety of diplomatic missions.

49. Charles Kendall Adams to James Burrill Angell, December 19, 1891, Angell Papers, box 4, folder 125.

50. Charles Eliot to James Burrill Angell, September 28, 1890, Angell Papers, box 3, folder 114.

51. James Burrill Angell to Charles Eliot, October 2, 1890, Angell Papers, box 3, folder 114.

52. James Burrill Angell to Charles Kendall Adams, October 9, 1890, Angell Papers, box 3, folder 114.

53. May Cheney to James Burrill Angell, September 4, 1893, Angell Papers, box 4, folder 134.

54. J. W. Anderson to James Burrill Angell, September 7, 1893, Angell Papers, box 4, folder 134.

55. *University of Michigan President's Report of the Board of Regents, 1889–90* (Ann Arbor, 1890).

56. Elmer Brown to James Burrill Angell, April 30, 1896, Angell Papers, box 4, folder 154.

57. Elmer Brown to James Burrill Angell, May 14, 1896, Angell Papers, box 4, folder 156.

58. Louis Webb to James Burrill Angell, June 6, 1896, Angell Papers, box 4, folder 157.

59. Louis Webb to James Burrill Angell, June 13, 1896, Angell Papers, box 4, folder 157.

60. California was not the only state to encounter slight difficulties while such programs were in their formative stages. A couple years before California's program was established, A. C. Horner, state examiner for northern Illinois, wrote Angell asking for a blank teacher's certificate. Horner claimed to have been presented a fraudulent certificate in the past year and suggested that this approach would discourage such false claims (A. C. Horner to James Burrill Angell, July 13, 1894, Angell Papers, box 4, folder 141).

61. T. C. Chamberlin to James Burrill Angell, October 21, 1895, Angell Papers, box 4, folder 147.

62. W. W. Campbell to James Burrill Angell, November 14, 1899, Angell Papers, box 5, folder 176.

63. Charles Eliot to James Burrill Angell, February 28, 1896, Angell Papers, box 4, folder 152.

64. Charles Harrison to James Burrill Angell, March 31 1897, Angell Papers, box 4, folder 163.

65. *University of Michigan President's Report to the Board of Regents, 1892–93* (Ann Arbor, 1893).

66. Hadley, *Baccalaureate Addresses.*

67. Charles Kendall Adams to James Burrill Angell, January 13, 1887, Angell Papers, box 3, folder 91.

68. *University of Michigan President's Report to the Board of Regents, 1885–86* (Ann Arbor, 1886).

69. Henry Wade Rogers to James Burrill Angell, March 18, 1885, Angell Papers, box 2, folder 83. Rogers would go on to serve as president of Northwestern University from 1890 to 1900 and as dean of Yale Law School from 1903 to 1916, as well as serving on the U.S. Circuit Court of Appeals for the Second District, as an appointee of Woodrow Wilson.

70. *University of Michigan President's Report to the Board of Regents, 1886–87* (Ann Arbor, 1887).

71. *University of Michigan President's Report to the Board of Regents, 1887–88* (Ann Arbor, 1888).

72. *University of Michigan President's Report to the Board of Regents, 1888–89* (Ann Arbor, 1889).

73. *University of Michigan President's Report to the Board of Regents, 1889–90* (Ann Arbor, 1890).

74. *Biennial Report of the President of the University on Behalf of the Regents to the Governor, 1896–98* (Berkeley, 1898).

75. Ibid.

Chapter 6

1. *Annals of Congress,* 13th Cong., 3rd sess., 14.

2. Hoyt recounted that George Washington was an active supporter of establishing a national university. As already mentioned in text, unfortunately for fellow supporters of this plan, Washington's fifty shares of the Potomac Company, left for "the endowment of a university to be established in the District of Columbia under the auspices of the General Government" (Hoyt 1892, 42), turned out to be worthless (ibid., 945).

3. John W. Hoyt, *Reports on the London and Paris Universal Expositions,* 6:397–98.

4. *Addresses and Proceedings of the National Education Association,* 1869, 23–25.

5. *Addresses and Proceedings of the National Education Association,* 1870.

6. *Addresses and Proceedings of the National Education Association,* 1871, 37.

7. Ibid., 41.

8. As the leading proponent of the movement, Hoyt was made chairman of the committee. Among those included in the committee's membership were Col. D. F. Boyd, president of the University of Louisiana, and Dr. Daniel Read, president of the University of Missouri. Seeking to incorporate all of the leading members of the educational policy domain, the committee also included the federal government's commissioner of education, the president of the NEA, the head of the National Academy of Sciences, the president of the National Association for the Advance-

ment of Sciences, and the president of the American Social Sciences Association, as ex officio, but active, members.

9. *Addresses and Proceedings of the National Education Association*, 1874, 73.

10. Ibid., 86.

11. John Hoyt, *Memorial in Regard to a National University* (Washington, DC: U.S. Government Printing Office, 1892).

12. *Congressional Record*, 45th Cong., 2nd sess., 1878, vol. 7, pt. I, 7.

13. U.S. Senate, *University of the United States*, 57th Cong., 1st sess., 1902, S. Rep. 945, 20–21.

14. In this era, it was Charles Eliot of Harvard, Timothy Dwight of Yale, Seth Low of Columbia, and Charles Harrison of Penn who most actively and publicly voiced their opposition to Hoyt's efforts.

15. John W. Hoyt to James Burrill Angell, April 10, 1895, Angell Papers, box 4, folder 144.

16. Ibid.

17. E. P. Powell to James Burrill Angell, November 28, 1895, Angell Papers, box 4, folder 148.

18. George Edmunds to James Burrill Angell, June 13, 1896, Angell Papers, box 4, folder 157.

19. U.S. Senate, *University of the United States*, 57th Cong., 1st sess., 1902, S. Rep. 945, 36.

20. Ibid., 36–37.

21. Charles Kendall Adams to James Burrill Angell, October 23, 1899, Angell Papers, box 5, folder 176. Needless to say, Adams's view can only be charitably described as a tad naive.

22. Benjamin Ide Wheeler to James Burrill Angell, October 24, 1899, Angell Papers, box 5, folder 176.

23. Henry Wade Rogers to James Burrill Angell, October 28, 1899, Angell Papers, box 5, folder 176.

24. John W. Hoyt to James Burrill Angell, February 14, 1900, Angell Papers, box 5, folder 177.

25. John W. Hoyt to Arthur Twining Hadley, April 6, 1900, Records of Arthur Twining Hadley as President of Yale University, RU 25, series I, box 45, Manuscripts and Archives, Yale University Library.

26. Charles W. Eliot to Daniel Coit Gilman, January 1, 1896, Gilman Papers, box 1.13.

27. Daniel Coit Gilman to Charles W. Eliot, January 3, 1896, Gilman Papers, box 1.13.

28. Arthur Twining Hadley to John W. Hoyt, May 15, 1900, Hadley Records, series II, box 98.

29. Ibid.

30. John W. Hoyt to Arthur Twining Hadley, May 21, 1900, Hadley Records, series I, box 45.

31. Arthur Twining Hadley to John W. Hoyt, June 1, 1900, Hadley Records, series II, box 98.

32. U.S. Senate, *University of the United States*, 57th Cong., 1st sess., 1902, S. Rep. 945, 29.

33. Ibid.

34. Ibid.

35. Ibid., 34.

36. *Proceedings of the Fifteenth Annual Convention of the Association of American Agricultural Colleges and Experiment Stations Held at Washington, DC, November 12–14, 1901*, Experimentation Station Bulletin 115, 1902.

37. Benjamin Ide Wheeler to Seth Low, October 6, 1899, Wheeler Papers.

38. In addition to the institutions of the signatories (the University of California, the University of Chicago, Columbia University, Harvard University, and Johns Hopkins University), the invitees were the Catholic University of America, Clark University, Cornell University, the University of Michigan, the University of Pennsylvania, Princeton University, Leland Stanford Junior University, the University of Wisconsin, and Yale University.

39. Benjamin Wheeler et al. to James Burrill Angell et al., January 1900, Angell Papers, box 5, folder 177.

40. Arthur Twining Hadley to Benjamin Wheeler et al., January 19, 1900, Hadley Records, series II, box 98.

41. Arthur Twining Hadley to Charles Eliot, January 19, 1900, Hadley Records, series II, box 98.

42. Arthur Twining Hadley to William Harper, February 5, 1900, Hadley Records, series II, box 98.

43. Arthur Twining Hadley to William Harper, February 21, 1900, Hadley Records, series II, box 98.

44. Arthur Twining Hadley to Benjamin Wheeler, February 24, 1900, Hadley Records, series II, box 98.

45. Ibid.

46. Ibid.

47. Arthur Twining Hadley to Benjamin Wheeler et al., March 22, 1900, Hadley Records, series II, box 98.

48. Association of American Universities, *Journal of Proceedings and Addresses* 1 (1900), 13.

49. William Harper to James Burrill Angell, March 25, 1900, Angell Papers, box 5, folder 178.

50. William Harper to James Burrill Angell, October 8, 1900, Angell Papers, box 5, folder 181.

51. Arthur Twining Hadley to John Simmons, March 15, 1901, Hadley Records, series II, box 98. Thankfully, Twining's daughter, Laura, would survive her bout with the disease.

52. James Burrill Angell to William Harper, October 10, 1900, Angell Papers, box 5, folder 181.

53. Hawkins, *Banding Together*, 13.

54. Nicholas Murray Butler to James Burrill Angell, July 16, 1901, Angell Papers, box 5, folder 184.

55. Association of American Universities, "Report of the Executive Committee of the Association Concerning the Scope of Membership Thereof," 1902, Hadley Records, series I, box 3.

56. Ibid.

57. While not irrelevant to the process, state governments were largely subservient to the desires and standards of local universities. In states with strong public universities, such as Michigan, governors and legislators invariably followed the lead of the university in regard to education and the regulation of professions. In states with strong private institutions, there was little that governors and others could do. For example, in November 1908, the New York State Board of Regents

proposed rating college degree programs, but Columbia's Butler and Yale's Hadley vociferously opposed the plan and refused to provide information deemed necessary for such an effort. Without the support of two of the region's leading institutions, the plan was abandoned.

58. Association of American Universities, "Report of the Executive Committee of the Association Concerning the Scope of Membership Thereof," 1902, Hadley Records, series I, box 3.

59. The merger failed that November, despite the efforts of NASU's chairman, University of Iowa president George MacLean, who had written Michigan's Angell explaining these efforts and asking for his assistance (George MacLean to James Burrill Angell, July 16, 1901, Angell Papers, box 5, folder 184).

60. Association of American Universities, "Report of the Executive Committee of the Association Concerning the Scope of Membership Thereof," 1902, Hadley Records, series I, box 3.

61. Ibid.

62. Ibid.

63. New York University Faculty to the Association of American Universities, December 9, 1902, Angell papers, box 5, folder 190. Twenty-three NYU faculty from such institutions as Chicago, Clark, Columbia, Cornell, Harvard, Johns Hopkins, Michigan, Princeton, and Yale signed the letter. The authors also noted: "many other professors of New York University, who hold degrees from one or another of the universities included in the Association withhold their signatures from this letter solely because invitations to the dinner have failed to reach them. They have in every case heard from, cordially endorsed the position above taken."

64. Ibid.

65. William Rainey Harper to Nicholas Murray Butler, October 3, 1904, Columbia University President's Papers.

66. Nicholas Murray Butler to William Rainey Harper, October 8, 1904, Columbia University President's Papers.

67. As Arthur Powell and others discuss, schools of education would not become fixtures on many campuses for another twenty years or so, and even those established were often thought of as "second-tier" institutions. Additionally, university-wide lectures were seen as a significantly more prestigious undertaking than a simple departmental appointment. See Arthur Powell, *The Uncertain Profession: Harvard and the Search for Educational Authority* (Cambridge: Harvard University Press, 1980).

68. When it was founded in 1817, the University of Michigan was modeled on the French system whereby the university incorporated not just education at all levels but public libraries and museums as well.

Chapter 7

1. The NEA had had a higher education division since 1870.

2. Hugh Hawkins, *Banding Together*, 141.

3. Benjamin Wheeler to James Burrill Angell, February 5, 1901, Angell Papers, box 5, folder 191.

4. Levi Barbour to James Burrill Angell, January 23, 1903, Angell Papers, box 5, folder 191.

5. Arthur Twining Hadley to J. Howard Rogers, November 26, 1899, Hadley Records, series II, box 98.

6. Gifford Pinchot to Arthur Twining Hadley, January 30, 1905, Hadley Records, series I, box 69.

7. Charles Eliot to James Burrill Angell, May 22, 1903, Angell Papers, box 5, folder 192.

8. Ibid.

9. *Michigan Alumnus,* May 1907, 2–3.

10. Ibid.

11. James Burrill Angell to Arthur Twining Hadley, July 10, 1909, Angell Papers, box 7, folder 247.

12. James Munoz to James Burrill Angell, December 7, 1908, Angell Papers, box 7, folder 238.

13. Nicholas Murray Butler to Arthur Twining Hadley, October 16, 1899, Hadley Records, series I, box 14.

14. Arthur Twining Hadley to Roger Sullivan, November 29, 1899, Hadley Records, series II, box 98.

15. Arthur Twining Hadley to Herbert Beecher, January 22, 1899, Hadley Records, series II, box 98. On a personal note, I faced a similar choice in the spring of 1987. Growing up in Los Angeles and choosing between Yale and the University of California at Berkeley, I chose to attend Yale.

16. Historians have generally referred to the organization as the College Entrance Examination Board. Butler and his colleagues tended to refer to the organization as the Middle States Board.

17. College Entrance Examination Board of the Middle States and Maryland Document 2, February 1, 1901, Hadley Records, series I, box 14. The founding members were Barnard, Bryn Mawr, Columbia, Cornell, Johns Hopkins, NYU, University of Pennsylvania, Rutgers, Swarthmore, Union, and the Women's College of Baltimore. Secondary school representatives from New York, Brooklyn, Newark, and Haverford were also present. Lehigh and Washington and Jefferson would join a little over a year later. The initial topics covered were to include botany, chemistry, English, French, German, Greek, history, Latin, math, physics, and zoology. Plans called for a conference to be held in December of each year, at which the board would name a chief examiner for each subject in addition to an established board of examiners. The exams were to be given in the first couple months of the following year, with exam books ranked (100–90, 90–75, 75–60, etc.). Students could have exams sent to any designated college upon request.

18. Statement of Princeton faculty to the College Entrance Examination Board of the Middle States and Maryland, May 30, 1901, Hadley Records, series I, box 14.

19. Nicholas Murray Butler to Arthur Twining Hadley, December 7, 1900, Hadley Records, series I, box 14.

20. Arthur Twining Hadley to Nicholas Murray Butler, December 9, 1900, Hadley Records, series II, box 98.

21. Nicholas Murray Butler to Arthur Twining Hadley, December 9, 1900, Hadley Records, series I, box 14.

22. Arthur Twining Hadley to Cromwell Childe, August 26, 1901, Hadley Records, series II, box 98.

23. Nicholas Murray Butler to Arthur Twining Hadley, November 27, 1901, Hadley Records, series I, box 14.

24. The mission of the NCA was stated as follows: "The purpose of the association shall be the development and maintenance of high standards of excellence for universities, colleges, and schools, the continued improvement of the educational

program and effectiveness of instruction on elementary, secondary, and college levels through a scientific and professional approach to the solution of educational
problems, the establishment of cooperative relationships between the schools and
colleges and universities within the territory of the association, and the maintenance
of effective working relationships with other educational organizations and accrediting agencies" (North Central Association, Articles of Incorporation, 1895), Angell
Papers, box 4, folder 148.

25. Represented on the commission were the University of Chicago, Colorado,
Iowa, Lewis Institute, Michigan State Normal School, Nebraska, Purdue, and Wisconsin, as well as the Chicago, Cleveland, and Indianapolis school boards.

26. A. S. Draper to James Burrill Angell, April 1, 1902, Angell Papers, box 5,
folder 187.

27. James Burrill Angell to A. S. Draper, April 3, 1902, Angell Papers, box 5,
folder 187.

28. R. H. Jesse to James Burrill Angell, February 27, 1905, Angell Papers, box 6,
folder 211.

29. *Yale Alumni Weekly,* May 26, 1911, 4.

30. Nicholas Murray Butler to James Burrill Angell, March 28, 1901, Angell
Papers, box 5, folder 178.

31. Ibid.

32. Daniel Coit Gilman to James Burrill Angell, March 21, 1906, Angell Papers,
box 6, folder 220.

33. The AAU's status is still apparent. An article in the *Chronicle of Higher Education* (February 4, 2000) describing the efforts of the University of Illinois at Chicago
to recruit top faculty summarized an interview with UIC provost Elizabeth Hoff-
man as follows: "What kind of institution will UIC become? Something akin to the
University of Michigan, she answers. In fact, she won't stop until she lands an invitation to the toniest club of them all: the 61-member Association of American Universities."

34. Arthur Twining Hadley to Henry Walcott, February 6, 1901, Hadley
Records, series II, box 98.

35. Though individual administrators and faculty may have expressed ambivalence about the university's relationship with its benefactor, there was no such concern institutionally. School letterhead even stated "Founded by John D. Rockefeller"
below the university's name. Thus, the my use of the possessive in text does not
seem excessive.

36. Henry Eddy to James Burrill Angell, July 8, 1905, Angell Papers, box 6, folder
214.

37. Ibid.

38. Ibid.

39. Cyrus Northrop to James Burrill Angell, July 11, 1905, Angell Papers, box 6,
folder 214.

40. R. S. Woodward to James Burrill Angell, July 28, 1905, Angell Papers, box 6,
folder 214.

41. Ellen Condliffe Lagemann, *Private Power for the Public Good: A History of the
Carnegie Foundation for the Advancement of Teaching* (Middletown, CT: Wesleyan University Press, 1983), 14.

42. Henry Prichett to James Burrill Angell, October 30, 1905, Angell Papers, box
6, folder 215.

43. The original forty-six schools included two institutions in Canada (Dal-
houise and McGill) and forty-four in the United States: Amherst, Beloit, Carleton,

Case (School of Applied Sciences), Clark, Clarkson, Colorado College, Columbia, Cornell, Dartmouth, George Washington University, Hamilton, Harvard, Hobart, Johns Hopkins, Knox, Iowa College (Grinell), Lawrence, Lehigh, Marietta, MIT, Middlebury, Mt. Holyoke, NYU, Oberlin, Pennsylvania, Poly (Brooklyn), Princeton, Radcliffe, Ripon, Smith, Stevens Institute, Trinity, Tulane, Union, Stanford, Vassar, Vermont, Wabash, Washington University, Wellesley, Wells, Western Reserve, Williams, the Western University of Pennsylvania (now the University of Pittsburgh), and Yale.

44. Announcement of the Carnegie Foundation for the Advancement of Teaching, July 9, 1906, Angell Papers, box 6, folder 215.

45. W. E. Stone to James Burrill Angell, October 9, 1906, Angell Papers, box 6, folder 230.

46. Charles Van Hise to James Burrill Angell, January 27, 1908, Angell Papers, box 6, folder 231.

47. Andrew Carnegie to Henry Prichett, March 31, 1908, Angell Papers, box 6, folder 234.

48. Charles Van Hise to Henry Prichett, April 16, 1908, Angell Papers, box 6, folder 234.

49. Announcement of the Carnegie Foundation for the Advancement of Teaching, May 27, 1908, Angell Papers, box 6, folder 235.

50. Henry Prichett to James Burrill Angell, June 11, 1909, Angell Papers, box 7, folder 245.

51. Nicholas Murray Butler to Arthur Twining Hadley, October 5, 1905, Hadley Records, series I, box 14.

52. Association of American Universities, *Journal of Proceedings and Addresses* 17 (1915), 22.

53. Report on university nomenclature, presented at the annual meeting of the Association of American Universities, Ithaca, NY, January 1909, Hadley Records, series I, box 3.

54. Report of the Committee on Academic and Professional Degrees, presented at the eighteenth annual conference of the Association of American Universities, Clark University, Worcester, MA, November 9–11, 1916, Hadley Records, series I, box 3.

55. Ibid.

56. Ibid. The Juris Doctor, or JD, also stems from this tradition.

57. Ibid.

58. Aaron Segerhamm to Arthur Twining Hadley, January 15, 1907, Hadley Records, series I, box 77; Phillip Twiling to James Burrill Angell, September 27, 1900, Angell Papers, box 5, folder 180.

59. Charles Van Hise to James Burrill Angell, April 19, 1906, Angell Papers, box 6, folder 220.

60. As discussed earlier, the letter of invitation issued by Wheeler et al. is quite clear in terms of invitees and prospective invitees. Northwestern is nowhere mentioned.

61. A. W. Harris to James Burrill Angell, February 26, 1908, Angell Papers, box 6, folder 232.

62. James Burrill Angell to A. W. Harris, February 26, 1908, Angell Papers, box 6, folder 232.

63. A. W. Harris to James Burrill Angell, March 2, 1908, Angell Papers, box 6, folder 233.

64. Edwin Alderman to Henry Higginson, February 18, 1909, available at

http://www.virginia.edu/publichistory/courses/readings/ald2hig1.html. At the time of the letter, Virginia had not been added to the list, but Alderman had received assurances that it would be added within "the next year or so."

65. "Criticises Universities: Dean Russell Says Standard of Scholarship Is Too German," *New York Times*, April 5, 1918, 8.

66. "Drafting Our Universities," *New York Times*, October 20, 1918, 72.

67. "Technical Training for Needs of War," *New York Times*, August 25, 1918, 77.

68. "Theories of Education," *New York Times*, December 1, 1918, 37.

69. Arthur Twining Hadley, *The Moral Basis of Democracy* (New Haven: Yale University Press, 1919), 10.

70. Among those who sent attendees were the U.S. Bureau of Education, the American Council on Education, the National Association of State Universities, the Association of American Colleges, the American Association of University Professors, the National Council of Normal School Presidents and Principals, the Institute of International Education, the Rhodes Scholarship Trust, the Western Electric Company, and the British Educational Mission (list of delegates and guests, annual conference of the Association of American Universities, New York, November 17–19, 1920), Hadley Records, series I, box 3.

Chapter 8

1. Gifford Pinchot to Arthur Twining Hadley, November 29, 1899, Hadley Records, series I, box 69.

2. Gifford Pinchot to Arthur Twining Hadley, December 6, 1899, Hadley Records, series I, box 69.

3. Arthur Twining Hadley to Gifford Pinchot, December 9, 1899, Hadley Records, series II, box 97.

4. Arthur Twining Hadley to Gifford Pinchot, March 6, 1900, Hadley Records, series II, box 97.

5. Gifford Pinchot to Arthur Twining Hadley, March 22, 1900, Hadley Records, series I, box 69.

6. Arthur Twining Hadley to Herbert Myrick, December 3, 1900, Hadley Records, series II, box 97.

7. Gifford Pinchot to Arthur Twining Hadley, June 12, 1903, Hadley Records, series I, box 69.

8. Gifford Pinchot to Arthur Twining Hadley, June 23, 1900, Hadley Records, series I, box 69.

9. Filbert Roth to James Burrill Angell, June 12, 1903, Angell Papers, box 5, folder 192.

10. James McLaughlin to James Burrill Angell, January 21, 1909, Angell Papers, box 7, folder 241.

11. Joint agreement of Cobbs & Mitchell, Mitchell Bros., Cadillac Handle Co., and Murphy & Diggins to James Burrill Angell, January 26, 1909, Angell Papers, box 7, folder 241.

12. Gifford Pinchot to James Burrill Angell, February 16, 1909, Angell Papers, box 7, folder 242.

13. Gifford Pinchot to James Burrill Angell, March 5, 1909, Angell Papers, box 7, folder 243.

14. Gifford Pinchot to James Burrill Angell, March 10, 1909, Angell Papers, box 7, folder 242.

15. Gifford Pinchot to Arthur Twining Hadley, June 17, 1909, Hadley Records,

series I, box 69. Topics for the conference included the objects and methods of forestry, the organization and standards of educational work, the coordination of work of different institutions, and the needs of the Forestry Service and other employers.

16. Gifford Pinchot to Arthur Twining Hadley, November 9, 1900, Hadley Records, series I, box 69.

17. Arthur Twining Hadley to William H. Taft, January 9, 1901, Hadley Records, series II, box 99.

18. C. R. Edwards to Arthur Twining Hadley, June 20, 1901, Hadley Records, series I, box 29; Arthur Twining Hadley to C. R. Edwards, June 29, 1901, Hadley Records, series II, box 99.

19. Arthur Twining Hadley to C. R. Edwards, August 26, 1901, Hadley Records, series II, box 99.

20. George Edmunds to James Burrill Angell, May 27, 1903, Angell Papers, box 5, folder 192.

21. James Burrill Angell to George Edmunds, June 3, 1903, Angell Papers, box 5, folder 192.

22. Paul Freer to James Burrill Angell, July 20, 1903, Angell Papers, box 5, folder 193.

23. Ibid.

24. For example, toward the end of Freer's tour of duty, Angell heard from Government Laboratories chief botanist E. D. Merrill, who reported that his office was preparing a series of "decades" cataloging Philippine plants and trees for the various forestry schools in the United States and that Michigan could expect to receive theirs within the next few months (U.S. Government Request form, seven endorsements, February 9–May 4, 1904, Angell Papers, box 6, folder 207).

25. Arthur Twining Hadley to William H. Taft, February 2, 1900, Hadley Records, series II, box 97.

26. Ibid.

27. Ibid.

28. Arthur Twining Hadley to William H. Taft, September 26, 1901, Hadley Records, series II, box 99.

29. Arthur Twining Hadley to Nicholas Murray Butler, November 9, 1905, Hadley Records, series II, box 108.

30. Nicholas Murray Butler to Arthur Twining Hadley, December 15, 1905, Hadley records, series I, box 14.

31. Ibid.

32. Nicholas Murray Butler to Arthur Twining Hadley, January 21, 1906, Hadley Records, series I, box 14.

33. *Report of the President of Yale University* (New Haven, 1906), 17–18.

34. Gifford Pinchot to Arthur Twining Hadley, September 23, 1905, Hadley Records, series I, box 69.

35. Charles Curtis to James Burrill Angell, August 19, 1908, Angell Papers, box 6, folder 237.

36. James Warren to James Burrill Angell, March 15, 1908, Angell Papers, box 6, folder 233.

37. Ibid.

38. L. S. Rowe to James Warren, April 27, 1908, Angell Papers, box 6, folder 234.

39. James Warren to James Burrill Angell, July 1, 1908, Angell Papers, box 6, folder 237.

40. Charles Curtis to James Burrill Angell, August 19, 1908, Angell Papers, box 6, folder 237.

41. Charles Curtis to James Burrill Angell, September 8, 1908, Angell Papers, box 6, folder 237.

42. James Warren to James Burrill Angell, January 22, 1908, Angell Papers, box 6, folder 231.

43. James Burrill Angell to James Warren, January 29, 1908, Angell Papers, box 6, folder 231.

44. "Yale Head Advocates Credit for Army Work," *New York Times,* October 22, 1915, 3.

45. Programme and list of delegates, eighteenth annual conference of the Association of American Universities, Clark University, Worcester, MA, November 9–11, 1916, Hadley Papers, series I, box 3.

46. Hawkins, *Banding Together,* 141.

47. Herman Ames to Arthur Twining Hadley, May 1, 1917, Hadley Records, series I, box 3.

48. Ibid.

49. Herman Ames to Wilbur Cross, November 12, 1917, copy, Hadley records, series I, box 3.

50. Armin Leuschner, Ray Wilbur, and Arthur Kennelly to Newton Baker, November 17, 1917, and attachment, Herman Ames to Arthur Twining Hadley, May 1, 1917, Hadley Records, series I, box 3.

51. Ibid.

52. Newton Baker to Ray Wilbur, November 21, 1917, and attachment, Herman Ames to Arthur Twining Hadley, May 1, 1917, Hadley Records, series I, box 3.

53. Ibid.

54. Pennsylvania law forbade Pinchot from succeeding himself as governor in 1926. In the interim, he ran for the Senate in 1926, again losing a highly disputed contest.

55. Pinchot was planning on visiting England, France, Holland, and Switzerland.

56. Gifford Pinchot to Arthur Twining Hadley, September 25, 1918, Hadley Records, series I, box 69.

57. Arthur Twining Hadley to Gifford Pinchot, September 29, 1918, Hadley Records, series II, box 97.

58. Gifford Pinchot to Arthur Twining Hadley, November 26, 1918, Hadley Records, series I, box 69.

59. Attachment, Alvey Adee to the National Board of Farm Organizations, October 10, 1918, Hadley Records, series I, box 69.

60. Attachment, Gifford Pinchot to Robert Lansing, October 15, 1918, Hadley Records, series I, box 69.

61. In the war period, debates raged over academic freedom and the proper relation of the university to the wartime government. As I discussed earlier, many academics would complain that research universities had not subjugated themselves enough.

62. James Burrill Angell had passed away in April 1916.

63. James Rowland Angell to Arthur Twining Hadley, May 14, 1918, Hadley Records, series I, box 3.

64. Arthur Twining Hadley, "The Colleges and the Nation," *Harper's Monthly,* June 1919.

65. Ibid.

Chapter 9

1. Cook, *Bureaucracy and Self-Government*, 157.

2. Ibid., 156.

3. Ibid.

4. Ibid., 158.

5. Ibid.

6. Ibid., 159.

7. Nicholas L. Henry, "Root and Branch: Public Administration's Travail toward the Future," in *Public Administration: The State of the Discipline*, ed. Naomi B. Lynn and Aaron Wildavsky (Chatham, NJ: Chatham House, 1990).

8. Cook, *Bureaucracy and Self-Government*, 159.

9. I must confess that my thinking has changed on Cook's call for revitalization. Upon completing much of the work presented herein for my dissertation in 2000, I characterized these hurdles as barriers that could not be overcome. However, upon further reflection, my thinking has evolved to recognize that university service will be more convenient at some times than at others, depending on how it maintains and maximizes its societal position and how effective its leaders are as policy entrepreneurs.

10. James Twitchell, "Higher Ed., Inc.," *Wilson Quarterly*, summer 2004, 50.

11. Arthur Twining Hadley to Herbert Beecher, January 22, 1899, Hadley Records, series II, box 98.

12. Eyal Press and Jennifer Washburn, "The Kept University," *Atlantic Monthly*, March 2000, 39–54.

13. Ibid., 40.

14. Ibid., 41.

15. One might characterize Press and Washburn as given to hyperbole. However, they offer the case of Petr Taborsky as an example of the depth of their concerns. As an undergraduate at the University of South Florida (USF), Taborsky worked as a research assistant on a project sponsored by the Florida Progress Corporation. Some time into his work, Taborsky pursued an approach different from that which his sponsors suggested for removing ammonia from wastewater. He met with success. The commercially viable nature of his discovery led both USF and Florida Progress to lay claim to his discovery, and USF pressed charges of grand theft when Taborsky went to its laboratory and removed his notebooks detailing his discovery. Though there certainly is dispute over whether Taborsky had received formal permission to pursue his alternative method and whether such permission, even if he had received it, would free him from his obligations to his corporate sponsor, there is no dispute over the fact that Taborsky himself made the crucial research discovery and intellectual breakthrough. In 1996, Taborsky found himself on a prison chain gang, having been convicted, by a jury, of grand larceny.

16. Jonathan Cohn, "Irrational Exuberance: When Did Political Science Forget about Politics?" *New Republic*, October 25, 1999, 26.

17. "Scientific Political Training," *New York Times*, July 23, 1881, 4.

18. Frank H. T. Rhodes, "The University and Its Critics," in *Universities and Their Leadership*, ed. William G. Bowen and Harold T. Shapiro (Princeton: Princeton University Press, 1998). Rhodes's essay is published along with pieces by Harold Shapiro, Hanna Gray, and Daniel Kevles as part of an interesting collection that offers a comprehensive overview of various leaders' and academics' visions for contemporary universities and their relationship to American society.

19. Beginning with William F. Buckley's *God and Man at Yale* (Chicago: Henry Regnery, 1951), the modern conservative movement has made almost a cottage industry out of critiquing the university. In this tradition, Dinesh D'Souza's *Illiberal Education* (New York: Free Press, 1991) and Martin Anderson's *Impostors in the Temple* (New York: Simon and Schuster, 1992) have been among the most well known. However, that conservatives are not alone in their negative appraisal is demonstrated by a quick perusal of current writings on higher education and of the writings of Rhodes's selection of critics—that is, Allen Bloom's *Closing of the American Mind* (New York: Simon and Schuster, 1987), Charles Sykes's *Profscam: Professors and the Demise of Higher Education* (Washington, DC: Regnery Gateway, 1988), Thomas Sowell's *Inside American Education* (New York: Free Press, 1993), and Page Smith's *Killing the Spirit: Higher Education in America* (New York: Viking Press, 1990).

20. Rhodes, "The University and Its Critics," 4–5.

21. Ibid., 5.

22. Skowronek, *Building a New American State*, 18.

23. Ibid., 15.

24. This duality—the intermingling of general acceptance of higher learning with attacks on its ideas, institutions, and individuals—can be traced throughout the history of education. Richard Hofstadter's *Anti-Intellectualism in American Life* (New York: Vintage Books, 1963) offers the seminal discussion of the social forces driving this phenomenon.

Bibliography

Adams, Herbert Baxter. *Thomas Jefferson and the University of Virginia.* U.S. Bureau of Education Circular 1. Washington, DC: Government Printing Office, 1888.

Adams, Henry Carter. "The Relation of the State to Industrial Action." In *Two Essays by Henry Carter Adams,* ed. Joseph Dorfman. New York: Augustus M. Kelley, 1969.

Anderson, Martin. *Impostors in the Temple.* New York: Simon and Schuster, 1992.

Annals of Congress, Thirteenth Congress, 3rd session. Washington, DC: United States Congress.

Axelrod, Robert, and Michael Cohen. *Harnessing Complexity.* New York: Free Press, 2000.

Barrow, Clyde. *Universities and the Capitalist State.* Madison: University of Wisconsin Press, 1990.

Bensel, Richard. *Sectionalism and American Political Development, 1880–1980.* Madison: University of Wisconsin Press, 1984.

———. *Yankee Leviathan: The Origins of Central State Authority in America, 1859–1877.* New York: Cambridge University Press, 1990.

Bishop, Morris. *A History of Cornell.* Ithaca: Cornell University Press, 1962.

Bloom, Allan. *Closing of the American Mind.* New York: Simon and Schuster, 1987.

Buckley, William F., Jr. *God and Man at Yale.* Chicago: Henry Regnery, 1951.

Carpenter, Daniel. "The Corporate Metaphor and Executive Department Centralization in the United States, 1888–1928." *Studies in American Political Development* 12, no. 1 (1998): 162–203.

Cohen, Michael, and James March. *Leadership and Ambiguity.* 2nd ed. Boston: Harvard Business School Press, 1986.

Cohen, Michael, James March, and Johan Olsen. "A Garbage Can Model of Organizational Choice." *Administrative Science Quarterly* 17 (1972): 1–25.

Cohn, Jonathan. "Irrational Exuberance: When Did Political Science Forget about Politics?" *New Republic,* October 25, 1999, 25–31.

Cook, Brian. *Bureaucracy and Self-Government.* Baltimore: Johns Hopkins University Press, 1996.

Croly, Herbert. *Progressive Democracy.* New York: Macmillan, 1914.

Dabney, Charles. *Universal Education in the South.* Vols. 1–2. Chapel Hill: University of North Carolina Press, 1936.

Dabney, Virginius. *Mr. Jefferson's University.* Charlottesville: University Press of Virginia, 1981.

Dahl, Robert. *Who Rules: Democracy and Power in an American City*. New Haven: Yale University Press, 1962.

Dennis, Michael. *Lessons in Progress: State Universities and Progressivism in the New South, 1880–1920*. Urbana: University of Illinois Press, 2000.

DiMaggio, Paul, and Walter Powell. "The Iron Cage Revisited: Institutional Isomorphism and Collective Rationality." In *The New Institutionalism in Organizational Analysis*, ed. Walter Powell and Paul DiMaggio. Chicago: University of Chicago Press, 1991.

Douglas, Mary. *How Institutions Think*. Syracuse: Syracuse University Press, 1986.

Douglass, John Aubrey. *The California Idea and American Higher Education: 1850 to the 1960 Master Plan*. Palo Alto: Stanford University Press, 2000.

D'Souza, Dinesh. *Illiberal Education*. New York: Free Press, 1991.

Dumenil, Lynn. *The Modern Temper*. New York: Hill and Wang, 1995.

Dyer, Thomas. *The University of Georgia: A Bicentennial History, 1785–1985*. Athens: University of Georgia Press, 1985.

Eckstein, Harry. "Case Study and Theory in Political Science." In *Handbook of Political Science*, vol. 7, ed. F. I. Greenstein and N. W. Polsby. Reading, MA: Addison-Wesley, 1975.

Eisenach, Eldon. *The Lost Promise of Progressivism*. Lawrence: University Press of Kansas, 1994.

Elazar, Daniel. *American Federalism: A View From the States*. New York: Thomas Crowell, 1972.

———. "The American Partnership: The Next Half Generation." In *The Politics of American Federalism*, ed. Daniel Elazar. Lexington, MA: D. C. Heath, 1969.

Evans, Peter, Dietrich Rueschemeyer, and Theda Skocpol. "Toward a More Adequate Understanding of the State." In *Bringing the State Back In*, ed. Peter Evans, Dietrich Rueschemeyer, and Theda Skocpol. New York: Cambridge University Press, 1985.

Farr, James, and Raymond Seidelman, eds. *Discipline and History: Political Science and History*. Ann Arbor: University of Michigan Press, 1993.

Franklin, Fabian. *The Life of Daniel Coit Gilman*. New York: Mead and Company, 1910.

Freidman, Lawrence. *A History of American Law*. New York: Simon and Schuster, 1973.

Geiger, Roger. *To Advance Knowledge: The Growth of American Research Universities, 1900–1940*. New York: Oxford University Press, 1986.

Gordon, Lynn D. *Gender and Higher Education in the Progressive Era*. New Haven: Yale University Press, 1990.

Gray, Hanna. "On the History of Giants." In *Universities and Their Leadership*, ed. William G. Bowen and Harold T. Shapiro. Princeton: Princeton University Press, 1998.

Hadley, Arthur Twining. *Baccalauerate Addresses and Talks on Kindred Themes*. New York: Scribner's and Sons, 1907.

———. "The Colleges and the Nation." *Harper's Monthly*, June 1919, 12–17.

———. *The Moral Basis of Democracy*. New Haven: Yale University Press, 1919.

Harris, William T. "The Necessity of Free Public High Schools." *New England Journal of Education* 11 (1880): 53.

Haskell, Thomas L. *The Emergence of the Professional Social Science*. Urbana: University of Illinois Press, 1977.

Hawkins, Hugh. *Banding Together: The Rise of National Associations in Higher Education, 1887–1950*. Baltimore: Johns Hopkins University Press, 1992.

Heise, Arthur. *The Brass Factories*. Washington, DC: Public Affairs Press, 1969.

Henry, Nicholas L. "Root and Branch: Public Administration's Travail toward the Future." In *Public Administration: The State of the Discipline*, ed. Naomi B. Lynn and Aaron Wildavsky. Chatham, NJ: Chatham House, 1990.

Herbst, Jurgen. "The Eighteenth Century Origins of the Split between Public and Private Higher Education." In *The Social History of American Education*, ed. B. Edward McClellan and William J. Reese. Urbana: University of Illinois Press, 1988.

Hochschild, Jennifer. *The New American Dilemma: Liberal Democracy and School Desegregation*. New Haven: Yale University Press, 1984.

Hofstadter, Richard. *The Age of Reform: From Bryan to FDR*. New York: Random House, 1960.

———. *Anti-Intellectualism in American Life*. New York: Vintage Books, 1963.

Hofstadter, Richard, and Wilson Smith, eds. *American Higher Education: A Documentary History*. 2 vols. Chicago: University of Chicago Press, 1961.

Hogan, Neal C. *Unhealed Wounds: Medical Malpractice in the Twentieth Century*. New York: LFB Scholarly Publishing, 2003.

Hoyt, John. *Reports on the London and Paris International Expositions of 1862 and 1867*. Madison, WI: Atwood & Rublee, 1869.

———. *Memorial in Regard to a National University*. Washington, DC: Government Printing Office, 1892.

Huntington, Samuel. *Political Order in Changing Societies*. New Haven: Yale University Press, 1968.

Jackman, Robert. *Power without Force: The Political Capacity of Nation-States*. Ann Arbor: University of Michigan Press, 1993.

Kahn, E. J. *Harvard: Through Calm and Storm*. New York: W. W. Norton, 1969.

Kaufman, Herbert. *The Forest Ranger: A Study in Administrative Behavior*. Baltimore: Johns Hopkins University Press, 1967.

Kelley, Brooks Mather. *Yale: A History*. New Haven: Yale University Press, 1974.

Kevles, Daniel. "A Time for Audacity: What the Past Has to Teach the Present about Science and the Federal Government." In *Universities and Their Leadership*, ed. William G. Bowen and Harold T. Shapiro. Princeton: Princeton University Press, 1998.

Key, V. O. *Southern Politics*. New York: A. A. Knopf, 1949.

Kingdon, John W. *Agendas, Alternatives, and Public Policies*. 2nd ed. New York: Harper Collins, 1995.

———. "Politicians, Self-Interest, and Ideas." In *Reconsidering the Democratic Public*, ed. George Marcus and Russell Hanson. University Park: Pennsylvania State University Press, 1993.

Lagemann, Ellen Condliffe. *Private Power for the Public Good: A History of the Carnegie Foundation for the Advancement of Teaching*. Middletown, CT: Wesleyan University Press, 1983.

Lester, Robin. *Stagg's University*. Urbana: University of Illinois Press, 1999.

Lieber, Frances. "An Inaugural Address Delivered on the 17th of February, 1858, on Assuming the Chair of History and Political Science in Columbia College, New York." In *Discipline and History: Political Science and History*, ed. James Farr and Raymond Seidelman. Ann Arbor: University of Michigan Press, 1993.

March, James, and Johan Olsen. *Rediscovering Institutions*. New York: Free Press, 1989.

Marsden, George. *The Soul of the American University*. New York: Oxford University Press, 1994.

McClellan, B. Edward, and William Reese. "The Nineteenth Century." In *The Social History of American Education,* ed. B. Edward McClellan and William J. Reese. Urbana: University of Illinois Press, 1988.

Meyer, John, and Brian Rowan. "Institutionalized Organizations: Formal Structure as Myth and Ceremony." *American Journal of Sociology* 83 (1977): 340–63.

Mills, C. Wright. *The Power Elite.* New York: Oxford University Press, 1956.

Monkkonen, Eric. *America Becomes Urban: The Development of U. S. Cities and Towns, 1780–1980.* Berkeley: University of California Press, 1988.

Morone, James. *The Democratic Wish: Popular Participation and the Limits of American Government.* New York: Basic Books, 1990.

Mumford, Frederick. *The Land Grant College Movement.* Columbia: University of Missouri, College of Agriculture, Agricultural Experiment Station, 1940.

National Education Association of the United States. *Addresses and Proceedings— National Education Association of the United States.* Washington, DC.

North, Douglass. *Institutions, Institutional Change, and Economic Performance.* New York: Cambridge University Press, 1990.

Oriard, Michael. *Reading Football: How the Popular Press Created an American Spectacle.* Chapel Hill: University of North Carolina Press, 1993.

Parks, Stephen. *The Elizabethan Club of Yale University and Its Collections.* New Haven: Yale University Press, 1986.

Peckham, Howard. *The Making of the University of Michigan.* Ann Arbor: Bentley Historical Library, 1992.

Pierson, George. *A Yale Book of Numbers: Historical Statistics of the College and University, 1701–1976.* New Haven: Yale University, 1983.

Poggi, Gianfranco. *The Development of the Modern State: A Sociological Introduction.* Stanford: Stanford University Press, 1978.

————. *The State: Its Nature, Development, and Prospects.* Stanford: Stanford University Press, 1990.

Powell, Arthur. *The Uncertain Profession: Harvard and the Search for Educational Authority.* Cambridge: Harvard University Press, 1980.

Powell, William. *The First State University.* Chapel Hill: University of North Carolina Press, 1992.

Press, Eyal, and Jennifer Washburn. "The Kept University." *Atlantic Monthly,* March 2000, 39–54.

Reese, William. *The Origins of the American High School.* New Haven: Yale University Press, 1995.

Reuben, Julie. *The Making of the Modern University.* Chicago: University of Chicago Press, 1996.

Rhodes, Frank H. T., "The University and Its Critics." In *Universities and Their Leadership.* ed. William G. Bowen and Harold T. Shapiro. Princeton: Princeton University Press, 1998.

Richardson, Leon Burr. *History of Dartmouth College.* Hanover, NH: Dartmouth College, 1932.

Roberts, Jon H., and James Turner. *The Sacred and the Secular University.* Princeton: Princeton University Press, 2000.

Rudolph, Frederick. *The American College and University: A History.* Athens: University of Georgia Press, 1990.

————. *Curriculum: A History of the Undergraduate Curriculum from 1635 to Present.* San Francisco: Jossey-Bass, 1992.

Sellers, Charles. *The Market Revolution: Jacksonian America, 1815–1846.* New York: Oxford University Press, 1991.

Shapiro, Harold T. "University Presidents Then and Now." In *Universities and Their Leadership*, ed. William G. Bowen and Harold T. Shapiro. Princeton: Princeton University Press, 1998.

Shaw, Wilfred, with assistance from James R. Angell. "James B. Angell." In *Michigan and the Cleveland Era*, ed. Earl Babst and Lewis G. Vander Velde. Ann Arbor: University of Michigan Press, 1948.

Skocpol, Theda. "Bringing the State Back In: Strategies of Analysis in Current Research." In *Bringing the State Back In*, ed. Peter Evans, Dietrich Rueschemeyer, and Theda Skocpol. New York: Cambridge University Press, 1985.

Skowronek, Stephen. *Building a New American State: The Expansion of National Administrative Capacities, 1877–1920*. New York: Cambridge University Press, 1987.

Smith, Charles. "Southern Colleges and Schools." *Atlantic Monthly*, October 1884, 548.

Smith, Page. *Killing the Spirit: Higher Education in America*. New York: Viking Press, 1990.

Sowell, Thomas. *Inside American Education*. New York: Free Press, 1993.

Stadtman, Verne. *The University of California, 1868–1968*. New York: McGraw-Hill, 1970.

Starr, Kevin. *Inventing the Dream: California through the Progressive Era*. New York: Oxford University Press, 1985.

Starr, Paul. *The Social Transformation of American Medicine*. New York: Basic Books, 1982.

Stinchcombe, Arthur. *Information and Organizations*. Berkeley: University of California Press, 1990.

Sykes, Charles. *Profscam: Professors and the Demise of Higher Education*. Washington, DC: Regnery Gateway, 1988.

Tappan, Henry Phillip. *University Education*. New York: G. P. Putnam, 1851.

Thelin, John. *Higher Education and Its Useful Past*. Cambridge, MA: Schenkman Publishing, 1982.

———. *Games Colleges Play*. Baltimore: Johns Hopkins University Press, 1994.

Thorsen, Niles Aage. *The Political Thought of Woodrow Wilson, 1875–1910*. Princeton: Princeton University Press, 1988.

Toma, J. Douglas. *Football U.* Ann Arbor: University of Michigan Press, 2003.

Twitchell, James. "Higher Ed., Inc." *Wilson Quarterly*, summer 2004, 46–59.

Turner, Paul Venable. *Campus: An American Planning Tradition*. Cambridge: MIT Press, 1984.

U.S. Senate. *University of the United States*. 57th Cong., 1st sess, 1902. S. Rep. 945.

Veysey, Lawrence. *The Emergence of the American University*. Chicago: University of Chicago Press, 1965.

Walker, Jack L. "The Diffusion of Innovation among the American States." *American Political Science Review* 68 (1968): 880–99.

Weber, Max. *Economy and Society*. Vols. 1–2. 1922. Reprint, Berkeley: University of California Press, 1978.

White, Andrew Dickson. *The Autobiography of Andrew Dickson White*. New York: Century Company, 1905.

———. "Scientific and Industrial Education." *Popular Science Monthly*, April 1874.

Wiebe, Robert. *The Search for Order*. New York: Hill and Wang, 1968.

———. *Self-Rule: A Cultural History of American Democracy*. Chicago: University of Chicago Press, 1995.

Williams, Brian A. *Thought and Action: John Dewey at the University of Michigan*. Ann Arbor: Bentley Historical Library, 1998.

Williams, Roger. *Origins of Federal Support for Higher Education.* University Park: Pennsylvania State University Press, 1991.

Wilson, James Q. *Bureaucracy: What Government Agencies Do and Why They Do It.* New York: Basic Books, 1989.

Wilson, Woodrow. "The Study of Administration." *Political Science Quarterly* 2 (1887): 197–222.

Wood, Gordon. *The Creation of the American Republic, 1776–1787.* New York: W. W. Norton, 1972.

Woodward, C. M., comp. *Opinions of Educators on the Value & Total Influence of Inter-collegiate & Inter-scholastic American Football as Played in 1903–1909.* St. Louis, 1910.

Index

Page numbers in italic refer to tables.

government service application of,
81–82, 100–101
influence of, 8, 21
nation-building requirement of, 2,
24–25
as nurtured by universities, 1, 3, 9,
11
universities providing government
with, 216, 228, 243
universities redefined in support
of, 123
Wilson, Woodrow, on, 81–83
extracurricular programs, university,
36–38, 182, 245

faculty. *See* professors
favoritism and patronage, 81, 83, 90,
99
federal government capacities, 2, 5,
7–9
federal government departments and
bureaus, 30–31
federal service of scholars, 78–83
federal university proposal. *See*
national university movement
Federation of Graduate Clubs, 37,
136, 144, 163, 165
fellowships, graduate, 92–93, 135
Filipino students, 221
football, 37–38, 182, 245
foreign students at American universities, *185t*, 221, 229–30
Forestry, Bureau of, 31, 216–20
forestry education, 31, 216–20, 227,
277n15
foundation support, 199–200
Freer, Paul, 223–24
Frieze, Henry Simmons, 105, 110–11,
265n3
Fulton, Robert, 154
fund-raising, 183
funds, federal, 219–20
funds for professor pensions, 201–4,
274n43

garbage can model of organizational
choice, 6
Geiger, Roger, 5, 15

gentleman scholar, 3
geology, 155–56
Georgia, University of, 19–20
German universities, 163–64, 205
Gilman, Daniel Coit
and AAU founding, 164–65
career of, 18
on definition of university, 126
graduate training of, 41
on growth in education, 44
and Johns Hopkins fellowship program, 92–93
and Johns Hopkins presidency,
59–60
and Morrill Act funds use for
research universities, 57–59
on national university proposal,
159
and University of California presidency, 57, 69, 71, 262n27
White, Andrew Dickson, ties with,
28, 51–53, 65
government service of scholars,
78–83, 105, 107
graduate education, 41
degree requirements for, 163–64,
169, 207–8
degree standards for, 134–40
and fellowships, 92–93, 135
funding for, 199–200
Graves, Henry, 217
Great War. *See* World War I

Hadley, Arthur Twining
on AAU founding, 165–68
on admissions standards, 188–93
on citizenship, 39–40
and colonial administration curriculum, 225–26
and Filipino student scholarships,
221–22
and fund-raising, 183–84
and government partnership,
226–27
graduate training of, 41
as Interstate Commerce Commission (ICC) advisor, 3
on military preparedness, 232